UNFIT
PARENT

UNFIT PARENT

A Disabled Mother Challenges an Inaccessible World

Jessica Slice

Beacon Press ▪ Boston

BEACON PRESS
Boston, Massachusetts
www.beacon.org

Beacon Press books
are published under the auspices of
the Unitarian Universalist Association of Congregations.

27 26 25 24   8 7 6 5 4 3 2 1

This book is printed on acid-free paper that meets the uncoated paper
ANSI/NISO specifications for permanence as revised in 1992.

Text design and compostion by Kim Arney

This book depicts real individuals and personal stories based on
interviews and text-based research. Some names and identifying
details have been changed and, when requested, some have been
anonymized to allow for transparency and to maintain privacy.

*Library of Congress Cataloguing-in-Publication
Data is available for this title.*
Hardcover ISBN: 978-0-8070-1324-3
E-book ISBN: 978-0-8070-1325-0
Audiobook: 978-0-8070-1821-7

To Amy and Heather, my first babies,
who grew up to take care of me. I love you.

And to Megan, Mama, and Sarah.
You were with me as I wrote.

CONTENTS

UNFIT
PARENT

INTRODUCTION

If my child were in charge, we would spend every hour of every day in matching floral nightgowns playing the late eighties version of Mario 3. I play; K narrates. She tells me which treasure chest to open and stops talking when it's time to fight Bowser so that I can concentrate. Our goal is to reach the part in level 5 when Mario jumps around in a sock. We are in an impenetrable bubble on our fluffy white sofa with that dated, pixelated game on the TV.

Another of "our" activities, which also must be done in our long twin nightgowns, is to shop for home furnishings online. K could, without exaggeration, look at rugs and light fixtures for an entire afternoon. I pick a store, and we scroll and scroll. Which is silliest? Which do we want to buy? Recently, I ordered a Benjamin Moore paint swatch fan, and we spent the evenings looking through the colors and laughing about the names—*"kitten whiskers"?!*

Sometimes, I feel insecure about which activities I do with her. My husband, David, is the one who is teaching her how to ride a bike. David drives her to school. David flies a kite and swims in the lake. If I want to spend more than a few minutes with K, I need to be reclined and stationary.

When I was considering the first paragraph of this book, the image that would introduce the reader to my relationship with my child, I considered the morning I sat with her in a lobby of a government building when she was a few weeks old. A security guard approached us and said that she had never seen a caregiver and baby so connected. That our bond brought tears to her eyes.

I thought about starting the book with the time our neighborhood caught on fire in California: how David drove our van down the hill away from the wall of flames with K on my lap. How tightly I held her and refused to let go until we were far away from danger. How we saved her life. Or maybe I could start the book by describing K's first asthma attack at eighteen months old. I was in bed and heard her first cry of the day and, without hesitation, told David that something was wrong and we needed a doctor. David looked at me, confused, but I was right. I know my baby. We are connected.

I'd tell those harrowing stories to prove that I am a real parent. A part of me wants to spend this whole book defending why I am just as worthy as a nondisabled parent. I want to convince you, the reader (and myself), that K's life isn't worse with me as her mom.

But I know, when I am calm and honest—that approach won't get us anywhere; you'll smell the defensiveness on me. My rule of writing, the reminder I write each morning before I start and repeat to myself when I edit, is this:

Tell the truth.

That's what I will do in this book. I will tell the truth about what it means to be a disabled parent. What our days are like, and how it feels to go out in the world when the world is not designed for you. About the barriers of our bodies and minds, of those imposed on our bodies and minds, and the pernicious barriers of our own internalized ableism. The absolute terror of parenting publicly while knowing that the vast majority of people who have their children removed by social welfare systems are disabled. How expensive and demoralizing it is when you're disabled and trying to find baby equipment that works. I'll tell the truth about medical care, selective abortions, and labor. About breastfeeding and imposter syndrome and community. I'll tell the truth even when it will make people think I'm a worse parent than someone who is not disabled. I'll tell the truth even when it makes people mad.

I will also share the lessons that my disabled body has taught me and how those lessons have helped me as a parent. I'll share the deep wisdom that disability culture offers and how it could alter parenthood for everyone. Being a disabled parent is hard, but in our isolated and productivity-driven society, being *any* parent is hard. I believe—not because I'm trying to prove my worth, but because I have lived it—that disabled parents have something powerful and transformative to offer. We have wrestled with misbehaving bodies and minds. We have navigated a world that rejects frailty and weakness.

Years before acquiring my disability and over a decade before becoming a parent myself, my dear friend Kate had four kids in five years. I spent hours at her house hanging out and observing what it took to care for children. She would try to update me on some aspect of her life, and in the course of one sentence of one story, she'd be interrupted by three different kids: a bottom that needed to be wiped, a request for a snack, a squabble over sharing. The needs were constant and variable—second-to-second demands. Sometimes, we'd be on the phone, and I'd overhear the complex tactical planning of finding a minute to step away to pee.

While I was not disabled at the time, I was considering having kids one day. It was our first decade out of college. Going about my day, I would try to imagine what it would be like to have kids. I'd consider my mornings—a run, breakfast, coffee, shower, work—and try to add in four small children with constant needs. I'd peek around my shower curtain and imagine a four-year-old digging through my toiletries, a two-year-old falling on the tile, and a newborn wailing with a dirty diaper. How could children possibly fit into life? I'm a parent now and write about parenting professionally, and I still don't know that they can.

Parenting, for everyone, when seen through the lens of their life before parenting, is unthinkable. Parenting two kids, through the lens of parenting one, is unimaginable. Every new stage of parenting is impossible to comprehend before you're there. And yet we do it. We keep our kids safe; we love them in a way we never imagined; we delight in their lives. Our capacities exceed our imagination—they grow from our creativity.

Disabled parenting is the same. If you look at my life through the lens of your body, it may seem unsustainable. But my capacity—for joy, for innovation, for community—is enough. Disabled parents, out of necessity, must reject the rules and standards that guide nondisabled parents.

And disabled people have learned important lessons living in an unreasonable world.

I have not written a comprehensive historical or cultural account of parenting in North America. Other authors are doing that brilliantly.

What I offer is my view from my own disabled body and from my place in the wider disability community. And, from here, I see how the lessons I've learned that help me survive in a world that was not designed for me also help me as a parent. I've witnessed how our family divides our labor differently and how much I value flexibility and reconsidering popular standards of parenting success.

Unfit Parent blends my own story of disability and parenting with interviews, social commentary, disability theory, and sociohistorical research. It cannot be a comprehensive account of every type of disability, nor can it cover the full history of being a disabled parent in the US and Canada. There are a few topics that I will gloss over or pause briefly on that, in fact, could take up a multivolume collection: the history of disabled sterilization, the financial reality of being disabled in the US, and the child welfare system. Disabled parenting deserves its own genre of books, and it's my wish that this will help spur the publication of many more. What I hope is that this book will start conversations and encourage other disabled parents to share their experiences.

By the nature of its topic, it discusses medical abuse, family separation, institutionalization, sexual violence, infertility, ableism, violence, racism, and loss. Take care of yourself while reading.

Being a disabled parent isn't easy—our needs and experiences are often overlooked, and, as I've mentioned, we never forget that the social welfare system can swoop in at any time and remove our children. Being disabled can feel lonely, and parenting while disabled can compound that feeling. The world was not designed for us. For example, my kid's former school was not wheelchair accessible, and, as a result, she spent her days in a building I had never been inside. I will describe the real, practical, and emotional experience of parenting in what philosophy professor Dr. Elizabeth Barnes calls "a minority body."[1] Through interviews and research, I will help you glimpse what it's like to be a parent with a minority body and mind.

If I find myself trying to defend myself, I will go back and try again. *Unfit Parent* isn't proof of my value. It doesn't need to be. The reality is this: this book is an offering. And I hope my fellow disabled parents will feel seen reading these stories.

If you are disabled and parenting or thinking about parenting, I offer this book as solidarity. You are doing something hard and real and, despite a total lack of representation, know that you are not the only one. Every time you feel like a fake or like you aren't a real parent, remember that you bring something deeply true and wise to your children and your family. You have survived in this world. That is huge. And you aren't doing this alone. There is a community of brilliant and creative disabled people cheering you on.

And, if you aren't disabled, I hope to give you the information you need to reconsider what disability means and what we owe one another. I hope you can start to understand why I believe that my body isn't the problem; it's our inaccessible world. The harm done to us by an individualistic and profit-driving culture is hurting nondisabled people, too.

If you are a parent—disabled or not—and you are exhausted and feel like you are drowning in inhumane policies and culture, I hope this book offers hope. My first message is this: you aren't wrong; you are doing something impossible. But the good news is that marginalized people are often the first to notice when something is broken, and, as such, are the first to establish reparative solutions. Disabled people are the canaries in the coal mine. We have seen the problem, and we have found answers.

Disability culture reframes the wider culture. It teaches creativity and acceptance. It rejects rabid capitalism and embraces mutual aid. It encourages rest. Just imagine what it would be like to be a parent in a society where parenthood didn't mean perfectionism and loneliness.

As disability activist Alice Wong brilliantly says, disabled people are "oracles."[2] Our needy minds and bodies slow us down, and, once humans stop moving so much, we can look around. We can see. These disabled bodies and minds give us perspective. Disabled parents have been omitted from mainstream parenting conversations, but it's our wisdom and culture that could transform the whole system.

This book isn't evidence that we deserve to parent. It's not a lament of how we suffer. It's centuries of disabled wisdom crafted into a gentle, transformative, magical map.

Chapter 1

DISABILITY & ME (& YOU)

I became disabled in 2011, though I wouldn't identify as disabled until 2018. On August 23, 2011, I was on the tenth day of a cruise, hiking on the Greek island of Santorini with my then-husband. I was twenty-eight and fit, striding along a brush-lined path between the towns of Fira and Oia. But, halfway between the cities, the mood changed—it was hot, and we ran out of water earlier than anticipated. The unobstructed sun beat down on us. And then, a mile from the end, about an hour since we had last seen another person, and with Fira just barely in view, a pack of large wild dogs blocked our path.

To our left, a rocky cliff dropped into the Mediterranean. To the right, the brush-covered hill stretched a couple of hundred yards. The dogs crouched, ready to lunge, and the leader let out a low growl. My husband and I both knew that we were in imminent danger. The world narrowed to the dogs, to us, to survival. With a head tilt and a nod, we agreed to scale the hill to our right. We scrambled up, the brush tearing at our skin, our ears cocked for pursuing dogs.

They didn't follow us. We reached the top of the hill and rested, breathless and bleeding, in our running shorts and backpacks. We avoided the path for the rest of the hike, adding considerable distance to our already fraught adventure. When we arrived in Fira, I was sick with heat exhaustion—my hands shook, my mind was scrambled, and I vomited. I tried to choke down some food but felt like I was losing consciousness.

Instead of an afternoon in the shops, I returned to our cruise ship and rested. I was a runner and extremely active. There was no reason to think that it would take any more than an afternoon to recover from heat-related illness. But when I woke up the next day, I was still dizzy and nauseated. I attempted to join a group tour of Olympus but spent the day in the snack bar, guzzling water and feeling my muscles grow numb and my legs weak.

I visited the ship's doctor, who found that I had critically low levels of sodium and potassium (if I had been on land, I would have been hospitalized). I took the doctor-provided supplements and went back to bed. Two days after the hike, I still felt sick. I could hardly stand, and it was like I was trapped behind glass—my surroundings felt far away and confusing. We had two weeks left on our trip, and I grew sicker each day. Giant blood blisters formed in my mouth, and my face became puffy. Every morning, I would try to walk to breakfast, and every morning, I had to stop and sit on the ground.

I spent the rest of the trip in bed. When we returned to North Carolina, I saw a few doctors. They all said the same thing: it might take a while to recover from my electrolyte imbalance and heat exhaustion, but that recovery was at hand.

It wasn't.

I had no idea then that I would see dozens of doctors over the next few years. That most of them would blame "stress" or "too much attention on my symptoms." I had no idea that my skin would yellow and tiny hairs would grow on my back and hands. That my bones would jut out, that at night I would run my hands over my changing body and wonder if I would disappear.

It took two years to get a diagnosis: a form of dysautonomia called Postural Orthostatic Tachycardia Syndrome (POTS). The hike had triggered a shift in my autonomic nervous system, which, mediated in part by the vagus nerve, controls heart rate, blood pressure, digestion, and temperature. Standing, getting warm, or eating now sends my body into fight-or-flight.

In 2014, a year after I received the diagnosis and started medication and cardiac rehab, my younger sister became ill. It was obvious that she also had POTS, and so our cardiologist suggested that we see a geneticist to look for a cause. The geneticist diagnosed us with hypermobile Ehlers-Danlos syndrome (hEDS), a connective tissue disorder that can cause POTS. EDS alters the structure of collagen, an essential component of joints, tendons, blood vessels, skin, and organs.

My sister and I don't have the life-shortening vascular version of EDS (vEDS) but experience a panoply of collagen-related symptoms. My joints and muscles ache every minute. Something as benign as rolling over in bed can injure my hips, ribs, and neck. Digestion is difficult for me, and I experience nerve and motor problems in my hands. A few days every month, I have migraines.

With POTS, I cannot tolerate temperatures above 73 degrees and develop heat exhaustion within minutes. I can only sit upright and unsupported briefly; I must spend my days reclined. After a minute of walking, I become lightheaded and can stand still for only around thirty seconds before I start to black out.

In the year after my diagnosis, I attempted a comprehensive cardiac rehabilitation program, desperate to be well. Dr. Benjamin Levine developed the Levine Protocol to help those with orthostatic intolerance (difficulty standing due to blood pressure and heart rate changes) slowly increase our ability to stay upright.[1] It's a six-month titrated exercise program that some patients complete at home. Due to the severity of my illness, I completed my therapy at a rehab center for, primarily, heart attack and lung transplant patients.

I was not able to progress through the protocol as quickly as prescribed, and I finished in just over one year. The cardiac rehab center was only a ten-minute drive from my North Carolina home, but I couldn't drive that far, so the thrice-weekly appointments required rides from friends. Getting from my apartment to the car was difficult, and then, once at the rehab center, I had trouble walking to my station. By the time I was saying hello to my PT, I was often so faint that I could barely communicate. At my first appointment, my therapist, Sean, helped me through thirty seconds of slow recumbent biking before I became too lightheaded to finish.

After a year, I was forced to admit that the protocol had not worked. I had increased my tolerance for standing, but merely from thirty seconds to a minute. I increased my ability to walk from one minute once a day to fifteen minutes, three times per week. However, these changes did almost nothing to change my daily life. I was and am still unable to sit at a restaurant or ride in a plane sitting upright. I plateaued. Every time I tried to build more tolerance, I would experience significant setbacks.

I was twenty-eight when I went on the hike on Santorini, and I turned forty while writing this book. I've been disabled for most of my adult life, but I still remember vividly what it was like to travel and go on runs and drink with friends until late. When I talk to people who became disabled as a child or were born with disabilities, I am struck by the sense of entitlement I retain as someone with an acquired disability—I am surprised when the world isn't designed for me.

Because I spent decades with the privilege of living in a body that was accepted and celebrated, the shift in external attitudes and treatment at twenty-eight was more striking. In all likelihood, I am more outraged than if I had spent my life believing that all I could expect was discrimination and ableism.

It was seven years before I started to identify as disabled. Until then, I thought I was "sick," which, in my mind, was a more superficial, more transient state. A year after the hike, I filed a claim with my private "disability" insurance company but considered the term a legal technicality. When a doctor diagnosed me with POTS, they sent me home with paperwork for a permanent "disability" parking placard. Still, the term didn't resonate.

Years later, in 2017, while in graduate school for social work, I encountered access obstacles while looking for a mandatory internship. I was referred to "disability" services. That word again. I thought that "disability" was a bureaucratic term under which my true identity—sick, fragile, weak—fell. When Columbia was unable to find a placement with air conditioning that could accommodate my mobility scooter, I delayed my internship for a semester to consider my options. When an administrator said I might be too sick to be a social worker, I worried they were right.

To stay enrolled in my program, I developed an independent study with a professor I admired. There must have been a kernel in me looking for answers because my proposed independent study was called "Disability, Chronic Illness, and Grief." My question was this: Does becoming chronically ill or disabled initiate the same internal process as losing a loved one does?

The syllabus was dense and rich. I read Eli Clare, Elizabeth Barnes, Julie Rehmeyer, Toni Bernhard, Jean-Dominique Bauby, Nasim Marie Jafry, Meghan O'Rourke, Leslie Jamison, Maya Dusenbery, Laura Hillenbrand, Rhoda Olkin, Cheri Blauwet, Erin Rafferty, Amy Berkowitz, Nancy Eiesland, and Madelyn Detloff. I interviewed scholars and watched documentaries. For four months, I inadvertently immersed myself in disability theory. This independent study would change everything.

During the first week, I read Dr. Elizabeth Barnes's *Minority Body*, a book of analytic philosophy that attempts to bridge the gap between the views of the disability rights movement and those of academic philosophers.[2] Dr. Barnes, with whom I went to college and was acquainted, wrote the book because she locates herself in that gap: she is a tenured philosophy professor with hEDS and young onset Parkinson's.

It would not be an exaggeration to say that *Minority Body* altered my life. I had not considered my shift from healthy to sick to be anything but a great loss until I picked it up. To start, Dr. Barnes challenged an assumption that I had internalized but had never examined: that sick bodies like mine create bias from which we cannot perceive ourselves or the world clearly. We must be told what is true by objective (healthy) sources. It's why I had believed the doctors who, for years, said I wasn't actually sick. It's why I believed Columbia when they doubted if I could complete my graduate program and if the field of social work was a fit for a disabled person. I believed that my view from what Susan Sontag calls "the kingdom of the sick" was too obstructed to have perspective.[3] I doubted my own authority.

In *Minority Body*, Dr. Barnes explains that she expects there may be other academics who object to her capacity to write a book on disability because she is disabled. She confronts that concern in the preface:

> I used to think I couldn't philosophize about disability precisely because the topic is so personal. But on reflection, that's absurd. Disability is a topic that's personal for everyone. The last time I checked, most non-disabled people are pretty personally invested in being non-disabled. The fact that this sort of personal investment is so easy to ignore is one of the more pernicious aspects of philosophy's obsession with objective neutrality. It's easy to confuse the view from normal with the view from nowhere. And then it's uniquely the minority voices which we single out as biased or lacking objectivity. When it comes to disability, I'm not objective. And neither are you. And that's true whether you're disabled or (temporarily) non-disabled.

That concept was a revelation to me. *There is no view from nowhere.* I have repeated that sentence to myself dozens of times since I first read it. Every person is biased about disability because we all have bodies, and all bodies, eventually, fail. It was the first time that I had considered that if we are lucky to live long enough, every single person will become disabled.

The next assumption that shifted for me was that my body and life were inherently inferior to what they had been before the Santorini hike. Using analytic philosophy, Dr. Barnes describes why it is not philosophically sound to assume that being disabled is worse than not being disabled. She defends this view using three arguments. First, the group of features that would result in someone being labeled as disabled is "strikingly heterogeneous." Any attempt to unify disabilities using physical characteristics crumbles, and one is forced to find another common quality. The definition of disability that makes the most sense, according to Dr. Barnes, is "people who have grouped themselves when organizing a civil rights struggle." Disability, without the ability to clearly delineate which bodies and minds have disabled characteristics, is defined by a social movement.

I started to learn about disability rights and its more recent iteration, disability justice. It's hard to believe that I had not connected my struggles navigating the medical system with disability advocacy, but I hadn't. Even though I had fought for years for disability income, I hadn't situated myself with others doing the same. Once I started to search online, I was floored by the decades of tireless work that had gone into each step toward disability equity. As I read about the 504 sit-ins and the resulting legislation that outlawed disabled employment discrimination, I considered that I had these advocates from decades before to thank for my right to attend graduate school.[4] When I saw photos of disabled people crawling on their bellies up the stairs of the Capitol to fight for the Americans with Disabilities Act, I realized that my identity and my life were shaped by this community that I had unknowingly joined in 2011.[5]

After Barnes defines disability by its social movement, she examines an alternative to the philosophical model of disability, called the "bad difference" model. Bad difference arguments are deeply flawed and make assumptions that cannot stand up to deeper investigation. For example, there are many people whose well-being is positively impacted by being disabled. She, instead, proposes a value-neutral approach or a "mere difference" construction of disability. She compares this approach to Sally Haslanger's account of race and gender: that being socially oppressed does not make an identity inherently worse.[6]

In other words, if life is harder for a disabled person, we should consider the possibility that it's not our bodies or minds that are to blame, but the social structures that we navigate with those bodies and minds. If life is harder for a disabled person, we must subtract the difficulties that emerge from socially mediated obstacles.

Many scholars, including Barnes, draw a comparison to queer people. Life is often difficult if you are a queer person in a culture that discriminates against and holds biases toward queer people. But very few people would argue that being queer is the thing that's "wrong"—it's the social oppression. Disability is the same. According to Barnes, disability is a way of having a minority body, not—despite what traditional society has told us for centuries—a moral failing or a fall from grace.

The analogy to queerness crystalized something for me, and I started to read other poets and scholars who had made similar parallels. In Eli Clare's poetic reflections on queer and crip theory, I discovered that disabled art offers a resonant wholeness and connection.[7] Clare, who is disabled and trans, was the first disability scholar to write about the "bodymind," and pushed against the common Western separation between the two. Even more resonant to me were his descriptions of what it feels like to be oppressed as a queer and disabled person. While I am in a relationship with a cis man, I identify as queer and was finally coming into my disabled identity during this course. Part of that homecoming came when I read my lived experiences in Clare's words.[8]

Through Alison Kafer's *Feminist, Queer, Crip*, I considered compulsory heterosexuality and, by extension, what she calls "compulsory able-bodiness and able-mindedness."[9] Kafer rejects the assumption that queerness and disability are deviations from some normal way of being a person but are, instead, groups advocating for a more just world. Through this lens, she considers environmental justice, reproductive justice, and transgender rights. Critically, she advocates for alliances between feminist, queer, and disabled advocates.

Reading her work, I realized that I had been deeply wrong in my assumption that there were ideal bodies and "others"—bodies that strayed from the ideal. I had thought that a cure was the goal and that being disabled was, by definition, worse than not. I was able to see that both queerness and disability are both based on normative assumptions and not based on objective truth.

What a feeling to have my mind change, to have my shame begin to fall away. To consider that on that hike in 2011, I had not transitioned from a good body to one that many would prefer not to exist, but to one that put me in alliance with powerful and brilliant thinkers and activists.

Dr. Barnes's third defense of her argument that disability must not be assumed to be a "bad difference" is the simple reason that most disabled people don't think it is. She argues for the testimonial integrity of disabled first-person accounts. Disability isn't worse if the people who are disabled don't see it that way. *Oh*, I thought, again, *I don't have to be ashamed.* A revelation.

In her book's final chapter, Dr. Barnes describes the importance of disability pride as a counterbalance to widespread assumptions and discrimination. Pride. This was also the first time that I considered that I had the right to feel proud of who I was. As a disabled person, I was developing new skills and perspectives that I might value. I felt newly honored to be grouped with the other disabled people with whom I was now affiliated.

As I've learned more about disability pride, I've witnessed how complicated it is. For many whose bodies endure a great deal of pain or who are unable to access adequate medical care, the concept of pride can feel like a blow. There are others who see a focus on pride as a distraction from the profound injustices that disabled people experience. They see pride as papering over structural cruelty and preventable poverty.[10] The criticisms are valid, of course, but to have pride be an option for me was expansive.

It was that semester, starting with Dr. Barnes's dense philosophy textbook, that I began to change how I thought about myself. That my body ceased to be a collection of limitations and pain, and my value was no longer a function of specific capacities. Deep in the academic jargon of analytic philosophy, I started to believe in magic.

In first-person narratives of others who had, in their twenties, become mysteriously ill, I felt less alone. Recognizing my story in the stories of Julie Rehmeyer, Meghan O'Rourke, Laura Hillenbrand, and Nasim Marie Jafry, I stopped blaming myself for becoming sick.[11] Sometimes, bodies change.

Reading Nancy Eiesland's explorations in *Disabled God*, I reconsidered my waning spirituality.[12] In Maya Dusenbery's *Doing Harm*, I realized that my own trouble with finding a diagnosis was not because I failed to advocate correctly but because I was part of a larger system in which female-presenting patients are ignored, and our problems minimized.[13]

Anyone who studies disability is confronted with the task of defining it. For the sake of this book, based on all that I learned that semester and since, I will define disability as having a body or mind that benefits from the disability justice movement. (Though I could immediately argue with myself and say that every person benefits from disability justice and that no one is free until we all are free and that every body and mind needs justice.) But, still, if you benefit from accommodations, from adaptive equipment, from more equitable employment and healthcare, from access, then, for the sake of this book, you are disabled. Or, at least, you have the right to claim it. The literal structures (houses, buildings, cars) and figurative structures (long work hours, extreme capitalism, inadequate sleep, isolation) in our world actually work for very few.

For so long, the term "disabled" has been used as an insult. In response, schools started to call their students "different" and "special." Well-meaning but misinformed advocates assured people, "You aren't disabled—you are handi-capable!" We call accessibility requirements "special needs." But it's not the term "disabled" that needed to change; it's that we have accepted the false and dangerous belief that there is a good way to have a body-mind and a bad way. Our needs aren't special, they are human.

Disability, like gender, race, and sexuality, is tricky to define because the reality is that all are based on social constructs. You can seek to define any of those identities, but all crumble when interrogated. Why is a dress feminine? What percentage of what ancestry makes someone Black? What version of capacity qualifies as disabled?

When "disabled" is used as an insult, people are eager to distance themselves from the label. But, as I learned, being disabled is not inherently worse than not being disabled. In fact, through *Unfit Parent*, I hope to explain that, when it comes to families, disability is a gift. In some ways, my book is an exploration of "disability gain." This term, coined by Rosemarie Garland-Thomson in reference to the benefits of being disabled, invites disabled and nondisabled people to consider that there is value in having a body that deviates from the norm.[14]

A central benefit of disability is that it forces a reckoning with our collective fragility and mortality. Disability teaches and reminds us that all bodies need. In fact, becoming a parent is making the decision to love the neediest version of a person. Follow this reasoning far enough, and one is forced to consider that it is not clear when and where disability ends. If all bodies need, where does a person cross over to pathologically needy?

So, if you're reading this book and hear yourself in the stories of disabled parents and start to wonder if maybe your ADHD or hearing impairment or joint pain or chronic migraines may be a disability, then welcome. We are happy to have you. If I celebrate mutual aid and crip time and reject corrosive perfectionism, and you feel something stir inside you, then *Unfit Parent* is for you.

If recovering from labor was more grueling than you expected and you felt your sanity ripple at 3 a.m. as your baby cried and thought that you are not made for this, disabled parenting welcomes you. If you feel so frazzled that you think you might leave your baby in a hot car, or you stare into your phone for hours after bedtime because it is the only time you can be alone and numb, disabled parenting has something for you. If you always feel like you are doing this wrong and think there must be some solution that you just haven't found or don't have the discipline to implement, we welcome you.

Chapter 2

WE, PARENTS

As I write this book, parents are exhausted. Most of my friends who are parents are not disabled, and, without exception, they are all barely hanging on. Early in the COVID pandemic, in opposite-gender couples, the burden of family illness management and homeschooling fell on the shoulders of women. We left our jobs in record numbers—decades of feminist professional progress halted and even reversed. Eighty-eight percent of the people who lost their jobs during the pandemic were women.[1] We haven't recovered.

One dear friend, after months of crying most days and losing her temper at work, confessed to her therapist that she was completely empty, emotionally and physically. Her children had spent the autumn home sick more days than they were at school, but she was still trying to work full-time as a professor and department head. Seeing no feasible, practical solutions, her therapist suggested increasing her dose of antidepressants.

Another friend, desperate for just one moment to breathe, has started telling her family she is showering, but instead, she puts her phone in a plastic bag, turns on Netflix, and sits on the floor while the water pounds against her back. Another, who works in a NICU, attends nursing school and is the parent of two young kids (arguably, three full-time gigs) and worries constantly that her kids will feel unloved because she is always so distracted. Every time one of her children struggles, she sees it as an indication that she has failed them. She must work long hours to support her family financially, but she aches to be with them, and to be present.

Before I start exploring the facets of being a disabled parent, in chapter 3, I want to spend some time considering the state of parenting for all of us. When I offer disability culture as a solution, it's important to have a shared understanding of the problem. Every parent I know feels like they are one minor logistical hiccup away from a breakdown. How did we get here? Why does parenting feel like an impossible feat that threatens to destroy any person who takes it on?

Katherine Goldstein, a Harvard fellow and journalist and founder of the Double Shift community for working mothers, doesn't know that she was present for a pivotal moment in both my career and my life as a disabled parent. In 2019, my family lived in Durham, North Carolina, on a yearlong layover between California and Canada. I grew up in North Carolina; Durham feels like home.

A friend mentioned that a podcast host she admired was speaking at a concert venue near my apartment, and a group of us, all mothers, decided to attend. On stage, Katherine, the parent of three boys, lamented the state of motherhood in the US—the inadequate social safety nets and the persistently unequal division of labor in two-parent opposite-gender families. The audience of (mostly) mothers murmured in agreement and, at times, cheered.

She recounted stories of what it is like to work and have young kids. and how it is, frankly, impossible to carry all we are handed. I was in the back row, my large wheelchair partially reclined, watching others in the crowd nudge each other with recognition. Something about how my body contrasted with the other bodies in the room made me feel like an interloper—like I was pretending to be a mother and pretending to recognize the struggles of these other women.

None of the examples she gave—pacing around the room with a crying baby or spending hours driving around the city to activities—fit my lived reality. I kept reminding myself that I really *was* a mother; I deserved to be there. After the event, a group of us returned to my apartment for wine and snacks. I stepped away to use the bathroom, and when I looked at myself in the mirror, I saw a fraud.

For weeks, the word "imposter" echoed in my head. Eventually, I wrote an essay exploring why I, despite parenting K from the time she was eight days old, felt that, because of my disability, I was only impersonating a mother.

I was new to writing, and the world of publishing was completely unfamiliar. One afternoon, I googled "how to submit essays to news outlets." A friend directed me to the "binders" Facebook groups where women, femmes, and nonbinary people share writing advice. I joined, tracked down email addresses for the *New York Times* and the *Washington Post*, and sent the essay to both.

To my surprise, an editor from the *Washington Post* responded and said she'd like to work with me on an essay. After a couple rounds of edits, the piece came out on September 4, 2019. A few months later, the inimitable disability activist Alice Wong emailed, asking if she could include the essay in her anthology *Disability Visibility*. I now realize how rare it is to be given a platform that quickly.[2] I attribute the early interest in my essays to a few things, but significant among them is that disabled parents are desperate for a voice in conversations about parenting and responded enthusiastically.

In the years since that first essay came out, I have been contacted by thousands of disabled parents, people who, because they never saw themselves reflected in parenting conversations, books, and podcasts, felt like they should hide. Emails come in from parents who have battled the social welfare system due to discriminatory medical professionals and others who had to go against medical advice to have kids—not because it was dangerous, but because doctors warned against creating more disabled people.

Disabled parents are everywhere—we make up at least 10 percent of parents—and we have been waiting to be included in mainstream conversations.[3] While few of the anecdotes at that event in 2019 reflected my lived reality, I acknowledged and then started to push against that feeling of alienation that disabled parenting brings. Maybe I am an imposter, I thought, but at least I'm going to talk about it. Maybe my view from the outside was important.

While writing this book, I reached out to Katherine, and we spoke on the phone. I knew that I wanted to apply disability culture to parenting culture but wanted an expert to weigh in on just what made parenting so impossible. I knew that just as my mind is tuned to disability culture and disabled parenting, hers stays dialed in to capitalism and caregiving. She swims in those waters, and I wanted to learn what she sees there.

I asked her to describe, from her decades of work, the cornerstones of what makes mothering (her focus) in the US so difficult. She answered without missing a beat: (1) minimal social safety nets; (2) a culture that prioritizes independence; (3) work cultures that do not support caregiving: and (4) gender inequality in the home.

Social safety nets are policy, but they also reflect ideology: a collective understanding that we cannot and are not supposed to tackle life alone. Medicaid, subsidized daycare, parental leave, and public schools all reiterate that one person cannot financially and practically provide all of a family's needs. Unfortunately, in the United States and, increasingly, Canada, the structures that make it possible to have a humane society are patently inadequate.

The US government does not guarantee a single day of paid parental leave.[4] Babies are, quite literally, essential for the continuation of society, and there is no law in place that gives new parents the time needed even to birth a baby and recover without taking a substantial financial hit. In 2019, 20 percent of workers in the private sector had paid time off to care for a new child.[5] The percentage lowers as wages go down.[6] The message is clear: if you have kids, you are on your own.

For many, childcare is cost-prohibitive, and there isn't enough of it. Most moderately affordable daycare options have limited hours and aren't adequate for those who work varied or nontraditional shifts. Also troubling: workers in the US are not guaranteed paid sick leave. Parents are forced to create their own Jenga-tower solution, which perpetually remains one illness or accident away from crumbling.

A dominant culture that prizes independence is both a cause and effect of our flimsy (or nonexistent) social safety nets for parents. As Angela Garbes (Katherine Goldstein's podcasting partner) writes in *Essential Labor*, Black, Indigenous, and other activists, including disabled people, have advocated for collectivism and interdependence for centuries, but the controlling (capitalistic) system still elevates independence above all.[7]

It's easy to see how families, without guaranteed parental leave and affordable childcare, are faced with scarcity, exhaustion, and desperation. To survive, we are forced to turn our attention to our own nuclear family and away from our community. And then, those who flourish are revered and lifted up and those who do not suffer, often silently.

I, and many others, hoped the pandemic would dislodge us from our obsession with individualism and independence. There were certainly glimpses. But then capitalism and profit and business prevailed; the threat of increased taxation trumped spending on public health. Those with means found workarounds. Those in between became too exhausted to do anything but survive. The most vulnerable retreated.

Without adequate social safety nets, people are forced to pursue individual capital and success to keep their families safe. Wealth is the only reliable method of ensuring the medical care and childcare that a family needs. It's a vicious cycle.

Katherine believes that unfriendly employment policies and cultures play a major role in how impossible it can feel to parent in the US. Any parent who has tried to work full-time while being the primary caregiver recognizes this reality in their bones. Pumping in storage closets, inadequate sick days, inflexible working hours. I asked Katherine about the genesis of this culture, and I was fascinated to learn that it was a post–World War II reaction to the presence of women and caregivers in the workforce.[8]

During the war, women, the primary caregivers at the time, joined the workforce out of necessity. When men returned from war, policies and culture made quick work of sending these once essential workers back home. Gender roles became more strict and enforced—employers demoted women who tried to continue working. Public figures lionized the nuclear family and homemaking for women, and their engagement in the workforce in the 1930s and 1940s was seen as a temporary and necessary evil. The "natural order" of things would be restored. Also, at that time, pensions, unions, and relatively better pay made it possible for one person working full-time to comfortably support a family, even in a blue-collar job. Women could stay home if they wanted, and that desire was strongly encouraged.[9]

Workplace inclusion of women, or any primary caregiver, has been a slow and halting process since the 1950s and still has a long way to go. For many families now, one wage earner is completely inadequate economically, but it remains almost impossible for both parents (in two-parent families) to work full-time.

And then there is home life. Despite feminism's powerful progress, domestic life has stayed unsustainably imbalanced in many opposite-gender couples. Entire brilliant books have been written on the subject, like *Fair Play* by Eve Rodsky, but the upshot is that, due to cultural habits and

antiquated policies, women carry more than their share of domestic responsibilities.[10] It starts with inadequate paternity leave: many men return
to work within days of a baby being born. As a result, women become the
experts on their children, and decisions and care fall to them naturally.
Without gender equality in the home, attaining it in the world at large
remains much more difficult. Women spend about twice as much time
each day on household-related tasks.[11]

A friend and I joke about how when you dig into an injustice or problem long enough, eventually you find capitalism at the root—capitalism
all the way down. But our quips are based in reality. We live in a culture
where so much of our collective time and energy is directed at economic
survival—a world in which we are caught in the sticky web of purchases
that masquerade as satisfaction. Where there are a few winners, and most
worry about meeting their basic needs. Where power is allocated based
on the capacity to labor or produce wealth.

In this system, which sucks all but a few into a vortex of flimsy promises,
waste, and poverty, disabled people are, at best, disparaged and, at worst,
collateral damage. (We are not the only ones.) Our bodies and brains are
often less economically productive. Corporations make less money from
our labor. We often require government aid, which is pulled from the taxes
that laboring people pay. We are the weakest links of capitalism.

And then, when we have the audacity to procreate and, even more gall-
ing, to exist in public with our messy bodies and minds, hyper-capitalism
and its henchmen can't help but push back—with family separation and
enforced poverty for disabled people. Our mere existence threatens the
system. The cruelty of it all is that *every* person threatens the system because every person has needs and fluctuating capacities. Parenting often
brings those needs to the surface.

The impossibility of parenting in the United States reaches beyond
policy and history. It digs its roots into the minds and spirits of parents.
Never has a title better reflected the state of parenting in the US than
Jessica Grose's 2022 book, *Screaming on the Inside: The Unsustainability of
American Motherhood.*[12] In her book, Grose examines the history of American motherhood. She considers how the history of modern parenting has
impacted the experience of pregnancy, balancing family and career, and

identity. But at the root of all these topics lie the same themes: shame, loneliness, and total exhaustion.

Parents in America (and, I would argue, Canada) are saddled with impossible expectations and pressures, which aren't new. Grose found Lysol advertisements from the 1930s that shamed mothers for their sick children: "Madam, you are to blame!" It's easy to feel that the health and well-being of our children is entirely up to us. We assume that, through the purity of our love and the diligence of our care, we should be able to prevent any harm from befalling our children. We carry this pressure from the very beginning of parenthood, from the first division of a zygote's cells.

For people who become pregnant, the fear of infertility and miscarriage looms large, and not just because of how devastating it can be to want a child and not have one but also because gestational parents are made to feel that being unable to carry a baby to term is a personal failing. Again, this isn't new. Pregnant people have been held responsible for the fate of their fetuses for centuries. The proposed explanations for miscarriages have changed over time but have consistently placed the blame on the shoulders of the pregnant person.

In 1939, influential—and deluded—psychiatrist brothers Karl and William Menninger came up with theories to explain unpleasant and dangerous pregnancy experiences: "despising one's femaleness" led to nausea, and "ambitious businesswomen" were more likely to die from pregnancy. The Menningers' peers blamed parents for miscarriages, which were caused by "bad marriages" and "weak fathers." Their troubling theories didn't confine themselves to books—during that time, psychiatrists served on "eugenics boards," which helped determine which people should be sterilized. While these attitudes and the subsequent sterilization may sound horrifying eighty years later, I think any person who has experienced infertility or pregnancy loss would attest that the sentiments remain familiar; if you experience a loss, you did something to cause it.[13]

The act of giving birth is also impossible. As Rachel Somerstein writes in her 2024 book, *Invisible Labor: The Untold Story of the Cesarean Section*, pregnant people are encouraged and often forced to relinquish bodily autonomy and reject their instincts in favor of poorly researched, fad-driven, and financially motivated birthing experiences.[14] Somerstein expertly deconstructs the overuse of C-sections in most US hospitals and explains just how often C-sections turn traumatic and painful for birthing people.

That said, as Somerstein clarifies, the solution to too many C-sections doesn't lie on the other end of the birthing spectrum (at home, unmedicated, in your bathroom, with candles lit); after all, most spectrums are actually loops. The idealization of an "all-natural mama" can be as detrimental as a dependence on the overmedicalized C-section experience. The truth is, every person, baby, and parent has different needs. And each deserves to understand their options, the associated risks, and to have their wishes honored throughout the birthing experience.

If you are a parent and feel like it's impossible to carry all you've been handed, it's because it is. Parenting, in this profit-driven facsimile of community, will break even the most durable person. It doesn't feel hard because you are weak; it feels hard because it's impossible.

From the earliest days of reproductive care to the herculean task of paying for higher education, parents are facing an uphill climb. The lies of consumerism tells us that if we purchase more and perform better, this would be easier, and we would all be happier. We are tired because childcare isn't affordable, healthcare isn't universal, education is underfunded, and parental leave is inconsistent at best. Relying on the systems that brought us here for solutions will only tighten their destructive hold on us. Instead, I believe, we should look to those whom these systems reject.

Chapter 3

DECIDING TO PARENT

I was thirty-one and newly diagnosed with Postural Orthostatic Tachycardia Syndrome when my new ob-gyn mentioned my T-shaped uterus. A few weeks prior, after months of severe pelvic pain, he had ordered a transvaginal ultrasound. It wasn't the first time an ultrasound technician had inserted a large wand into my vagina. In college, the right side of my abdomen had grown swollen; I hunched over at work waiting tables, curled in with pain. At that time, an emergency room doctor found a grapefruit-sized cyst but didn't mention the shape of my uterus. Ten years later, I was back at my doctor's office to discuss the most recent results and to undergo a pelvic exam.

Before we talked, he performed the Pap smear. It was painful, as always, and after he left the room, I wiped away the blood that the speculum drew. He returned after I was dressed, my vagina aching, gel still caked on my thighs. He mentioned that the amount of free fluid in my pelvis indicated a recently ruptured cyst. "That explains the pain," he said. And then, as an afterthought, "That T-shaped uterus sure isn't compatible with pregnancy."[1]

I was not in a relationship and, at that point, not all that interested in having children. Plus, the way he said it gave the impression that he had not, in fact, shared important information. I always assumed that when I found out something life-changing, the moment would be obvious.

That evening, as I drank wine with my friend Jenna, a physician's assistant, I talked about the appointment. She knew about my pelvic pain. Her eyes became glassy when I mentioned the shape of my uterus, and a few days later, a card arrived in my mailbox. She was thinking about me and was so sorry to hear the news about my fertility. It was when I read her card that I realized that I had received news about my fertility.

The realization that pregnancy might be impossible for me didn't have a large impact until a few years later, when I was in my thirties and in a serious relationship with Christopher. Together, we started to plan our future. During those years, I had been diagnosed with Ehlers-Danlos syndrome, and with hard-fought explanations for my pain and fluctuating health, I had begun to imagine the rest of my life. Both Christopher and I wanted kids. But, unlike Christopher, I didn't feel a strong attachment to pregnancy or to children to whom I was genetically linked. I loved Christopher, though, and worried that if I couldn't become pregnant and carry a baby to term, our relationship might not survive. I asked my primary care doctor for advice, and she referred me to a high-risk ob-gyn.

The office was above a Chipotle and a UPS Store, less than five minutes from the tiny and slanted house that Christopher and I shared. I went to the appointment alone. The ob-gyn had reviewed my medical records before the appointment. As she entered the room, she handed me a thick folder of medical journal articles, printed and stapled. She was kind and forthright and said that if I decided to pursue pregnancy, she could help me, but that, in my case, it would be quite dangerous. After listing the potential complications, she predicted what would result from my genetic condition and my specific physiology. My fragile vaginal skin, which tore during Pap smears, foretold how my organs could respond to pregnancy. It was statistically improbable that both the baby and I would come out alive.

I worried more about Christopher's reaction than my own. I still didn't feel that strong internal pull toward pregnancy. I craved parenting but felt no less excited about adoption. (It would be years before I learned the complicated and often unjust reality of adoption and the fraught relationship between disabled people and the child welfare system.)

At that point in my life, I spent an hour or more reading poetry and journaling in the mornings. My changed body and new diagnoses required significant adjustment, and I had the space in my days to spend time resting and reflecting. During those quiet mornings, I stayed open to a latent pregnancy desire. Curled up with my notebooks, I searched for a kernel inside that craved pregnancy and couldn't find it. I only found peace. If pregnancy was safe, then, sure, it sounded nice. Since it wasn't, I could let it go.

Christopher did not feel the same way. When I told him about the doctor's visit, he was visibly disappointed, and that disappointment didn't fade. It would be one of the main factors in our breakup a year later.

Single, again, I considered what I wanted for my future family and found that my desire to be a foster parent was growing. I fell asleep thinking about the kids who needed consistency and safety and knew that I could provide that. I felt impatient and certain. My body had needs and limitations, sure, but I never doubted that I could find a way to parent well. I understood, finally, the need that many friends had felt to become pregnant. The specifics of our desires differed, but the thoughts and sensations were the same—we were made for this, our brains echo. Our lives are missing a critical piece without it.

When my now-husband David and I started dating and our relationship grew serious, we discussed kids. I told him I felt a pull in my chest toward foster parenting that I could not ignore. I looked at our second bedroom, and it felt undeniable that we should make our lives and our home available to children who needed a home. In many circumstances, including this one, David is ruled by pragmatism and thoughtfulness. His chest didn't ache for foster parenting, but he understood my points and respected my passion, and so, after only nine months of dating, we signed up for foster parenting classes.

I use a wheelchair for a few reasons, the primary of which is my fluctuating blood pressure. When I stand, walk, or sit upright, my blood pressure drops, bringing on light-headedness and a loss of consciousness. Early in the morning, before my medication, water, and salt have kicked in, I can hardly walk at all. In the evenings, I can sometimes walk for up to five minutes. Standing still is harder, and I must sit after thirty seconds. When in a chair, I do all I can to imitate lying flat—elevating my feet and reclining my torso. The farther I am from horizontal, the quicker I become clammy, and my vision tunnels.

When we started the process of becoming foster parents, I had an old manual wheelchair in my trunk that I was unable to propel on my own. If I wanted to do anything that required more than a couple of minutes of walking, I had to bring someone who could push me in my wheelchair. I didn't love being pushed. I missed autonomy, and it was hard to carry on conversations with someone behind me. I avoided situations that involved long, or even moderate, distances.

We lived in Oakland, California, and the first fostering step was to attend an orientation at a county building downtown. We parked near the door. I walked inside, forgoing my wheelchair. In the bright lobby, I sat on the floor while David arranged chairs so that I could recline and elevate my feet. Five years after becoming disabled, I had grown accustomed to sidelong glances and quips about "making myself at home." I looked around the room and was struck by the demographic cross-section represented: Black couples and queer couples and a range of socioeconomic presentations. I couldn't spot another disabled person, although my own disability wasn't apparent.

Two people gave the presentation, and the content was scattered. It was in part a warning (*fostering is HARD*) and in part a procedural overview, but it wasn't all that effective at either. David scribbled notes and asked questions: "Can you explain the difference between a licensing worker and a welfare worker?" Instead of answering, the presenters seemed to just pick an adjacent topic and meander there. David's notepad was full of question marks, crossed-out words, and flow charts that went nowhere.

Less than an hour in, I needed a break from the fluorescent lights and the municipal chairs and went to the bathroom, where, as I often did, I lay on the floor. When we left about ninety minutes after we arrived, we had a stack of paperwork, an application packet, and more questions than when we entered the room. I was undeterred.

Since that day, I have uncovered a great deal more about the foster system, including the specific ways that it harms disabled people, which I describe in the chapter on child protective services. I've also learned more about the demographic makeup of the children placed into foster care and the makeup of those who become foster parents. Black kids are overrepresented in the system—22 percent of children in foster care are Black, but only 13 percent of children in the US are.[2]

The race and ethnicity of foster parents are not tracked as consistently as that of foster children, but we do know that between 2017 and 2019, 28 percent of all adoptions in the US were transracial and, of those, 90 percent of the parents were white.[3] Transracial adoption—in which the race or ethnicity of the adoptive family does not match that of the child—is common but has vocal critics. In fact, in 1972, the National Association of Black Social Workers published a position statement calling for an end to transracial adoption.[4]

On the other hand, the motivations of foster parents have been well studied. Researchers across the US interviewed single foster parents in 2021 and found that they became foster parents because of their personal beliefs, connection to the foster system, other personal experiences, and family-building goals.[5] A 2006 study of Canadian foster parents found that they were motivated to be foster parents by a desire to give back and to grow their family, as well as, in small part, by financial reimbursement.[6] While I am sure that there are some people motivated by the monthly payments that foster parents receive (usually $600–$1,000), I observed that most foster parents spend far more on their foster children than the monthly stipend.

In my experience, many foster parents prefer to take care of babies, particularly the parents who are fostering in order to expand their families. Anecdotally, social workers told me that it's much harder to find a home for anyone older than a toddler, which is unfortunate because the average age of a child in foster care is eight.[7] During the licensing process, the people we met had one or more of the following characteristics. One, they had tried to become pregnant and, facing infertility, were exploring other options. Two, they were part of a religious community and felt a moral obligation to "care for orphans." (Worth noting that foster children are not usually orphans.) Three, they had personal experience in foster care and wanted to provide home and care for children like themselves.

Regardless of one's motivation, the application and licensing process is complex. David and I took it on as we do most things—with a shared spreadsheet. The application involved recommendations from friends, background checks, detailed financial reporting, and short essays. I plodded through each step but avoided one page: the doctor's note. We both needed a doctor to attest to our capacity to parent. David is mostly blind in one eye, but his other eye compensates well, and his doctor didn't hesitate to vouch for David's capacities.

On the other hand, I had been seeing my doctor for years, and he knew the depth and breadth of my health concerns. He knew I was usually too sick to prepare my own food and could rarely drive. He knew I couldn't make it through my visits with him sitting up and that a simple cold could knock me out for weeks. He was kind and attentive and respected my perspective regarding my care, but I worried that he would only view my capacity to parent through the lens of my symptoms and complications. I continued to put off the conversation.

At that time, before COVID introduced widespread virtual (accessible) options, prospective foster parents attended four, six-hour days of what most foster systems call PRIDE training (which stands for Parent Resources for Information, Development, and Education). PRIDE was established in the 1990s as a method of ensuring foster and adoptive parents had a baseline level of education and skill.[8]

For my disabled body, the PRIDE course had a few obstacles. One, sitting upright for six hours in one day is impossible for me, and, two, many buildings in Oakland are not air conditioned. I cannot effectively regulate my temperature. In rooms over 73 degrees, I quickly develop heat exhaustion, which presents as nausea, confusion, clamminess, and vomiting.

We signed up anyway, and my access solution was to "figure it out"— an approach that David, a look-before-you-leap-er, will always find aggravating. We packed an entire duffle of snacks and drinks to help sustain me and arrived early at the church where the training was held. I rested on a hallway sofa while David surveyed the available seating. He walked from room to room in the long fellowship building and eventually tracked down some large, cushioned seats. He set two in the cramped room where prospective foster parents would meet. The chairs faced each other, making a version of a shortened bed on which I could, in theory, arrange my body to a position as close to horizontal as possible.

We huddled together and whispered as the instructors arrived, plotting how to subtly open doors and windows to increase airflow and keep the room as cool as possible. I was balancing my physical requirements with the need to appear competent. I didn't want the instructors to think I was too weak to parent. I started the class self-conscious that I had already arranged new chairs and positioned a tiny fan in front of me, next to a small thermometer to monitor the ambient temperature.

The class met from 9 a.m. to 3 p.m., and on the first day, I stayed for the duration. The room stayed cool (enough), and my chairs were suitable.

I left exhausted and in wrenching pain. Any time I'm forced to sit in a new chair without the cushions I need to support my back and hip, I have pain and injuries for days after. Suffering aside, I had done it. Eighteen hours to go. The material we covered was a longer version of the orientation—chaotic and inefficient. Were I not dizzy and in pain, I might have been more able to go along with the disorganization and contradictory information. As it was, I saw every peculiar worksheet and meaningless acronym as a hurdle between me and comfort. I wanted so badly to learn more about fostering but felt like I was stuck, instead, in a DMV.

As we walked from the parking lot on the second day, I noted it was already warmer outside. My stomach dropped. We, again, arranged the makeshift recliner, positioned my fan, and set a cooling towel next to me. By 10 a.m., my thermometer said 71.5 degrees. I knew 3 p.m. would be impossible. My thermoregulation difficulties are made trickier by the fact that I cannot always *feel* that I am warm. I often become ill before I've noticed that I am too hot. Giving up on staying for the full six hours, I decided to try to leave at noon. The thermometer hit 73 at 11:30, and David held a cool drink on my neck. Finally, we took a break for lunch, and I walked directly to the car, where we pointed all the vents on me to lower my core temperature.

David went inside and explained to the instructors that I had to leave because I could not tolerate warm temperatures. As we had feared, they said that if I could not attend all twenty-four hours, I could not be a foster parent. They also mentioned that not being able to make it through the classes was a decent litmus test for parenting capacities.

It's reasonable to wonder if the difficulty in getting my license may have dissuaded me from trying to be a foster parent. To ask if being unable to even sit through a class would be a good sign that I was poorly equipped for the arduous task of caring for children.

It didn't. It wasn't.

I had been sick for five years when we started those classes. I didn't yet identify as disabled, but the creativity and ingenuity of living in a disabled body were already a part of me. In the years between losing my ability to sit, stand, or walk and starting fostering classes, I had moved to France, left an unhealthy marriage, moved to California alone, started graduate school, and formed a robust and caring group of friends. Every decision had moments that seemed impossible, but I was starting to trust my ability to surmount obstacles one step at a time. I knew, at my core, that parenting would be the same. I would love the kids we parented, and I would keep them safe. I never doubted it.

Confidence aside, I still needed to get my twenty-four hours. Even if the final two days were cool enough, I wouldn't graduate without the missing three hours from day 2. We looked at future sessions of PRIDE and found one in the winter that met at a community college. I called the campus and confirmed that the room where it was held had air conditioning in case of an unseasonably warm day. We asked about the chair options.

While we waited for our next class, we pulled out the list of safety requirements for our home. Our two-bed one-bath ranch was perched on the side of a hill, and we needed a way to ensure that kids could not go on the deck without supervision. We also needed to secure the door to the basement and block all windows. Our next-door neighbors came over, and we brainstormed solutions together. For two consecutive weekends, David, Laura, and Andy installed locks, fortified railings with plywood, and built a crib. I threw away my (medical) marijuana.

The final step of the application still haunted me. The doctor's note. When the rest of the application was complete, and we had signed up for the last of the twenty-four hours of training, I made an appointment. I went alone—an attempt to present myself as autonomous and capable.

My stomach roiled with anxiety. My cheerful demeanor and can-do attitude were less convincing for someone who had seen my entire medical record. Dr. Stern came into our appointment, and I forced myself to sit upright in a chair instead of reclining on the exam table. "So, you want to be a foster parent?" he asked. I spoke slowly and confidently. I had practiced not being defensive. "I do," I said. "I have thought a lot about it."

"As you know, you will encounter obstacles that other parents won't," he replied. "How do you plan to approach those?" I was ready. I explained that the money we had saved for childcare, David's work schedule, and parental leave options. I talked about ready-made meal services and our robust community. He thought for a few seconds, and I held my breath.

"It sounds like a child would be lucky to have you as their mom," he declared.

I wept.

Two months later, we finished our PRIDE classes, and a social worker scheduled a visit to inspect our house. He approved us within fifteen minutes. All that was left was waiting for the phone to ring. We knew that at any moment, a social worker would call about a child that needed a temporary home.

All disabled parents share certain experiences: external skepticism about our capacity and internalized shame about our identity. That said, becoming a parent was easier for me than it is for many disabled people. In fact, many facets of my experience as a disabled person are easier. Among other unearned privileges, I can present, for short periods of time, as nondisabled, and I have the means to pay for help. My choices were less fraught because I never had the deep desire to be a gestational parent. If I had, I likely would have encountered additional hurdles in receiving adequate medical care, which I will discuss in more detail in chapter 7.

For many disabled people, the decision to carry a baby is thorny. In her late twenties, Jessie Owen was in a car accident with her family.[9] Her parents died, and she broke her neck between two cervical vertebrae. She is quadriplegic, and she needs assistance with activities that require strength and fine motor movement.

In 2018, Jessie met Alan on Bumble. Jessie is white and was born in the US; Alan is Taiwanese American. Early in their conversations, they talked about kids, but neither was sure if they wanted to be parents. Years later, after traveling and getting engaged, they had the conversation again in earnest and realized they both wanted kids. They felt overwhelmed with their love for each other and saw kids as an extension of that—another adventure.

Two months after getting married, they found out that Jessie was pregnant with twins. They were shocked, initially, but then their primary reaction was excitement. Jessie says Alan is stable, kind, funny, and emotionally mature. Their relationship makes her feel safe and like she isn't a burden to him. Any concern about her pregnancy and parenting came from outside their relationship. Loved ones asked lots of questions about the practical function of their family. How much help would they have? What would Alan do? Would her mother-in-law move in?

Jessie heard the subtext: *How will you take care of babies when you need help taking care of yourself?* She didn't entertain the skepticism and answered, every time, "We are thrilled. We will figure it out as a family. We do lots of hard things, and this is the best one yet."

Even doctors with disabilities (as rare as they are) are not immune from parenting and fertility discrimination. Dr. Paige Church, from Vermont, is a neonatologist and developmental-behavioral pediatrician. In 2017, at age forty-five, she wrote an editorial for the *Journal of the American Medical Association* (JAMA) *Pediatrics* in which, in her words, she "came out" as having spina bifida.[10] In her piece, she describes the complications of her diagnosis and the daily exercises and medical interventions that her condition requires. She also examines the medical system's approach to disability and pregnancy counseling with a critical eye. While in medical school and residency, she had covered up her condition, arriving to her shifts early and working extra hard to guard against any negative judgment when she needed to take time away.

In her thirties, Dr. Church considered becoming pregnant, but ultimately decided that the probable complications that pregnancy would bring were not desirable for her. She stresses that every person with spina bifida makes a different calculation. Like me, she didn't have a strong internal drive to carry a child and felt equally drawn to adoption. Dr. Church's adoption agency expressed concern about her disability, and she was asked to have a doctor write a letter stating that she was "fit to parent," just as I had to. Her neurosurgeon wrote the letter. For Dr. Church, seeing her right to parent hinge on one person's opinion crystallized the impossible challenges disabled parents must face. She felt an even deeper commitment to advocate for other disabled parents. Still, she kept her own diagnosis hidden at work.

Later, in her forties, Dr. Church found herself consulting with a pregnant patient whose fetus was diagnosed with the same form of spina bifida that Dr. Church has. The patient had been told by other providers that the baby would have profound limitations that would negatively impact quality of life. Dr. Church bristled at hearing her own condition described in this way and decided to reveal her own diagnosis. The patient did decide to terminate her pregnancy, but the emotional fallout of that experience instigated a shift in how Dr. Church's diagnosis intersects with her profession, which I explore more in chapter 9. She finds that this advocacy is not without tremendous pushback because of a deeply entrenched mindset within the medical system—the number of limitations a person has is directly correlated with reduced quality of life. According to Dr. Church, for doctors, "death and disability are considered conjoined outcomes."

Because of the widespread assumption that a disabled life is inherently harder and not worth living, some disabled people worry about becoming pregnant, because they will have a baby that shares their condition. Society can cause us to absorb the belief that our lives are less valuable, and that it's cruel to subject another to the same fate.

Hope B. is one person who internalized that lesson.[11] When she is in the midst of a hard health season, Hope faints weekly. Like me, she has Ehlers-Danlos syndrome (EDS) and dysautonomia. Until 2020, she worked as an assistant manager at a daycare in Texas. While working there, she knew she wanted to be a parent but assumed she would adopt. She was terrified of passing along Ehlers-Danlos syndrome, which, according to some studies, her biological children would have a 50 percent chance of inheriting.[12]

For years, she agonized over her precarious health and worried that she might one day become "more disabled." She never escaped that dread and didn't want to subject her children to the same uncertain fate. Her fears about her own body were realized in 2020 when she caught COVID and developed long COVID. When we spoke in late 2022, she still hadn't fully recovered, and she was no longer able to work. She is now mostly housebound and subsists on federal disability payments.

After her capacities shifted in 2020, she was surprised to realize that, following a period of adjustment, she is still happy in her life and inside her healthy and loving marriage. Just as I discovered in my own life, Hope learned that many of us underestimate the joy that's possible in a disabled body. She now lives the life she had dreaded for so long, but instead of feeling depressed, she experiences deep purpose and satisfaction. She says that her future children could also have full and beautiful lives if they inherit her genetic condition. She no longer fears passing on a body like hers. Hope and her husband wish to be pregnant within the year.

Hope does not know how her body will handle pregnancy. She has relied on patient support groups, the limited medical research, and her doctor, who, when she expressed her concerns, assured her that they would "figure it out." She trusts herself to take it one step at a time.

Disabled people who do pursue pregnancy do so following decades of medical trauma. We are accustomed to a system that does not know how to handle us and to care providers who fail to listen. We have, regularly, been disbelieved and ignored. Some nondisabled people receive more medical care while pregnant than they have up until that point. Disabled people, on the other hand, are accustomed to the pitfalls and shortcomings of the medical systems in the US and Canada. Some disabled people, like me, determine that our desire to carry a child is not enough to override our bodies' physiology and the medical system's paltry disability resources. For us, the risk of pregnancy is not worth taking.

Even for nondisabled people, becoming pregnant and staying pregnant can be arduous and traumatic. Furthermore, pregnancy care in the United States (which I discuss more in chapter 7) is unnecessarily risky and dehumanizing.

The trauma of pregnancy and loss can be magnified by our own shame. For those who have not had to confront the fragility of our bodies, complications often feel like a personal indictment.

In 2015, when Jourdan F. was thirty-one, she and her husband, Andrew, a medical resident, decided to start a family.[13] Jourdan, who is white, cisgender, straight, financially secure, and not disabled, was accustomed to a body that followed instructions. In fact, until 2015, she felt that she *was* her body. Through early adulthood, Jourdan was a ballet dancer and had always felt comfortable in her skin. She is thin and experiences the advantages that come with meeting society's narrow conventional beauty standards. Without a history of chronic illness or mental health diagnoses, she had no reason to doubt that discipline and intention would bring results. And, if she encountered obstacles, doctors, like her husband, were there to help.

Within a few months of trying, Jourdan became pregnant. During the first trimester, when she went for a heartbeat scan at her ob-gyn's large and busy practice, the technician found something concerning. He mentioned that he thought she might lose the pregnancy and then, without further explanation, exited the room. Jourdan was left alone on the table, gel on her abdomen, for two full hours. It was during those 120 minutes that the illusion of control and predictability of her body began to change and her faith in the medical system started to falter.

The technician finally returned, and because the embryo still had a heartbeat, they said they would monitor it, but she should understand that the rate of cell growth was not promising. Jourdan returned a few days later, and they confirmed that her pregnancy was not viable but that she was not yet eligible for a dilation and curettage (D&C), which would terminate the pregnancy. Jourdan and Andrew left Chicago a few days later for a residency rotation out of town; she had to seek follow-up care at an unfamiliar clinic.

While away from home, she visited this new clinic every few days until, finally, they declared that she could undergo the D&C. Her miscarriage had, at this point, lasted for many weeks. She was devastated, and, without adequate information from medical providers, she felt convinced that she had somehow caused her pregnancy to end. At that point, she didn't know anyone who had experienced a miscarriage, and the only reasonable explanation for the aberration was some failure or shortcoming on her part. In Jourdan's mind, bodies, especially her own, were predictable and controllable.

Jourdan and Andrew tried again to get pregnant, which took longer than she expected. She had turned thirty-two and felt like a different person than she had one year earlier. She spent hours online researching fertility. Now, all the ways that a body can fail crowded out any other information in her mind. For so long, she had no idea that her body was fragile. And now it was all she could know.

She finally became pregnant again, and, this time, she carried her baby Sloane to term. Sloane was born in November 2016, and Jourdan spent the duration of her pregnancy and labor terrified. Where she once believed nothing could go wrong, she now believed everything could. She couldn't stop thinking about how something might happen, and she would fail her baby. It wasn't until she held Sloane in the hospital that she believed Sloane might actually be OK.

When Sloane was a few months old, Jourdan and Andrew started trying again. Jourdan got pregnant, but a few months later, as Jourdan bathed a one-year-old Sloane, she started to bleed. She was having her second miscarriage. She became fully convinced that something in her body was flawed, and she saved the tissue from the miscarriage and brought it to her doctor for investigation. She assumed they would want to understand her losses as much as she did. Instead, they acted as if she "had fourteen heads" when she carried the tissue in.

After she recovered from her second miscarriage, she tried to get pregnant again, which took two demoralizing years. She finally got pregnant again. And then, when she thought she couldn't bear another disappointment, she miscarried again.

In December 2019, when she realized she was pregnant for the fifth time, she barely had the energy to hope. The confusion and loneliness of the past years had whittled away her ability to expect good things to happen. When COVID hit, she felt like the whole world was finally as sad and scared as she was. She now believes that it was privilege and luck that allowed her to stay ignorant of life's pain until her fourth decade, but in 2015, when she started to experience how unpredictable and hard life can be, she had no context for this new reality.

Jourdan gave birth to Dylan in September 2020 and says that when she held Dylan for the first time, she felt joy and relief unlike any she had experienced. Perhaps they will have a third; she is not sure. But she now knows that nothing is promised.

Jourdan is a vivid example of someone insulated from life's pain until pregnancy, which is why I've shared her story here. Though Jourdan's shift was blunt, many pregnant people experience a degree of what Jourdan did: pregnancy is the first time they regularly interact with the medical system and experience the true fragility and unpredictability of their bodies.

Miscarriage is deeply painful. It's a loss that is poorly recognized and often hidden. Pregnancy loss deserves more research and support. I have grieved with friends after they lost babies. And that suffering is often compounded by outside messaging that life is predictable and that we are in control. Losing a baby that you wanted is a tremendous loss, and it can also feel like something has gone off course—that this isn't how this is supposed to go. But, in fact, the truth of our lives is that we will all lose the people we love the most. We will all suffer.

All bodies fail, always. It's what we share. We are all fragile, and as much as we want to shut our eyes to it, we are also mortal. We can do everything right, and things can still go terribly wrong. We don't have the agency we'd like to think we have. The family and era we were born into and the bodies we inhabit dictate an enormous amount.

Life is unpredictable and sometimes miraculous, and the more we try to understand, the more mystery we find. Someone called at just the right time or the wrong time. Someone heard the fall in the bathroom, or didn't. The other car swerved.

Disabled people spend their lives claiming their power and independence while working to accept life's transience. As I discuss in chapter 7, we exist in a society that attempts to strip us of our bodily autonomy, and we will never stop fighting to hold on to what is ours. Meanwhile, our own fragility reminds us that our lives are, at least in large part, dictated by luck and privilege. That we should not feel ashamed of our pain and loss—when we stop blaming ourselves for our suffering, we find that we can carry a bit more.

Years before I decided that I wanted to be a mom and began what is always an unpredictable process, I had been confronted with my inability to control outcomes and comforted by my capacity to withstand the in-between times (that, in fact, make up most of our lives). Those painful years in my twenties fortified me for parenthood.

When my body shifted at twenty-eight—from one that could run, work long hours, and travel internationally to one that must mostly rest—I believed that I would go back to my old life once I solved the puzzle of my body. Until the hike in Greece during which I became disabled, I had the false belief that the life I wanted was a matter of sufficient effort and prudent decision-making. I don't know how I would have defined my worldview then, but I know now that I believed in individualism, hard work, and power over one's destiny.

Sure, I had experienced tragedies as a kid, but, as an adult, I had started a successful company, married the first person I loved, and earned more money in real estate than anyone in their twenties should expect. I attended the college I had dreamed of since middle school and, after graduating, interned at the White House. The life I wanted was a function of setting goals and working for them. Roadblocks were a chance to recalibrate. And then, in the course of one day in 2011, I found myself living in a body that could no longer stand or walk and no one knew why.

I became obsessed with retracing my steps. I played over the long workouts of the year prior and my lack of hydration on the hike. I wondered which singular decision had tipped me into becoming sick. I made detailed spreadsheets with lab results, symptom progression, and treatment options—convinced that diligent effort would bring healing. If I wasn't better, it was because I hadn't yet uncovered the solution.

As I've mentioned, it took two painful years to get my diagnosis of POTS, a form of dysautonomia. I was determined to recover, and so, still holding tight to the illusion of control, I embraced every suggested treatment, including the arduous cardiac rehab program.

It was after that program was unsuccessful that I finally started the process of untangling what I can and cannot control. Ultimate control had been an illusion that I used to help me feel safe, but it had never been real. I can control some things, sometimes, but the function of my body—of any body—is more complicated than I had realized.

Before I became disabled, I thought I knew what an ideal life looked like: a vibrant social life and a certain amount of money, professional success and a sparkling marriage, travel and beauty. I could measure almost all of it quantitatively. I worked harder and longer and became more successful and connected. And I was deeply unhappy. My marriage was corrosive, and I held destructive beliefs about myself. I tried new solutions: therapists and longer runs, and more time volunteering with local nonprofits. And still I carried around a deep sense of rottenness that I could only ignore for minutes at a time.

In 2014, when I realized that I would likely be sick for the rest of my life, I had to come to terms with how much of my body and future will remain a mystery. It would take years to accept my new reality and to live within my physical boundaries, but, once I did, I was surprised to find out that I was experiencing the joy and freedom that I had yearned for during my years of rabid achievement.

I think our attempt to control outcomes is motivated by the assumption that we know what makes a life good and worthy. When we acknowledge our limited ability to orchestrate our future, we soon realize that our ability to design it is also tiny.

Eventually, I began to apply these standards to my body. I cannot change what I did in those months leading up to the hike. I cannot control the structure of my connective tissue. I cannot change how other people react to my body. Starting to let go gave me the space and energy to feel more power over the parts of my life that I can control. Reckoning with the inability to control outcomes does not leave us with hopelessness or apathy. Instead, surprisingly, awe awaits on the other side. We can love with fervor despite the truth of our collective fragility. Hurt still hurts, of course, but pain without shame is bearable.

The sense that doing life "right" would satisfy me and the fear that one misstep could crumble it all had blocked me from looking at myself and the world with a sense of openness and honesty. I still tend to hold on to the flimsy comfort that control offers. The work of my life will be figuring out what is and is not up to me. But, because my disabled body reminds me every minute of every day that life is an unpredictable miracle, my disability pulls me out of my shame.

When David and I decided to become foster parents, I was able to start the process with the sense of openness that disability had brought me. I noticed that the other parents I met in training or in support groups agonized over exactly how long it would take for an adoption to be finalized. The uncertainty and in-between time felt impossible. A naturally anxious person, I was surprised to find that my own level of anxiety was manageable. My friends who were becoming pregnant were often distraught over fertility and timelines. As I experienced when I got sick, people experiencing fertility setbacks have reached the limit of what good decision-making and discipline can do.

Many who miscarry, or don't conceive when they want to, perseverate on what they may have done wrong, just like I did when I became sick. It's this illusion that suffering is always, at least indirectly, because of our mistakes. It can also be a comfort to think that outcomes and decisions are predictable and merit-based. That sense of failure can lead to shame so deep that many people drown there for years. This isn't to say that disability somehow inoculates us against loss and grief, and there are times that internalized ableism compounds our shame. However, disability forges new trails on which we can experience pain without regret.

Grief and loss and disappointment are brutal and often lonely. But, in my experience, it's the worry that I could have done something to change the outcome that becomes quicksand. Time does not heal the wounds we continue to give ourselves.

The acceptance of what we cannot orchestrate can bring a sense of freedom and awe, not of complacency. Disabled people, with our bodies and minds that change and shift unpredictably and our evolving needs, offer wisdom to those who want to be parents. We have had the illusion of control pried from our hands and found ways out of the shame the suffering can bring. In its place, we are left holding heart-shattering awe. This mystery doesn't corrode, it fortifies.

Once we were approved as foster parents, and waiting for a call, I slept with my phone under my pillow, ringer turned up. I was ready and excited and scared. But I also felt peaceful. I didn't know what would happen next, but I knew it was not up to me; I knew I could figure it out.

Chapter 4

THE FIRST WEEK

K loves the story of how we met. Twelve hours before we first saw each other, her social worker called to tell us about a baby in the NICU. My phone rang at 9 p.m. on March 14 and we fell asleep talking about the newborn who needed a place to stay temporarily. In the morning, David went to work, and I went to the hospital to meet K.

I was able to find parking on Fifty-Second Street, right outside the entrance to the dated concrete Children's Hospital in Oakland. I was alone and, at that point, only had a heavy manual wheelchair, which I could not self-propel. With no other options, I was on foot. I walked into the lobby and rested on the first chair I saw, elevating my feet. At reception, I told the uniformed guard that I was there to meet a baby in the NICU. He took my photo for security clearance and directed me to the elevators, which would take me to the third floor.

In the elevator, I sat on the floor and took a selfie—my face is lined and pale in the harsh overhead lights, and my expression looks scared. We weren't sure if we were ready to bring another foster child into our home. It had only been a few days since two-year-old Moses had left, and we were still reeling. But I had agreed to at least meet the eight-day-old baby. From the elevator floor, I texted David at work. *I'll let you know how it goes.*

I was in my first year of graduate school but didn't have classes that day. I wasn't in a hurry. When I got off the elevator, a nurse directed me to a locker where I should leave my purse and jewelry. I pinned the locker key to my belt loop and met her at the giant metal sinks, where she opened a fresh loofah-like sponge and told me to scrub for three minutes, every nail, every finger, all the way up to my elbows.

Paper booties stretched over my shoes, and a large paper gown covered my T-shirt and jeans. Once I was adequately sterile, I followed her into a large room with over a dozen tiny plastic beds. Little babies lined both walls, and a command center of nurses in the center kept watch. I asked if I could sit and rest, and she motioned to a chair next to the third bed on the right.

Inside the plastic box, with tubes and wires stretching from her tiny body, lay a Black baby with feathery hair, long delicate fingers, and dancing dark eyes.

"This is K," the nurse said. I leaned in.

"Hi, my little potato," I whispered.

And, impossibly, I loved her.

Her social worker ushered me to a back office where K's neurologist, pediatrician, physical therapist, and nurse waited. They talked me through K's first week (the details of which belong to her) and described all we did not yet know about her future. The doctors handed me a three-inch binder already stuffed with records and instructed me on feeding and possible complications and when we should bring her in next. But what I kept noticing was the way their eyes lit up when they talked about her. Every single person said something along the lines of "K really *is* special" with a bit of wonder in their voice. They already knew something that David and I are now reminded of daily: she is magic.

I texted David. *I think we should take care of her for the next few weeks until she can return to her family.* He agreed. Before leaving the hospital, I needed to demonstrate that I could feed and change K. Our first bottle together is her favorite part of the story. The nurse handed me a plastic bottle of premixed formula, and I lifted her from her bed, nestling her head against my chest and in the crook of my elbow. I put the nipple in her mouth, and she rooted around impatiently. She opened wider. *More.* She demanded (and still does). I pushed the bottle in deeper until the entire nipple was inside her tiny baby mouth. It looked ridiculous. Her body relaxed, and she drank the 1.5 ounces quickly. The nurse looked on, smiling.

I changed her tiny diaper, and the nurse put her in a too-big yellow onesie from the lost and found; I hadn't even considered bringing a going-home outfit. I explained that I needed to rest before driving and left the NICU to sit on the floor in a walkway stretching across Fifty-Second Street. While I recovered from the morning of activity, I ate some almonds and texted with David. I then pulled my car up to the front of the hospital, where the paramedics ensured that K's car seat was installed correctly.

When I saw K inside a few minutes later, I didn't have to scrub in or put on a gown. For the first time in her life, she was out of the NICU—sitting in a too-big stroller in her too-big onesie, looking around and crying. The nurse and I pushed her stroller down the long hallways and to the entrance, where she helped me load K into the car seat. K stopped crying and looked at me, stunned by the changes. I started the car and pulled out, turning right on Fifty-Second Street to begin the ten-minute drive home. At the first light, I looked in the rearview mirror at K's little feet.

"We love you already, little bug, and we will do our very best."

Because we were approved to foster a broader range of ages, we weren't prepared to parent a newborn. We had been told that because so many people want *only* to foster newborns, it was unlikely that we would receive a call about one. As a result, our collection of baby supplies was haphazard. We had butt paste and a swing but no clothes or diapers. We had two bottles and four baby wraps, and no stroller. We didn't have a changing pad or table or wipes. In our tiny second bedroom, a bite-marked craigslist crib sat in one corner, and, barely a foot away, we had crammed a queen-sized mattress.

Arriving home from the hospital, I brought K inside and placed her inside the crib and called my friend Kate. "Are you allowed to get stuff from the car if a baby is in a crib inside alone?" She said it was legal, so I urged K to stay put and brought in the formula, medicine, and diapers that the hospital had given me. I set a timer on my phone for the next time K would eat and another for her next diaper change. Filling a bowl with kettle chips, I returned to K's bedroom and placed her next to me on the mattress. I propped myself on pillows, dizzy and fatigued from my morning out. It wasn't even noon. K slept.

I googled: *How do you take care of a newborn?*

I decided the first task should be supplies, so I posted on our Oakland neighborhood email list that I was taking care of a baby, unexpectedly, and needed some newborn outfits and other gear. Within minutes, neighbors were at the door with bags of clothes, blankets, diapers, and toys. While I coordinated the collection, another message came in. A night doula, who has since trained as a therapist, Renée Racik, had seen my message and offered to come and meet with me and give a free consultation. An hour later, she was sitting on the mattress with me, exuding comfort and certainty. She looked at K, and her eyes filled. "She is perfect, huh?" she said.

Renée was still at our house a few hours later. She had set up a bottle sanitizing station in our kitchen, made a few trips from her own house with her own stockpile of baby goods, and set up K's room to facilitate easy feeding, changing, and sleeping. We practiced swaddling and wrote down a sample daily schedule. She warned me that I shouldn't let her head flop forward or back. I hadn't texted David for hours when he walked in the front door to meet K for the first time. His eyes were wide with all that had changed while he was at work.

The three of us talked, and Renée offered to come back a few hours later to help us with our first night with a newborn. She said she could reduce her rate and cover nights for us for a bit while we got our sea legs. Shell-shocked and dazed by our transformed life, we agreed. And a woman who had been a stranger the day before left to prepare to stay up all night with a baby who, a day earlier, we didn't know existed.

I remember only some of the details of that first week with K. I have photos, emails, and texts that fill in what I've forgotten. But I do remember how happy I felt. I remember the peace that filled my chest and how my love for K blossomed, and how I couldn't imagine not knowing her. I know we tried a bunch of different bottles before finding some with giant nipples that would work for her cavernous mouth. I remember the downy hair covering her body. I remember going to grad school classes online and positioning my computer so my professors couldn't see K's head on my chest. I remember nights, waking briefly to hear Renée and K pacing the halls.

I've wondered if I will ever feel as at home as I did at the beginning with K. Our days existed in a vacuum, removed from the future and past. We didn't know when she would leave, so I let go of long-term worries. I had the individual moments, and they were delicious. Looking back, I can see that K and I loved each other immediately. I knew her. Every sound and wiggle and scrunch of her face was a language, and I was fluent. My early ease with K is one of the greatest gifts of my life.

And, of course, those early days are complicated. She was taken away from her first mom. Our first seven days with K will always contain heartbreak and loss. Her body had spent nine months held by a woman who loved her, named her K, and whom she had to leave. For K and her first mama, those early days are when their family shattered.

The complex reality of transracial foster care and adoption merits its own book, and I am not the one to write it. Adoptees and foster children deserve the platforms to share their stories and what it feels like to have your identity split apart. But know that as I talk about becoming a parent, it is from the perspective of our disabled family changing and adapting, and there are other stories that I'm not telling—that aren't mine to tell. Adoption and fostering are never purely good.

When K was a few months old, and we realized she would stay with us for at least a bit longer, I joined a group for new moms. We met on Wednesdays and brought our babies, talking for a couple of hours in a community center on Grand Avenue in Oakland. I was the only parent who had not been pregnant and the only one not breastfeeding at least some of the time. As far as I know, I was also the only disabled person.

There, I began to acknowledge that my experience of the first week of caring for a newborn was unusual. The other women talked about the absolute torture of the first seven days. The worst week of their lives, they said. I explained, to myself, that it was probably because they had been recovering from giving birth, and I had not. They were also enduring hormone fluctuations that I was not.

But it's not like parenting inside a body that gets injured from rolling over in bed is easy—or managing graduate school and caring for a newborn without daytime childcare. Or twice-weekly trips to the downtown Oakland social services office when it's hard to stand up for longer than thirty seconds. I could tally and compare the daily challenges in their lives and mine, but that's no way to live. We all lived in nice-enough houses and drove nice-enough cars. The group was racially and ethnically diverse but not socioeconomically so. We were also all cis women married to cis men.

Despite our economic similarities, I noticed that my parenting choices were different from theirs. I used a thirty-dollar umbrella stroller that I could lift and unfold from my car without injuring myself. They had very expensive strollers that all looked alike. They breastfed, and those that needed to use formula imported it from Germany because the ingredients were supposed to be healthier. It was four times the cost of the formula David and I used (which K's doctors had recommended and the county paid for).

It's not the amount of money they were spending that struck me, but a general sense that they felt that these choices, which seemed small to me, were critical. If I imagine the person I was before becoming disabled and think about her parenting, I can see that I would have been much more like the other women in my group. In my twenties, I thought I could achieve perfection, and that goodness was a matter of the right choices and hard work. Judging by my "healthy" eating during those years, I almost certainly would have imported organic European formula.

At twenty-eight, when my body changed and I could not regain my old capacities, despite doing absolutely everything in my power, my worldview started to shift. My relationship with control changed and, by extension, my capacity for flexibility. By the time I met K, five years after becoming disabled, I had accepted that bodies are unpredictable and that it's impossible to know what they will need and how they will feel. I didn't yet identify as disabled, but I had learned to live with uncertainty.

To be clear, I will never be laid back. I am, at my core, an uptight person. Anyone who looks at my methodically arranged sweater shelf or watches me select paint colors would agree. But becoming disabled has dismantled something corrosive about my perfectionism. Despite certain behaviors, I don't actually believe that I can control the outcome of my life or anyone else's. My job is to be as loving and just as I can. My other job is to believe my own experience.

In 2017, Thomas Curran, a social psychologist at the London School of Economics, conducted a meta-analysis of perfectionism research and found that the rate of perfectionism had been, indisputably, rising since the 1980s.[1] He also examined the health impacts of perfectionism and found that they were profound. When people fail to be perfect—which is inevitable—they experience deep shame and guilt.[2] His research has also found that perfectionism impedes performance.

In his 2023 book, *The Perfection Trap*, Curran credits capitalism for a great deal of perfectionism's rise. He explains that while competitive markets, materialism, and consumer culture are not new, the increase in globalization means that we are always competing against the entire world. In many ways, capitalism has become more powerful. Social media also serves to reinforce perceived shortcomings by distorting our perceptions of how other people live.[3] Wealth disparity also drives perfectionism; with the middle class vanishing, one has to work much harder to achieve financial stability. But, too often, an individual feels as if their financial struggle is due to insufficient "hustle" and not a reflection of a complex knot of economic obstacles and legislative failures.

All of that is to say, it's no wonder we bring perfectionism into parenting. We have been training our whole lives to see having a baby as a measure of our goodness. If our babies suffer, or if we suffer, it's surely because we failed in some way.

While writing this chapter, I interviewed Renée, our beloved night doula, who, thanks to a generous family member, ended up spending a few nights per week with K for her first few months.[4] Near the end of our call, I asked her about my own first week. "I worry that I have painted a rosy picture of it in my mind. What do you remember about our family during those days?" I held my breath as I waited for her answer. All of these years, I have remembered those days as the week I came home to myself, as the hours that K and I first loved each other. What if Renée had witnessed something far more complicated and fraught? She has also been with hundreds of families. What if she didn't remember us?

"Of course I remember," Renée said. "I have never seen a family exude so much peace. I loved arriving at your house.

"I remember all the poetry on your walls. How thoughtfully you decorated and arranged your space to honor comfort, expression, and beauty. The most overwhelming feeling in your home was awe and sweetness. You were all living in the present. K's doctors were worried about the size of her head, and you had to bring her in frequently that first week. When I asked you about it, you just said that you thought her body would probably catch up. I had never seen a parent respond that way to medical uncertainty.

"I took note of how you weren't abandoning yourself. I walked in, and you were sitting on the floor making bottles because you couldn't stand at the counter. You never pretended that you didn't have needs. I have come to believe that accepting your own needs in the early days is a good predictor of how well you will adjust to parenthood."

The evening after I talked to Renée, David and I lay in bed, and I told him about the conversation. We both got a little teary. What a gift to have those magical moments witnessed and to have someone affirm our fuzzy memories. *Yes, it was as good as you remember.*

So, why was it good? As I've said, I am not naturally relaxed. I'm hard on myself. I'm only slightly less hard on others. I am a firstborn, overachieving, and relentless striver. So why did I float around those early months with K in a gauzy fog of peace, acceptance, and confidence? How, when K's health and future were completely uncertain, was I able to be present in the moments?

To develop a hypothesis, I needed to hear more stories about what others experienced during those first days of parenting. What did those who struggled have in common? What helped ease the transition to parenthood for those who found moments of peace? Which qualities were predictors of struggle, and which predicted ease? How did the experience of disabled parents, who are more prone to medical complications, differ from nondisabled parents?

I spoke to about a dozen parents from various racial, ethnic, and socioeconomic backgrounds. I spoke with queer parents and single parents by choice. I spoke with the same number of disabled and nondisabled parents. What I heard floored me.

Nondisabled parents described the first week as some of the most challenging days of their lives: harrowing, destabilizing, and terrifying. In all but one case, disabled parents had different responses: their first weeks were . . . fine.

There were other trends, too. Nondisabled parents who had endured adversity and unpredictability in their early life were generally less destabilized by caring for a newborn. They seemed to know, going into that first week, that life is often unpredictable and hard.

Across the board, disabled parents had more medically complicated birth and recovery experiences, but the emotional adjustment to caring for a newborn was far easier.[5] When I asked disabled parents about recovering from C-sections, they echoed Jessie Owen, the woman who became quadriplegic after a car accident in her twenties and gave birth to twins via C-section. "Dealing with recovery was pretty breezy. I didn't feel great, for sure, but it wasn't all that bad."[6]

On the other hand, nondisabled parents who gave birth via C-section often described profound fear and uncertainty as their bodies were unable to move and function in the manner they had hoped for after birth. One interviewee described falling asleep on the floor and getting trapped there for twenty minutes because her stomach muscles were so damaged that she couldn't find a way to get herself up.

One way to think about the first week is that it's the time during which a large portion of a family is or becomes disabled. As Jennifer Natalya Fink writes in *All Our Families: Disability Lineage and the Future of Kinship*, our society has established a deep and abiding fear of disability. Disability, when seen as a shift away from an ideal body and mind, is by definition further from perfection.

Fink posits that a fear of disability is, actually, a fear of care. She traces the racist and sexist underpinnings of care structures in the United States and theorizes that because these structures are unjust, flimsy, and inadequate, any evidence that a person will need additional care is terrifying. She reframes the common and destructive incantation about babies "As long as they are healthy" as "As long as they don't need additional care." In fact, a euphemism for disabled is "high care needs."

The first week of parenting is a cold plunge of care. Not only does a new baby need unpredictable and relentless attention, but the birthing person often also does. A family shifts from one with established independence to one oriented around profound care needs. In a society that values perfection and independence above all, that experience can feel life-threatening.

As the nondisabled parents told me in the interviews, some of their darkest moments were when their bodies didn't obey: when stomach muscles couldn't contract, and exhaustion prevented walking. The other dire moments were when their babies' needs exceeded expectations and the specter of a future that would be oriented around those needs felt impossible.

Fear, as a feeling, isn't always born from logic, and if we agree with Fink that our culture fears disability and therefore care, then how much of the distress from that first week is because it pulls us closer to the truth of our endless need?

The author of *Invisible Labor*, Rachel Somerstein, talked about her C-section recovery and how she kept expecting to be able to do more than she was.[7] She walked the half-mile in the cold to the pediatrician with her husband and new baby during her first week of recovery and was frightened and surprised by how difficult it was.

Rachel's experience in the hospital had been uniquely terrifying—the anesthesia during her C-section had not worked, and she endured excruciating pain on the table. She was, literally, strapped down and tortured while giving birth. Returning home with a new baby, while recovering from that trauma, was profoundly destabilizing, particularly because she had expected to have an epidural-free vaginal birth.

The usual hurdles that the first week of parenting brings were magnified by the medical trauma Rachel had endured. When her new baby cried, Rachel, an unflappable journalism professor with a PhD, was certain that her baby would cry for eighteen years without stopping. Her ability to trust her own instincts and judgments was suffering.

When her baby couldn't latch, and her nipples grew scabbed and bloody, Rachel staunchly resisted using formula. After a few days of her baby's stalled weight gain, her pediatrician explained firmly that she had no choice but to introduce formula. Meanwhile, small worries ballooned in her mind—she became certain that her (shoulder-length) hair would strangle her baby and would not take it out of a bun in her child's presence. Risks had taken on an Alice in Wonderland magic potion quality: some grew to ten times their size, and some shrank, with a tenuous connection to actual danger. She says, in retrospect, "I was losing my mind."

I asked Jessie Owen what she credits with the smooth transition into parenthood. Jessie has minimal use of her hands and legs, and it's not hard to imagine that parenting twins could feel insurmountable. Plus, Jessie had preeclampsia and prolonged high blood pressure after giving birth, which could have easily pushed her beyond her ability to cope.

She reminded herself that she already knew what it was like to have life flipped upside-down. She had practiced asking for help and navigating change. She had learned to be creative and take care of her own needs. She also thinks that realistic expectations were important. "Well, it was very much what I expected," she explained. "I knew my body, knew my relationship with my husband, and knew what my challenges would be."

She and her husband had many long conversations about that first week. They wanted their relationship to be as stable as possible before everything changed. They devised plans for the potential challenges and even hung reminders to each other around the house.

Their (printed) mantras included:

"Lean into the uncomfortable. Strength is standing in it and breathing."

"We are strong enough to stand alone and wise enough to ask for help."

"Let go of what you think this is supposed to be; let go and embrace the love and support that we have; it takes a village."

"Me and you against the problem, not each other. We are on the same team."

My call with Jessie made me think more about how disabled expectations impact those first parenting days. Disabled people have years of living in bodies that rebel and fail. We have, in many cases, learned the hard way that recovery from surgery is long and arduous and that bodies, in general, are impossible to predict. Even when parenting is a totally novel experience, we have exercised the muscles that the early days with a newborn demand.

Dr. Jessi Elana Aaron is a Florida professor with arthrogryposis multiplex congenita (AMC), with greatly reduced use of the muscles in her limbs. She relies on her mouth for most tasks. She is also a single parent by choice to a son who was born in 2018. While I was writing this book, Jessi Elana and I spoke regularly.

When I asked about her first week of parenting, she explained that the hardest part was that the practical support she had put into place fell through. Her mother had said she would take nights while Jessi Elana recovered from surgery, but her mother was unable to do so, and Jessi Elana was forced to find a way to care for her newborn on her own while recovering from a C-section.

And she did it. She fed him and changed his diapers and comforted him when he cried. She set up bottles next to her bed with ice packs while her son rested in a bassinet nearby that she could access from the side. Rolling over with her temporary catheter tubing was difficult, but she found a way to make it work.

"Did it feel impossible?" I asked.

"Parenting was the least of my concerns," she said, a reference to painful family dynamics.

When she thinks about the first week of being a parent, she remembers snuggling in bed together and long days just getting to know each other and not trying to do much else. Just like Jessie, she was ready for the challenge.

Each new conversation I had drove home the reality that something special happens when a disabled person becomes a parent. Somehow, being disabled eases the transition to parenthood, even when the physical and practical challenges are particularly difficult.

I talked to my dear friend Tianna, a mother of two who works in racial equity at an elite university in Canada.[8] Tianna is Black and nondisabled. Both of her experiences giving birth were traumatic—the first because, like with Rachel, the anesthesia didn't work, and she felt the entire C-section. The second because prolonged elevated blood pressure meant she had to return to the hospital three times in her first week of parenting.

When I asked if she believes racial discrimination impacted the quality of her medical care, she was quick to affirm that she thinks she would have been believed more if she were not Black. In fact, she had a midwife who visited after her first daughter was born who disregarded Tianna's suspicions about a tongue tie. The midwife worked with many of Tianna's (white) friends, all of whom had great experiences, but she had a totally dismissive approach with Tianna and her daughter. A second opinion did reveal a tongue tie, and it's hard for Tianna not to wonder what role racial prejudice played in that mistake.

Even more traumatic, when Tianna was on the operating table for her first C-section, she repeatedly told them that she could feel everything, and they said it was just a "slight pressure" and not to worry. It wasn't until she described the exact location of the scalpel that they believed her. At that point, it was too late, and she had to endure the full procedure without anesthesia.

Some early childhood adversity and traumas had taught Tianna that to survive, she needed to push through pain. So, when she returned home with her first daughter, she did just that, to her own detriment. When extended family visited only days after she gave birth, instead of resting in bed, she felt pressured to host a lunch. It took over an hour to set the table, but she didn't ask for help. She hoped that if she ignored the trauma from the hospital and her surgery, it would fade. Each time her body's needs demanded attention, she felt terrified. She didn't recognize herself.

When I asked about her mental health that week, she said it was hard, but she said she was not shaken to her core. Deep down, she knew she could figure it out—she always had. Early struggles had increased her resilience. At the same time, without direct experience with disability, she found the change in her physical capacity quite jarring.

While Rachel and Tianna both had particularly traumatic C-section experiences (though anesthesia fails more often than you might think), the nondisabled people I interviewed with uncomplicated vaginal births still had very difficult first weeks.[9] All labors are traumatic—tearing and bleeding and pain. Even the nondisabled people I interviewed who left the hospital as planned, were able to breastfeed without much complication, and had adequate support systems at home found those early days impossible.

A friend, Lee, who had a vaginal birth, explained it like this:

In the first week and beyond, I kept having this feeling of *how*. Like, how is this possible? How do people do this? I don't think I was prepared for the level of physical trauma birth would wreak on my body. Maybe this is an exaggeration but at the time it sort of felt like—you get hit by a truck and then instead of having a chance to rest and recover, someone hands you a tiny, vulnerable creature who didn't ask to be born and who is confused and hungry and needy and tells you to keep it safe and alive. Like, how?[10]

And Lee is right; it's natural to feel that the shift from not being a parent to being a parent is grueling. Becoming responsible for another person is wild. It's not that nondisabled people are wrong to find it difficult; the question is, what about our culture makes it so disabled people are more equipped for this insurmountable challenge?

As I interviewed more people from different socioeconomic and racial backgrounds and with different family structures, the same story kept repeating itself. Those who had endured great personal hardship and found equilibrium already in their lives were, on the whole, more suited for the early days of parenting. But, if the hardship had not included illness or disability, people who had given birth often found the *physical* recovery to be particularly terrifying and destabilizing.

I couldn't help concluding that disabled people with adequate resources and support are, as a group, particularly equipped to weather the adjustment to parenthood. Physical weakness and change do not scare us as they do others. We have spent years decoupling joy from physical or mental function.

I shared my findings with Dr. Lisa Iezzoni, the Harvard doctor who studies disabled healthcare access. She was not surprised. "Disabled people have years of figuring out how to get along," she told me. She has found that disabled people have an inherent practicality, and that, to her, it makes sense that after spending every day navigating a world not designed for them, they would be particularly well equipped to navigate something new, like parenthood. On the other hand, many nondisabled parents haven't yet been forced to reject the larger capitalist narrative that correlates effort and success.

I also talked through my observations with Renée, our former doula, and she added that the parents who suffer the most are those who deny their own needs and aren't able to ask for or receive help.[11] She thinks disabled people are more likely to honor our own needs because we haven't had the option to ignore them and have years of practice with accepting bodies and minds that vary from the norm.

In her practice, she has also noticed that parents with a firm vision of how things *should* be with a new baby are often the most devastated when reality deviates from that expectation. Along the same lines, flexibility is particularly protective during that first week. When parents can adjust their plans based on their own needs and those of their babies, everyone is more likely to thrive. In some cases, this means switching to formula. In others, it means asking for more help at night. It's important to remember here that inadequate social supports for new parents mean that these resources are out of reach.

Between my conversation with Renée and hearing firsthand from non-disabled parents how horrible the first seven days are, a thesis began to solidify in my mind: the first week lays bare that we cannot, through the force of our wills and our perfect behavior, make our babies and our bodies do what we want them to.

So, what is the solution? The answer, surely, is not that everyone just needs to be disabled so that they can eventually adjust well to parenthood.

And it's not as if the people who have trouble acclimating to parenthood are doing something wrong. Their reactions are valid—labor is punishing, and feeding a baby is much harder than it looks on TV, and not sleeping destroys our sanity. Finding the first week hard is not a personal failure, but it's worth considering what wisdom and skills disabled people can share to make it easier for everyone.

If nondisabled parents entered that first week with a disability-informed understanding of what makes a life good, what an individual's efforts can yield, and the fragility of all bodies, perhaps those seven days would not feel as destabilizing. The dream of perfection corrodes.

My therapist says I am a perfectionist. I always argue that I'm not because I don't do anything well enough. I can see the irony here. I have not, historically, forgiven myself easily. But I am changing because, thankfully, disability has forced me to confront and accept my limits and to see my worth as separate from my performance and strength. It's taught me that something (or someone) can be good without being all-the-way-good, including me.

I think these hard lessons about (not) being perfect have helped me parent K. I have been able to look at our parenting choices or mistakes (formula, inadequate tummy time, a chaotic approach to sleep schedules, maybe too much TV on in the background) as minor and not distract me from the ways that we were providing exactly what they needed. I had been training to forgive myself.

For disabled people who have confronted internalized ableism and have rejected the world's false hierarchy of bodies and minds, the failures or uncertainties during that first week can feel less dire. Say, for example, breastfeeding isn't possible. We may know that some studies show that outcomes are better for babies who breastfeed, but we also know that the metrics by which studies judge "better" or "worse" are flawed.[12] We have worked hard to reject the idea that there is a right way to have a body, to be OK. We know that, no matter what, there will never be a perfect person or perfect life.

And, while disabled people plan (goodness do we plan), we, typically, plan in a different way from nondisabled people—with zero expectation that everything (or even most things) will work out. Before I was disabled, failed plans led to disappointment. Take a week in Paris in my late twenties. I plotted every meal, every garden, every shop. I didn't account for the intractable migraine and the vague ennui that descended when I realized that, even in Paris, I was still my same neurotic self. I see that all now through Curran's perfectionism lens. I had become convinced that there was a way to effort myself into happiness.

Now, when our family travels, I forget to look up restaurants, shops, or galleries. I have no illusion that I can craft an ideal experience. I know that how much we enjoy the trip comes down to how flexible we are and our capacity to meet each person's physical and emotional needs. I am never surprised when we have to cancel a trip or end it early. I am also never surprised when the most joyful moments are the ones that I couldn't have anticipated. The in-between times when everyone is fed and comfortable and able to connect and laugh.

I used to think that I could create the very best experience if I prepared enough. My disabled body has taught me that joy doesn't work that way. Planning for the first week of parenthood is similar. In my interviews, I found that disabled people made very practical plans—Jessi Elana considered how she could keep bottles cool next to her bed so that she didn't have to transfer in the middle of the night. But the disabled parents were rarely surprised when they had to adjust. Most importantly, they didn't blame themselves when something went wrong.

Most new parents, disabled and not, plan every last detail of birth and the first week, but I think experience has taught disabled people that there will likely be complications. We are not surprised when plans fail. In the decade-plus that I've been disabled, I've learned, through repeated disappointments, that I should expect problems. It's not pessimism; it's the absence of denial. We know that bodies and people and buildings and basically everything is fallible. When one thing falls apart, I don't automatically assume that everything will. Some things/bodies/brains work, sometimes. That's just the way life is. Disabled people know that we cannot predict the future but also know that we can survive it.

But flexibility and self-compassion are not *exclusive* to or *inherent* in disabled people. It's disability *culture* that has allowed us to grow and develop in an alternative context to the rest of society. Flexibility and compassion are protective countercultural survival techniques that disabled people pass to each other. But one doesn't need to be disabled to learn the lessons.

Capitalism and popular culture reinforce the (false) narrative that we are responsible for our destinies. That the right products will make the first days beautiful. That satisfaction is directly correlated with effort. That perfection is attainable. Those aren't values that people automatically have, but they are what emerge when we aren't forced to question the culture we are surrounded by.

Disabled people cannot rely on the dominant narrative of individualism and bootstrap-ism. Our bodies and minds dispel the myth of optimization. We could not survive with that worldview. And so, together, we create a new template. It's much more complicated and far less aspirational. But flexibility and compassion are exactly what you need when your body is sore from labor, and your family dynamic has shifted beyond recognition.

Disability culture offers a solution that is gentle and soft and, most importantly, true.

Chapter 5

PARENTING AT HOME

B efore I became a parent, I watched friends, newborns in their arms, skip-walk around the room until their babies fell asleep. Others sat on exercise balls, rocking and bouncing to ease out one last burp. I can stand for about thirty seconds before my vision starts tunneling. I can sit upright, unsupported, for three to five minutes. *What will I do when my baby cries?* I wondered.

When K was a newborn, a neighbor gave us a swing that jiggled and rocked. I thought this could imitate what other parents did on foot, but I only used it on occasion—while getting dressed or feeding the dog. What K craved, more than a parent who could pace endless laps around the family room, was my still and warm chest. Fortunately, I am an expert at being still.

Our house has always been filled with places to sit and lie down. In every spot that K needed to eat or sleep, I built another where I could recline, supported. When K was a baby, an orthopedic mattress rested on the hardwood floor up against her crib. I could take her out of bed and lie down to cuddle, feed her, or change her diaper. When she started eating solids, instead of a high chair, we purchased a booster-style seat and put it on the floor so that I could feed her and lay flat on the floor when my body demanded.

We never had a changing table; I can't stand up long enough to use one. I moved a small pad around the house with me. During potty train-ing, when she needed help wiping, instead of standing and leaning over the potty, I taught her to get down and bend over so I could clean her up while sitting on the floor. We made up a song. "Look at my butttt!" she hollered. "Boooooooty!" I sang.

Now that she is six, we have cushioned spots where I can recline by our ancient Nintendo, in her playroom, at the dining table, and outside. A padded swivel chair near the kitchen counter helps me to prepare food. A padded bench by the front door allows me to rest while I hug her good-bye before school and greet her after.

As I've described in earlier chapters, becoming a parent as a disabled person is fraught. We must invite (or force) gatekeepers to adjust their understanding of what it means to be a capable parent. As disabled care-givers, we invite judgment when we leave the house with our children and, in some cases, those judgments can threaten custody of our children.[1] The outside world is full of accessibility obstacles: stairs, heavy doors, and unnavigable crowds.

But at home, where we can mold our environment to fit our needs, we thrive. Many of us have been honing our creativity and resourcefulness for decades, and we flex those muscles while parenting. We consider the needs of our kids, our own requirements, and the available tools, then create systems that keep everyone safe. We arrange our environments and our schedules so that our needs and our kids' needs overlap. Construct-ing a living space that is safe and functional can be complex and involves constant innovation and creative thinking, but, as disabled people, we are practiced in problem-solving.

Before becoming disabled, I assumed that if I didn't function well in the world, the problem was with my discipline or perspective. I told my-self that I should be able to sit in an airplane seat, wait in a line, or drive a car. When my pain shouted, every second of the day, I tried to ignore it. I assumed, for twenty-eight years, that every person felt like I did but that they didn't complain.

While driving, I used to curl one leg under me, and stuff tiny rub-ber balls behind my back, rolling them over the knots of pain along my spine. Waiting in lines, I shifted back and forth, trying to relieve the throbbing in my feet, my hips, my back. I took yoga, got massages, tried new shoes, bought new cars, and still I hurt. Once, after a neighborhood board meeting, I leaned against a knobby banister for some pressure against my screaming back. I swayed back and forth while chatting with an acquaintance until they finally asked what I was doing. I was doing what I always did, quietly looking for a moment of relief. For all those years, I blamed myself for not adapting.

At twenty-eight, when my yet-undiagnosed genetic condition, Ehlers-Danlos syndrome, led to a secondary neurological condition, dysautonomia, I could no longer ignore my body's sensations. I became lightheaded, feverish, and nauseated in addition to aching. My body simply refused to stand up. But, even then, despite fluctuating blood pressure, a rapid heart rate, tunneled vision, and faded hearing, it took years to accept my new reality. Every day, I woke up and thought I might be better. Every new doctor, supplement, or test might have a solution.

I didn't get better, and, eventually, I started the process of accepting my body as it was, not as I thought it should be.

As I've discussed, it was years after I became sick that I began identifying as disabled. For me, *sick* came with assumptions—that the goal was to become well, that there was a way that I *should* be and a way that I *was*. That something was temporary about the way that I felt. Learning about disability culture and the hard work of the disabled people who came before me shifted the way I looked at my body.

Instead of considering every new episode of weakness or nausea a fluke or failure, I considered these sensations part of what it means to live inside my body. I stopped being surprised. I stopped waking up each morning thinking: *Today is the day. My body will fit in again.* Instead of believing that I should be able to walk but growing too dizzy to do so, I accepted that my body, as it is, cannot walk.

This is not the same thing as giving up.

My acceptance and identity as disabled brought tremendous freedom. I stopped trying to shoehorn my body into the world and started to adapt my world to my body. For years, every time I drove, I became so dizzy that I feared for my life and the safety of other drivers. And, so, I stopped driving. There was freedom in admitting that I am too disabled to drive.

When I developed dysautonomia, I became incredibly sensitive to heat, suffering from heat exhaustion anytime ambient temperatures exceeded 73 degrees. Despite the frequency of those scary episodes, I regularly put myself in situations in which I became too warm. *Maybe this time will be different*, I thought. Identifying as disabled allowed me to accept that my body simply cannot thermoregulate well. It's not a matter of willpower. I now ask about the temperature in advance. I no longer sacrifice my safety because I think I *should* be able to handle 74 degrees.

Identifying as disabled altered my view of the world. I no longer looked at its structures and assumed that they were made for me. I considered everything with fresh eyes: chairs, cars, buses, airplanes, beds, shoes, showers, toilets, dishes. When I ride in a bumpy car, my ribs dislocate. I've accepted that. Cars aren't made for bodies like mine. There is a lightness in acknowledging that another person's experience of potholes is vastly different from my own. But mine is not the only body that doesn't work in a car—products are designed for one type of person, usually a thin white man, and everyone else has to adapt. For example, my short nondisabled friends have implemented a variety of creative solutions so that they can see the road and reach the pedals when driving. Cars don't work for them either.

My identity as disabled introduced me to disability culture, which brought with it some of the greatest gifts of my life. Among them, a spirit of ingenuity and creativity. Because disabled people live in a world that does not work naturally with our bodies and minds, we become inventors and collaborators. We are constantly reexamining objects, routines, expectations, and equipment. We start at the beginning. What do I need? What is available? What can I create?

Even getting my wheelchair was a process of innovation. First, I accepted that I could not walk. After years in cardiac rehab, trying to train my heart and brain to support extended time upright, I accepted that I could not willpower myself out of my disability.

It was the spring of 2014, and I wanted to visit the botanical gardens near my house. I had tried the week before but only made it a few feet from the parking lot before lying down on the path. It was the flowers I couldn't walk to that motivated me to purchase my first wheelchair, manual and inexpensive. That evening, my boyfriend pushed me around the tulips. That moment was a revelation—there were ways to bridge the gap between the world and my body.

Two years later, in Trader Joe's with the same wheelchair, I bickered with my (new) boyfriend, David. I am not strong enough to propel my own manual wheelchair, so he was pushing me. I wanted to stop and look at the cereal, but he didn't know that and couldn't hear me over the din of the store because I faced forward, away from him. "Stop here," I kept shouting, while other shoppers turned to stare.

Museums were the same. I craved independence—to stop and take in art at my own pace. I was tired of watching my desires float by because I was too fatigued to verbalize them. I wanted to wander a store on my own and pick up items and put them back and go at my own pace. That night, after Trader Joe's, David and I talked. I said that it was important to me to find a way to visit a store alone. I needed a mobility device that could propel itself and that I was strong enough to remove from the car and set up.

I started to ask the questions that I have grown used to asking daily: What do I need? What can my body do? What is the world like? What are the options?

We found a lightweight electric scooter that, on a good day, I could lift and assemble without help. Because of my dysautonomia, I must elevate my feet, and every lightweight scooter positioned a rider's feet well below waist level. I can only sit in that position for five to ten minutes. We decided that it was worth a try, and that I could wander a store for a few minutes and then pull over and elevate my feet. It was an improvement, at least.

The scooter arrived and I was elated. For the very first time, I could wander Piedmont Avenue in Oakland, window-shopping. I found a way to prop my feet on the handlebars when the scooter was parked. Sadly, it wasn't long before I started to notice ways in which my body and the scooter were not compatible. The scooter's light weight meant that it jostled over every sidewalk bump. I ended each excursion bruised and injured. The backrest reached my lower back, and my shoulders and neck aren't strong enough to support me for very long. Within months, I had passed it along to another disabled person with different needs from my own.

Years later, when David and I were parents and had signed K up for a baby dance class at the local studio, I considered mobility equipment again. Parking at the studio was sparse, and the interior lacked seating that my body could manage for more than a minute or two. I realized I would miss her first lesson. David and I, again, lay in bed talking about what my body needed and what the world had. I said that I wanted to take K to the zoo when she was older. And attend her school concerts. I wanted to be there. "There has to be a way to drive around on a mobile bed," David said.

I started to research reclining power wheelchairs. My scooter had weighed less than thirty-five pounds and the chairs I was considering exceeded four hundred. A new chair would mean a new car—one that had been adapted to load and transport adaptive equipment. But, at this point, I had fully accepted that I was disabled. Medicare would pay for the wheelchair, but the van to transport it would cost over $50,000.

David had a well-paying job and I had, after years of fighting, received backpay for a disability claim. We could afford it, but it was hard. We had planned on saving that money for K. My wheelchair changed my life. It is well cushioned, reclines fully, and has facilitated countless memories and moments with my family.

Granted, a power wheelchair for someone who cannot walk for more than a minute or two is not an outside-the-box idea. In retrospect, it's quite obvious. But the process of accepting my needs and seeking solutions has been a training in disabled innovation. Disabled people, through advice from peers and daily practice, develop the ability to bridge the gap between our environment and our needs. We learn to ask the questions and find the answers.

What do I need? What can my body do? What is the world like? What are the options?

When a disabled person becomes a parent, we are prepared to problem-solve. When parenting feels impossible, when the solution isn't obvious, we draw on our years of experience to take it one step at a time. We start at the beginning; we make no assumptions.

Disabled creativity is beautiful. It is also, often, communal.

Once a disabled person accepts their own needs, they can consider and accept the varied needs of others. Aislinn Thomas, a disabled artist, wrote about her experience of communal disabled creativity and gave examples of ways that her community has adapted, together: "Because we each understand the pain of exclusion, there is usually a commitment to the importance of each person's presence in the room. I've had Skype meetings over text, eaten meals with others in the dark, and shared fragrance-free personal care products ahead of a meeting, just so that we could be together. Doing the dance of figuring out access stuff with other disabled people is one of my favorite things to do."[2] Thomas highlights the joy of being creative and accepting needs. Surrendering to our bodies can be a celebration.

When nondisabled parents imagine parenting as a blind person, or in a wheelchair, or with only the use of their mouth, they can get stuck on the logistical conundrums. They imagine doing what they themselves do every day and then removing sight, hands, or their ability to walk. But that's not how creative adaptation works. Disabled people have honed creativity and often have cultivated communities that help devise solutions from the ground up. We don't implement a nondisabled routine and do a worse job—we create our own routines and solutions that are safe, loving, and beautiful in their own right. We create our lives from scratch.

Unlike nondisabled parents, we can't reference most baby books or parenting blogs and check off the list of "must-have" parenting supplies. Standard baby gear rarely meets our needs. It's worth noting that there are enough disabled people to justify producing more accessible baby gear. In fact, the 1990s saw a wave of reporting on "handicapitalism" or the celebration of the untapped market of disabled people. Companies know that we exist.[3]

However, in the US, labor and social security laws restrict disabled income to such a degree that despite the vast number of disabled people, our spending power remains limited. For example, as of 2023, SSI—that is, the disability income for those who were unable to work full-time before becoming disabled—is $10,900 per year, which is far below the poverty line.[4] The rate of poverty in the disabled population is twice as high as in the nondisabled population.[5] Disabled parents simply don't have the money to incentivize companies to design products for us. Instead, we think through what our children require and our own capacities and then alter and invent until we amass a functional supply arsenal. We connect with other disabled parents and learn from their experiences.

The research on disabled parents and innovation is limited, but, in 2018, a group of public health researchers summarized ten years of interviews with twenty-five physically disabled mothers about parenting at home.[6] They found that their parenting strategies fell into five categories: acquiring or modifying baby care equipment, adapting the home environment and mobility equipment, accessing information and support, developing communication strategies to facilitate safety, and receiving assistance from others. Their findings have been borne out in my own parenting and those who I interviewed.

Dr. Jessi Elana Aaron, forty-three, is the professor in Florida with greatly reduced use of the muscles in her limbs.[7] She relies on her mouth for most tasks and is a single parent by choice to a four-year-old. She uses a wheelchair inside and outside the house. An assistant visits the house for a few hours each day, but parenting tasks fall to Jessi Elana. When insurance pays for personal assistants, these assistants are legally prohibited from helping with childcare. They can only aid with the disabled person's tasks of daily living.

She knows that people must wonder how she manages her son's care. Like many disabled parents, Dr. Aaron takes the same ingenuity and creativity that have served her until this point—that helped her through Stanford and allowed her to travel the world—and applies them to her parenting. While at home, she is able to perform most parenting functions with her mouth.

When her son was a newborn, Dr. Aaron found a Pack-n-Play with a zipper on the side, to which she attached a loop large enough for her mouth to operate. She hooked this bed to the top of a sturdy table using boat ties, and then pushed the table and bed next to her own bed, placing her son in reach and at eye level for nighttime feedings. His premade bottles waited in a durable and insulated cooler close by, to save her from needing to access the kitchen at night. To move her son, she used her head to roll him onto a blanket with handles, called a Snuggle Bundle. She could then position him inside the blanket.

When we spoke on the phone, her now-four-year-old son made a few requests: a different snack, a new show, and to start the episode at the beginning. Using Alexa and other smart home tools, Dr. Aaron responded to each request promptly. She continues to create systems that allow her to provide for her son.

For sighted parents, it can be hard to imagine taking care of kids without the constant visual scanning of one's surroundings. But, for Stacy Cervenka and Greg DeWall, both forty-three and blind, parenting without sight feels completely natural.[8] In fact, when I first asked Stacy for examples of adaptive equipment that they utilized, she was unable to delineate her baby gear along those lines. It would be like asking an abled person to describe which baby equipment they purchased because they cannot levitate. Blindness is an integrated and essential part of their identities, and it informs every decision, big and small. Though, as we talked, she started to reframe some of their early decisions through the lens of adaptation.

Stacy and Greg's kids are now eight and four and are both sighted. When their kids were newborns, Stacy and Greg picked out car seats that could be removed and installed multiple times a day since they rely on public transportation and rideshares. Like Dr. Aaron, Stacy and Greg utilize smart home features—technology that wasn't initially developed with accessibility in mind but that often serves to bolster independence. Instead of a digital readout, their thermometer reads the temperature out loud so they can identify when their kids have a fever.

Stacy bought a variety of baby carriers so that they could keep their babies close by and safe throughout the day. She explained that having her children on her chest or back allowed her to be more aware of their needs and that as they grew, the carriers allowed her to keep herself and her babies comfortable.

The first question that many sighted people have about blind parenting is: How do you handle diaper changes? Stacy said that, for the most part, changing her kids' diapers went smoothly. Cues of a full diaper are not only visible but also palpable—the diapers sag and become heavy. Occasionally, when her kids had a particularly gnarly blowout, she would take the operation to the bathroom. There, she could crouch in the bathtub and turn on the faucet, holding her baby's bare bottom under the stream of water and wiping down every inch. This way, she could ensure that they both were completely clean and that any remaining spots of poop didn't cause a rash.

Stacy was so comfortable at home in the early days of parenting that she found it difficult to leave. She often wonders if the stark difference between the accessibility at home and the obstacles in the world contributed to her postpartum depression. She was more deliberate about leaving the house with her second baby and found that, despite the not insignificant obstacles, more variation in their days improved her mental health. She took her creativity outside of the home.

Unlike Stacy and Greg, whose kids are not disabled, Kelly Peterson and her husband adopted a daughter who was diagnosed at birth with the same disability that they share: spina bifida, which Kelly describes as "a neural tube defect that occurs in utero."[9] All three are wheelchair users. They built their house before becoming parents and were able to make it wheelchair accessible. Like many disabled people, when they adopted their daughter, they found themselves filtering baby supply lists through their own accessibility needs.

Many nondisabled people prefer newborn car seats that click in and out of a base so that they can carry their babies around in the car seat while in stores or out in public. Kelly and her husband knew that managing an unruly carrier from a wheelchair was impractical and installed a car seat that remains in the car and from which they could easily remove their daughter while in their wheelchairs.

An aside: it's not only disabled people who struggle with car seats. Many of my friends who had difficult births or C-sections had difficulty getting their babies in and out of the car, particularly in those first months. Car seats are heavy and unwieldy and require acrobatic twisting to manipulate. All parents would be served by user-based product adaptations. The "normal" bodies that baby gear is designed for are rare.

Instead of a crib, Kelly and Greg purchased a bassinet that allowed them to lift their baby in and out easily. There are cribs designed for disabled parents that open from the side but start around $16,000, so a bassinet was the more affordable option. Many wheelchair users would love an accessible crib, but the expense is unworkable.

Kelly describes bath time as a dance. She first situates herself on the floor next to the tub while her husband brings their daughter in. They alternate tasks with an eye on safety. Dinnertime is the same. Some of the disabled families I interviewed rely primarily on innovation for their adaptive parenting, but in Kelly and Greg's case, they also rely on communication and cooperation.

Every family I spoke to has utilized the creative resources they have developed as disabled people. Like me, they have grown used to a world that does not function in a way that supports them, and so they create their own buttresses. What a gift for children to witness a parent advocate and invent and stay open to a diversity of needs and capacities. This type of innovation can be further strengthened by community and information sharing.

Unfortunately, there are very few official resources for disabled parents. Through the Looking Glass (TLG), an organization in Berkeley that our family utilized, offers rental equipment for disabled parents as well as in-home accessibility consultations. Dr. Megan Kirshbaum founded TLG in 1982 after working as a family therapist with parents with disabilities at Berkeley's Center for Independent Living.[10] Dr. Kirshbaum witnessed the creativity and ingenuity of disabled parents and sought to create an organization that could amplify those strengths. The focus, from the beginning, was on creating a more accessible society for disabled parents.

TLG, while innovative and invaluable for the disabled families who can access its services, has, unfortunately, not spawned other similar organizations. Decades after its founding, it's still unique. The Disabled Parenting Project, an essential online resource for information about disabled parenting, lists no other active organizations advocating for disabled parents and, on the sections of their page offering accessible baby gear advice, the resources are woefully out-of-date. The most comprehensive guide that I could find, from the University of Idaho, was last updated in 1999.[11] There are very few disability-specific pieces of childcare equipment. Disabled parents cobble together their kids' highchairs, beds, bathtubs, and carriers—expertly accounting for capacities, both physical and financial.

With a lack of official local support for disabled parents, we create our own, primarily through online support groups. In those conversations, we can troubleshoot and ask other parents for information about how they managed certain tasks. Knowledge sharing is a vital form of mutual aid, and these communities help us maintain our independence and keep our children safe. Often, disabled people draw on community resources to compensate for reduced financial ones.

As I've mentioned, a disabled person is twice as likely to experience poverty as a nondisabled person. Social Security Disability benefits are not sufficient to cover living expenses, and disabled people are trapped in a catch-22 of poverty because benefits cease if a disabled person saves more than $2,000.[12] Outdated and exploitative labor practices allow employers to pay disabled people less than minimum wage.[13]

Being disabled is expensive, too. Often, we rely on more costly prepared food because extensive food preparation is outside of our physical capacities. Our housing needs are more inflexible because accessible design is exceedingly uncommon. Insurance—private, Medicare, or Medicaid—rarely covers all our needed mobility and adaptive equipment.

For many, becoming a disabled parent pushes up against an already stretched and precarious budget. For those lucky enough to live in Northern California, Through the Looking Glass offers affordable adaptive equipment. But for everyone else, the baby care equipment that fosters independence and safety is cost-prohibitive. There are regional and national organizations that offer grants for home modifications, but they don't include parenting gear.[14] Instead, disabled parents create online fundraisers to get the supplies that they need.

For everyone, figuring out how to parent at home can be a slippery slope into the capitalist lie: we are just a purchase away from contentment. Parents often feel the need to mimic an idealized version of some attractive and maximally safe home environment. It's easy to be lured by the ubiquitous message of consumerism that you can be a good parent if you buy the right things. In reality, we fill our homes with these empty promises that solve very little. Even the very architecture of single-family homes, which isolates us from other families, perpetuates our loneliness and exhaustion.

Parents suffocate inside the impossible demands, expectations, and promises of consumerism-driven parenting. In nearly every aspect of parenting, you can find a profitable, institutionalized solution (e.g., formula) and then an equally polarized reactive and "natural" response (e.g., breastfeeding). Savvy businesses eventually find a way of monetizing both ends of the spectrum. It's worth noting that none of these choices need to be binary, and, in many cases, we have falsely defined the spectrum.

How to feed babies is a particularly fraught conversation. Victoria Facelli, whose book *Feed the Baby: An Inclusive Guide to Nursing, Bottle Feeding, and Everything in Between* came out in 2023, explained to me that we have evidence that babies have always (truly, always) relied on a combination of chest milk, substitutions to chest milk, and on members of their community for nourishment.[15] The gestational parent's supply has not ever been the only nutritional source.

Formula became more reliable in the 1940s, and the 1950s advertising boom began touting it as the superior option. Facelli described how white women were the first to switch to formula; Black women took decades to make the change due to a combination of income inequality and culture. The story of formula versus chest milk is long and complicated, but a major backlash occurred in the 1990s during the "Breast Is Best" movement.

During the decades following the pro-breast-milk campaign, the health benefits of breast milk were so widely touted and had permeated medical schools and hospitals to the degree that formula became taboo in middle- and upper-class white communities. And, as was the case with formula manufacturers, corporations found a way to make money off of breastfeeding people. This time: by selling breast pumps.

But after a California mother named Jillian Johnson lost her son, Landon, at nineteen days old, from accidental starvation due to her limited breastmilk production, the pendulum began to swing again. With Dr. Christie del Castillo-Hegyi, Jillian created the "Fed Is Best" organization in 2016, which aims to teach parents about the signs of starvation and dehydration in newborns. She blames the collective obsession with the superiority of breastmilk for her medical providers' failure to see the signs that her son was not receiving enough nutrition.[16]

We are at an inflection point—breastfeeding is still pushed in nearly all medical settings. In what are called "baby-friendly hospitals," babies are not given formula unless a doctor writes a prescription, but more people are acknowledging that breastfeeding isn't always the best option. For parents who do use formula, the pressure around which formula to choose can be intense.

What all these arguments ignore, and what Victoria Facelli said so beautifully when we spoke, is that food is not a test of goodness, of morality. Babies need safe nourishment, but what they are given and how they are given it depends on countless individual factors. As with how we give birth, a false dichotomy harms parents and babies. The pressure to feed a baby "right" perpetuates the belief that our children's well-being is entirely up to our good choices and smart purchases. Disabled creativity is an antidote.

How to carry your young baby—wraps versus strollers—is another early example of what can feel like an impossible dilemma for new parents but is, in reality, a way for businesses to make money. In the early 2000s, strollers became cultural luxury items and aspirational purchases, starting with the introduction of the now ubiquitous Bugaboo.[17] Granted, certain features can make using a particular stroller accessible for some people: controllable with one hand, easy to fold, and able to fit in a trunk. But strollers became more than just features; they became social status indicators and moral objects. They have been, according to some parents, a physical token of how much you love your child. By 2007, every new Bugaboo model had months-long waitlists. The market has continued to grow so that there's now a market in reselling luxury strollers.

And, as these things always go, an anti-stroller reactive wave began with the trend of "baby wearing." Around ten years after the Bugaboo arrived in the US, organizations that touted the importance of keeping one's baby close began to vocalize their concerns about a stroller-focused culture. In my early days of parenting, I heard more than once that a stroller shows your baby that you want to "push them away from you." Wearing indicates that you will protect them and hold them close. Who doesn't want that?

Obviously, baby wraps are not new, and their use dates back millennia. But the social media and image-focused use of them has increased exponentially over the last decade, and, with that, opportunities for companies to make money by selling cloth that wraps around you and holds your baby in place. But it's not just material; according to baby-wearing advocates, it's a lifestyle.[18]

Just like C-section versus home birth and formula versus breast milk, how to carry our babies around has become a polarized conversation bound up in a feeling of personal powerlessness, fomented by the market forces that influence us. These false, pervasive, and capitalistic binaries persist through our children's adulthoods and distract us from the personal and social realities of parenting: we actually control very little, every person (adult or infant) has different needs, and no product can fix a broken society. How to birth, how to feed, how to carry. The winners are corporations.

Disabled people are systematically excluded from these false dichotomies; for example, I cannot breastfeed or use a baby wrap, and it's impossible to push a stroller in my wheelchair. But our exclusion from mainstream conversation isn't merely unjust. It actually hurts everyone, because our outsider's perspective offers solutions and new approaches that would benefit all parents. It's when we are willing to accept and adapt to our individual needs that solutions become sustainable. Our creativity and compassion are assets.

K's requirements while at home have evolved over time. During her first nine months, I could lift her without injury and provide for nearly all her daily needs without assistance. On occasion, a woman in my neighborhood whose kids were teenagers helped with some errands or heavier lifting. David fed K overnight, during those hours that my medication had worn off, and standing or sitting was nearly impossible.

K started daycare at nine months. Her level of activity at home had become difficult for me to manage alone. She was crawling, and while at any given moment I could keep up with her, the sustained physical effort of keeping her away from danger was outside of my capacity. It wasn't until she was around eighteen months old that the division of household labor shifted significantly. With K running, walking, and looking for a type of play that I could not sustain, David started to do more of the hands-on parenting, and I leaned into the behind-the-scenes household management: coordinating daycare, doctors' appointments, groceries, cleaning, home repairs, budgets, gifts, supplies, etc.

At the time of this writing, K is six, and that allocation of responsibility is starting to shift again. In most heteronormative two-parent families, the female-socialized parent manages more than her share of hands-on tasks as well as nearly all the behind-the-scenes mental labor. In our case, my physical needs mean that more of the hands-on work gets allocated to David while I gladly embrace my role as project manager.

Yesterday, K was home from school for the day. David brought her a snack first thing to tide her over until breakfast at 7 a.m. Around 6 a.m., I took my medication, which allows me to sit up and interact. Around 6:30, K crawled into bed with me to do a miniature crossword puzzle, which she loves. David then fed K breakfast and cleaned up, gave K her medication, fed our dog, and played with K for an hour. While they played, I ordered groceries, talked to her teacher about a missed school day, coordinated paperwork with her occupational therapist, scheduled a dentist appointment, and purchased a gift for a birthday party. I also worked on a chapter of this book.

K and I made birthday cards together later in the morning before I had to rest again. David and K played an active and enthusiastic balloon game. While resting, I ordered dinners for an upcoming trip, contacted our accountant, and emailed our financial planner about some issues that came up when filing our taxes.

The day continued in this way. I go in and out of time with K, but, right now, the needs of K's body do not work for sustained periods of time with the needs of my body. Though we are compatible, alone, for longer and longer stretches as K gets older and can sit still for longer. Over time, David's and my responsibilities continue to evolve.

David is leaving town to visit a sick relative in a few weeks. A friend is coming to help with K while David is gone, particularly school drop-off and pickup since I cannot drive. I do not consider this reliance on community to be a weakness. It's how all people thrive—in a web of giving and receiving.

I wonder, sometimes, how I would parent K if I were single, living alone. It's hard to imagine, but I believe that I'd figure it out. Like disabled people everywhere, I would call on my deep resourcefulness and well-practiced innovation. K and I would adapt to each other. In the spaces where I'd need help, I would find help. We'd take the city bus to school. Instead of a homemade lunch each day, I'd pay for the school-made meals. K would rely on me for companionship with puzzles and books but would learn to play with neighbors when she needs to run and jump.

But, in this family, which I am thankful for every day, we have a routine that works. I make this family better. Even though I must remind myself of that often. Despite my hard-fought beliefs about my value as a disabled person, I still carry a deep feeling of inadequacy around when it comes to parenting. I feel guilty for needing to rest. When I start to get lost in those feelings, I force myself to think about the internalized messages that breed them.

Is my sense of failure based in reality, or on the tired archetype of the superhero mother? In the day-to-day waves of inadequacy, I try to check in with myself to find the root of my fear. I try to imagine myself talking to another disabled parent the way I can talk to myself.

Sometimes, I have enough perspective to consider how the creativity that I have developed as a disabled person has helped me as a parent—has helped K as a child. I wonder what a nondisabled person might find, if they had the freedom and practice of starting at the beginning. If everyone considered that maybe our society wasn't designed for our comfort or survival. If, instead of thinking that it *should* be possible to parent without a community, work full-time while breastfeeding, and manage months of sleepless nights without relief, parents could really consider:

What can I handle?

What can I change?

I wonder how much time nondisabled parents spend making the assumptions that I did when I was in pain for decades. That life is easier for everyone else and that they just aren't tough enough. What would happen if we had the space to express what it's really like, make no assumptions, and invent solutions that really work? How would parenting shift if we finally admitted something must change?

Disabled parents are experts at telling the truth about what we need and what we can handle. And from that place of honesty, we are skilled at finding answers. We research, we consider, we make no assumptions. We ask for help and advice and share what we've learned. We create a life.

Chapter 6

IN THE WORLD

Before K was born, I had a few safe places to land when I left my house—my friend Nataly's apartment, where she always had the sofa fluffed for me, with a fan positioned to keep me cool, and where she cooked elaborate dinners that fit my evolving dietary restrictions (currently not tolerating cinnamon, oatmeal, and chocolate). I frequented the downtown movie theater, featuring a full dinner menu and thrifted sofas. I could park in an accessible spot right out front and knew to arrive early so that I could get the worn leather sofa on the top row all the way to the right that was high enough to allow me to lean back and close enough to the railing so that I could rest my feet. A coffee shop on Alcatraz Avenue had a black sofa in front of a wooden ledge where I could recline and do my grad school coursework for hours while elevating my legs.

I had my wheelchair in my trunk, but, because it was manual then and too heavy for me to propel, I restricted my adventures to the spots where I could find parking and sit reclined with my feet elevated. When I had to visit my specialists at Stanford, an hour away, a friend would drive me and push me down the long hospital hallways.

Before I was a parent, when David left each day for San Francisco, I was happy to spend my days at home in Oakland and venture out periodically to the few places where I could stay safe. And in the first months after K was born, I stayed home even more than before, but it felt natural. We were getting to know one another. It was easier to be at home than pack up our baby gear—bottles and formula and diapers and blankets. But I left sometimes; the nature of K's personality and my disability meant I could still visit some of my usual haunts. As a newborn, all K needed to be soothed was my proximity. The coffee shop on Alcatraz was across from her pediatrician. Before appointments, I drank my macchiato on my usual sofa with K's tiny body tucked beside me, calm and drowsy. I even, once or twice, saw afternoon movies with K, her little body curled up on my chest as I rested on my favorite worn couch.

After a few months, as David and I learned that we would be K's foster parents for the foreseeable future, we started to make plans. The first was a trip to a small island called Lummi off the coast of Washington State. After getting permission from K's social worker and a judge, our adventure began. We flew out of Oakland; a friend drove us to the airport and helped us check the bags. David pushed me in my wheelchair, and I carried K on my lap. Once in the air, we learned the hard way that air pressure changes can contribute to diaper blowouts, but the flight was, generally, fine.

When we arrived in Seattle, David pushed K and me to the corner of the baggage claim area and returned to watch for our bags while I bottle-fed her. Once David had our suitcases, he dropped them off with us in the corner and left to get our rental car. Returning an hour later with the car, he parked out front, came in and retrieved the bags, and then, finally, two hours after landing, brought K and me to the car. A few extra steps, but manageable.

Our week on Lummi was heaven. I read so many books that I joined the local library so that I could check out more. At night, I drank IPA and ate Oreos under the stars. During the afternoons, K and I lounged on a picnic blanket, listening to the waves.

The return trip was the first time I felt what would become a familiar sinking shame about my disability complicating our life as parents. We had passed the final day in Bellingham, Washington, reading in bookstores and visiting coffee shops. When we left for the airport, we had plenty of time to return our rental car and check in for our flight, but, due to a few car complications, by the time we were walking in the door of the airport, we were cutting it close. I suggested to David that we ask someone at the airport to push me while I carried K so that David could manage our bags. There was no curbside bag check. At that point, I had been using a wheelchair in airports for years and knew that all I needed to do was ask, and an airport attendant would push me to the gate.

When the person arrived, they told me I couldn't carry K on my lap. They said it was airport policy that a baby couldn't ride on a wheelchair (never mind that it was my wheelchair, my lap, and my baby). So, now, David needed to find a way to push our suitcases and carry K simultaneously. That is impossible, and our flight would be leaving soon. The attendant left, and we scrambled for solutions.

We called the attendant back and asked him to push me, and I would drag our suitcases, and David would carry K. And so we inched our way through the airport. I am not strong enough to hold my arms out to the side and push suitcases; before long, I had moved the bags in front of me, pushing them with my feet. It's difficult to navigate suitcases with your feet, so they zigged and zagged, unwieldy and slow. We made our flight. We made it home. But the humiliation of not being allowed to carry my baby continued to burn.

As K grew older, the list of places she needed or wanted to go expanded. The short list of my safe places was no longer enough for her. She started ballet, and I couldn't last an hour propped on the hard wooden floor. She started daycare, and dropping her off required a long walk up a steep driveway. She wanted to visit the zoo and the playground and the children's discovery museum.

As I've discussed, part of how I adapted to her expanding world was to get a power wheelchair. This allowed me to essentially tote the recliner that I need to sit in around with me. And, in many ways, it was effective. I attended ballet classes. We went to the playground. We fed the cows at the little farm in the Berkeley Hills. But a 450-pound wheelchair only works in spaces that are wheelchair accessible. When we go somewhere with stairs, I can't bring my chair, and even though I can walk up a few stairs if the seating at the top isn't accessible, I must leave after only a few minutes. For some disabled or chronically ill people, leaving the house simply isn't possible. But for others, the barriers are structural.

K is now six, and below is a non-exhaustive list of the places that she has gone where, because of inaccessibility, I haven't been about to join:

Her kindergarten classroom. In fact, the entirety of the school she attended for two years.

Countless hikes.

Multiple preschool tours—so many schools in California,
North Carolina, and Ontario are up or down stairs.

Field trips—the other parents were often asked to chaperone.
I never was.

Nearly every shop and restaurant in Montreal while on a
family vacation.

Birthday and holiday parties.

Most playgrounds with sand or gravel.

To visit a sick relative.

In an ambulance, twice.

Being separated on the ambulance rides devastated me. The first time
we called 911, K wasn't yet two and had been sick with pneumonia; the
EMTs arrived quickly, assessed K's status, and said K needed to get to
Oakland's Children's Hospital urgently. "Who's coming?" they asked,
looking between David and me, as they attached sensors to my tiny baby.
Saying I couldn't go with K to the hospital as she struggled to breathe
felt like tearing an organ from my body. But my wheelchair wouldn't fit
inside the ambulance.

David is a kind and attentive dad. K did not suffer for having David
in the ambulance. But I did. I walked with her outside as they loaded my
baby and turned on the sirens. Shaking, I went back inside to figure out
how to get myself to the hospital with my wheelchair. Our house, which
had, minutes before, been loud and busy with equipment and people and
uniforms and alarms, was silent. The sirens faded as they sped down the
hill. I called my neighbor and could barely speak through my tears. He
answered, and within minutes, we were en route to the hospital.

About a year later, K again became sick with a minor cold that turned
to pneumonia and worsened quickly. We were different parents by that
point; after a year of monitoring respiratory rate, oxygen percentage, and
trachea tugs, we knew exactly what to watch for. K had been admitted a year
prior, and we had learned about the risks of prolonged labored breathing.
We were paying attention.

And, even with all our vigilance, K experienced a rapid decline only
hours after visiting her pediatrician for pneumonia. Like the first time, my

gut knew before my brain, and by the time I was calling the after-hours nurse's line, I knew what they would say. "Call 911 immediately." Just like the time before, our apartment went from quiet and tense to brimming with noise and commotion. David, K, and I were on our king-sized bed, with thermometers and oxygen monitors surrounding us, when the EMTs entered.

The paramedics checked K's vital signs, and their demeanors changed. "Signs of sepsis," one reported. "Hurry." And, just like that, they were running, K on a stretcher, David hurrying behind. The silence they left behind was eerie. I knew what sepsis could mean for a baby, and all I wanted was to be with my child to ensure that no one made a life-threatening mistake. To demand that every person pay undivided attention to K.

Alone in my apartment, I remembered that, in my twenties, I had helped the chief of emergency medicine at the closest major hospital buy a home. He and I had connected in the process, and I had joined him and his wife, an infectious disease doctor, on their boat to celebrate after. It had been years since we had talked, and a lot had changed, including my disability and becoming a parent. I picked up my phone, found his contact, and called.

"It's Jessica—your old realtor. I have a child now, and she is in an ambulance on the way to the emergency room, and the paramedics said it might be sepsis. K is in respiratory distress." I was weeping, and my hands shook, but I got the words out. He was calm and kind and said he would call the attending on duty to make sure everyone acted quickly and would keep me in the loop. I was doing all I could to save my baby. I would have done anything.

Hanging up the phone, the adrenaline took over, and I barely made it to the bathroom before vomiting. I crouched over the toilet while looking at my phone every few seconds, waiting for news. Watching the minutes pass and knowing my baby was in danger felt physically intolerable. It wasn't long before the doctor was calling back. He was home with his family but had stayed on the phone with the emergency room to monitor K's care.

"K is in a room—she is stable, her oxygen is steady, and we are checking for sepsis. In the meantime, we are giving her IV antibiotics to fight the potential sepsis and pneumonia. She is OK." K *was* OK, thank goodness. But the feeling of having to leave her side while she was in danger still makes me cry. I can picture myself doing what I wanted and needed in that moment: to run alongside the stretcher, holding K's hand. I want to be there for the banal moments but I need to be there for the critical ones.

As chapter 5 explored, disabled parents use our ingenuity and creativity to build home environments that support our needs and keep our kids safe. Our caregiving abilities are optimized in our homes. But when we leave the house, the obstacles multiply. For one, the built environment is often inaccessible and inhospitable for individual bodies and minds. Secondly, when not in our homes we see other people, and people, through words and actions, create a different kind of hostile environment.

Jessie Owen, who you met in earlier chapters, is quadriplegic and has twins.[1] Her babies are not yet walking but are quite mobile. While she can provide the care her kids need at home, when she is out of the house with them, she needs assistance. Her family has a full-time nanny who accompanies her and the twins on outings. She and the nanny have a great working relationship, and she said that she never feels like the nanny is infantilizing or patronizing her.

That isn't the case for the strangers she encounters. She knows she is bound to receive comments when people witness her parent. "Well, I sure couldn't do what you do!" and "Oh, look at you! What an inspiration!" She tries to let the comments roll off and keep living her life, but it impacts her. Social media is much worse. She posts some videos about parenting on TikTok and Instagram, and the comments can be brutal.

I told her that sometimes I feel the need to be an especially good parent in public because of my disability—that I know people are judging, so I try to overperform. She said she does the same, and it's even worse when her husband is around because he garners so many compliments. "What an amazing dad and husband!" people offer, which can make Jessie feel inadequate, and she finds herself trying to demonstrate her worth as a mom.

Also worth noting: all dads, not only those with disabled partners, receive heaps of praise for basic parenting tasks. Parenting in public, for everyone, is something of a spectacle and a magnet for judgment, both positive and negative. Expectations around the performance of parenting hurt us all.

Jessie has adapted to her disability by thinking positively whenever possible. But optimism can't alter an inaccessible built world. With her babies and the nanny, she attends a music class where the parents and the babies all sing together. The building has a step at the entrance—something that a nondisabled parent might not even notice.

For Jessie, that step is a much more substantial hurdle. When they arrive, she must slide out of her wheelchair and then wriggle on the ground over the threshold and into the building while she waits for help. I have been stuck on the ground waiting for help, and I know: it is an awful feeling. Her nanny then hands the babies to whoever happens to be walking by, so she can heft the chair into the building. She then helps Jessie off the ground and back into her chair.

When they visit the park, Jessie wants her kids to explore, but they are too young to listen to instructions, so, with her husband, they created harnesses that she can grab with her level of dexterity. Ski enthusiasts designed the harnesses for parents to hold onto toddlers while they raced down the slope. Jessie purchased them and had them altered so that the handles were large enough that she could grip them with her mostly paralyzed hands. When her kids wander away and into danger, she leans forward in her wheelchair and loops her wrist through the handle on the back of the harness, halting one of her babies' progress. She can then, with a combination of her arms, mouth, and core strength, pull her child up into her lap and onto the wheelchair.

Jessie drives but cannot, without assistance, take her twins out of their car seats. She does, when needed, drive alone with them, but not without substantial planning. First, someone at her trip's origin buckles the twins in and positions the back seat camera so Jessie can see them as she drives. She makes sure her phone is accessible and voice control is enabled. Multiple people track her location and know where she is going and when she should arrive. And then she's off. She is on the road alone with two babies who, in the case of an emergency, she could not extract from their car seats. While someone is always waiting at her destination, there is inherent risk to being alone on the road with her kids.

I have made similar decisions, and so I asked, without judgment, how she determines which risks to take. She replied, "Yes, I do get nervous. But I've learned to adapt and use all of my skills. I got good at it. Keeping my kids safe is a bit more cerebral. At this point, I just try to manage my anxiety. I try to have a plan." She also reminded me that any time a parent gets behind the wheel with a kid, there is risk. We can't avoid it. She, more than anyone, knows this is true. She became disabled in a car accident that killed her parents. And she's reckoned with our fragility and has determined that it will not rule her. "As humans, we are meant to live big stories."

Jessie's calculations are familiar. Every parent, disabled or not, navigates the balance of safety and freedom. We want our kids to have expansive and interesting lives, and we also want, more than anything, to keep them completely and totally safe. It's hard to know which voices are our better angels when considering which risks to take and which to avoid.

Also, many parents my age remember our childhoods in the '80s and '90s and compare the risks of our childhoods to the safety expectations of parents today. It's hard to imagine a child today being tossed around in the trunk of a station wagon or roaming the neighborhood for hours before the age of ten. Risk calculation is complex, and I am certainly not one to elevate the experience of the good old days (Good? For who?), but it's hard to deny that parents are expected to insulate their children from many harms (at least those that we can purchase solutions for).

Personally, I am always wrestling with safety. I live in a body that is proof that bodies are fragile. I never forget, not for a moment, that life is ephemeral. So, then, how shall we live? How do I find the space between extending my life to the last possible second and squeezing every last drop from the moments?

For disabled parents in wheelchairs or on crutches, leaving the house brings risk. We cannot, despite our deepest desires, run after our kids. We cannot lift a car in a feat of superhuman strength. We cannot dive into the ocean to snatch our grade-schooler from a riptide. But we want to have, as Jessie says, big lives. We want to join our kids for music class and school drop-off and at the beach. We want access.

Accessibility is, simply, adjusting the environment to allow disabled people to participate. In Emily Ladau's brilliant book *Demystifying Disability*, she offers examples of ways that a location or event can be accessible, including:[2]

Quiet rooms with dim lights at events that may induce
    sensory overwhelm.

Sign language interpreters.

Closed captions.

Text descriptions of images.

Braille or large print options for written material.

And this is what accessibility is like for me: K has a friend at school who is having a birthday party in two weeks. The mom texted me yesterday and described the party location, the bathroom, and the height of the steps from the yard to the house. She said she would send photos so I could make sure she didn't forget to tell me anything. I explained that my wheelchair might tear up her yard. She assured me that she didn't mind.

In a few weeks, a friend is hosting our book club. She has already sent photos of the entrance to their house, and I will stop by the week before book club to make sure my chair can get in and out without issue. One of my oldest friends, Casey, turns the temperature down before I come over, clears off the sofa, and offers me food and drink immediately. Once I'm seated, she always asks if there is anything else I need to be safe and comfortable.

This is what access *feels* like to me: when I am sad or lonely or scared, and my therapist asks me to shut my eyes and think of a place where I am happiest and safe—to smell and touch and really imagine that I am there—I picture Casey's sofa. Being seen, believed, and cared for is life-giving.

Conversely, not being included or accommodated for can feel deeply painful. As Rebekah Taussig, who uses a wheelchair, wrote in *Sitting Pretty*:

> Many days, I feel too vulnerable to leave my house, too fed up to subject myself to the gamble of strangers interacting with me, too tired to fight to occupy a corner of space. Inaccessibility over time tells me that I do not matter, I'm not wanted, do not belong. This land wasn't made for me. So I stay in, keep to myself, avoid, cancel plans, carry anxiety in each fold and bend of my body, feel very alone, trapped, and helpless.[3]

I relate to Taussig's sentiments. A few weeks ago, I was spending a weekend alone to rest after experiencing some parenting burnout. I woke up the first morning and felt like a morning outing. The Airbnb I was staying at had no stairs, but a significant threshold at the entrance made coming and going unwieldy. I made it out with only a few issues and left to visit the neighborhood coffee shop. When I arrived, I realized there was a step at the entrance.

Not all steps have the same emotional impact. In fact, where the front door to a restaurant or shop is up a few steps and on a crowded street, I understand how challenging it would be to build a ramp to fit the space. To meet safety requirements, commercial ramps may only have one inch of lift for every twelve inches of length.[4] So, for a building with five average-height steps, they would need about thirty-five *feet* of ramp. Many city blocks have no space to accommodate a thirty-five-foot ramp. That's not to say there aren't other solutions, but when I see an older building with an entrance up a few stairs, I understand that the current occupants may have few options.

On the other hand, as is the case for this coffee shop, the one step at the entrance is about six inches—about four inches more than my wheelchair can climb—and the front of the building has plenty of space to accommodate a ramp. The owners renovated the shop recently and added a back patio onto which, incidentally, they installed a four-inch threshold to enter. While in my wheelchair, I cannot enter the back patio or the front of the restaurant, despite the availability of affordable and straightforward access solutions. In this case, a short ramp in the front and a gate in the back without a metal threshold would have allowed me to go inside.

Pulling up alone and realizing that I couldn't get inside felt humiliating. I waited out front, hoping an employee would see me, but no one came. I worried that people inside were watching me, and I felt self-conscious. I looked at my outfit and checked my teeth in my phone camera. I could feel that I was being watched. After a few minutes, a woman about my age walked by and looked inside. "Are you getting coffee?" I asked her, and she looked at me, surprised. "Actually, no," she said, "but do you need me to open the door for you?"

I explained that I couldn't get inside, even if she opened the door, and asked if she could get my coffee for me. It felt awkward. She agreed, I gave her cash, and she returned a few minutes later with my macchiato. I could overhear her inside, talking to the barista. "Yeah, she's just sitting out there. I wasn't even going to come in, but I thought I would help." I had imagined that I would go inside, order a coffee, and read on the patio. Instead, I spent twenty minutes on the sidewalk, excluded—a spectacle.

Dr. Jessi Elana Aaron, whom I've discussed in earlier chapters, has been living in the same town in Florida for years.[5] She has grown used to being watched. Her son is five, and for the first two years of his life, when they left the house, he rode in a camping carrier attached to her front. Starting around age two, his height made it so she couldn't see over his head, and they needed to find another option.

Dr. Aaron had set up her home with the ingenious adaptations that enable her to care for her son, but, like many disabled people, entering an inaccessible and judgmental world brings complications. She could drive an adapted van, but to do so would require well over $100,000 to cover the van itself plus the essential training, conducted only in Georgia. Without the funds to cover an accessible vehicle, she and her son rely on public buses.

Once his height began obstructing her view, they tried different positions that could keep them both safe and comfortable. At first, they thought he might tuck behind her, between her body and the backrest of her wheelchair, but she didn't like not being able to see him. They considered a trailer or cart attached to the back of the chair, but it wouldn't work on the city buses they use for transportation. Eventually, they discovered that if he knelt on her footrest while facing her shins and hugged her lower body, he could ride for miles. He crosses his ankles, and the position of the body makes it so that if he begins to slip, she senses it immediately and stops her chair.

We spoke over video one evening so that they could demonstrate the position. I had trouble imagining where his body would go but looking at them in their living room on my iPhone screen, it made sense. He tucks into his mom perfectly. Their bodies mold together. It looks natural.

When they first found this position, they practiced—first a half block, then a full block on a quiet street. Now, three years later, they travel for miles. Dr. Aaron has always prioritized and reiterated traffic safety with him since she can't reach out her arms to stop him from running into the street. He has internalized the message. During a recent playdate, when his friend got too close to the street, he yelled, "Be careful! Do you want to die?!"

In the three years he's been riding on her footrest, they have become accustomed to strangers commenting, sometimes quite aggressively, on their transportation. Recently, as they rode down the sidewalk, a woman in a car pulled up beside them, slowing down to their speed.

"GET HIM OFF OF THERE RIGHT NOW!!! THAT IS NOT SAFE," she shouted.

"Driving with your head out the window on the wrong side of the road is not safe," Dr. Aaron replied.

"HE IS GOING TO DIE," the driver shouted back before leaving.

Thanks to technology, opinions about how she exists in public follow her home. Not too long ago, Dr. Aaron logged into the Nextdoor app to find a post about her. "Have you all seen the poor woman in a wheelchair with her son? I want to help her." Comments poured in. "I've seen that little boy hanging on to dear life." And "We need to do something, so he isn't taken away."

Dr. Aaron replied to the original poster and explained that she is a tenured professor and doing fine, but, if they want to help, what she needs is the funds for a van. The "concerned" poster never replied.

She regularly catches people taking videos of her. She glares and shakes her head, but, of course, she doesn't always notice. A friend was on Instagram early in 2023 and came across a video of Dr. Aaron and her son backing down an overly steep curb cut. It felt invasive to know that her daily life was being recorded and widely commented on, without her permission.

When her son was a baby, her doctor asked her to stop bringing him to appointments, explaining that it wasn't safe for her to carry him on her chest. Her son's PT said she couldn't allow Dr. Aaron to leave appointments with her son in her wheelchair with her. That was the only way for her to leave, so they had to switch physical therapists.

I asked her how she understands the impulse of nondisabled bystanders to correct the choices that disabled people make. After all, their judgments can be quite consequential, as disabled people face an increased risk of child protective services involvement. Dr. Aaron believes that strangers assume that she cannot have a complex experience of human life because of her disability, and, from that restricted perspective, she cannot make full and educated decisions. She thinks people see it as their responsibility to explain how the world really works—that her view is too obstructed.

"Every single person is biased!" I couldn't help but reply when Dr. Aaron offered her explanation. The sentence that repeats in my brain came out: there is no view from normal. She agreed. She wished people could see that their bodies and minds didn't make them objective. That their perspective was also limited by experience. This is what I want people to know about disabled parenting.

The third time Dr. Aaron and I spoke, she and her son were settling in at home after a long day at work and school. His sweet little voice chirped into the phone: "Hi, Jessica!" And then, to his mom: "May I have a popsicle?" She said yes and asked if he needed help reaching it. He did. She asked where his step stool was. He didn't know. She said she would help lift him up.

"Did that hurt?" he asked after leaning on her to prop himself up.

"It did not hurt," she replied.

With him behind her back, she approached the freezer, backing into position.

"OK, mom! You're doing so good!" he said, and my heart melted.

Dr. Aaron had assumed she would need to use her chair's elevate feature, to raise him closer to the height of the freezer, but he could reach without it. She offered careful instructions—how to pull the popsicle out slowly without disrupting all the other food in the freezer. Once he had it in hand and the freezer door was shut, she suggested he toss the popsicle to the floor so that he had both hands to get off her chair. He did, and climbed down, thanking his mom and skipping away to play while Dr. Aaron and I finished our conversation.

Improved access is vital for all parents, not only those with disabilities. In 2019, Malaysia Goodson, a twenty-two-year-old mother, died after falling while trying to carry her baby in a stroller on the stairs at the Seventh Avenue stop on Fifty-Third Street in Manhattan.[6] Her baby was OK. The public response was intense, but brief, outrage. Disabled people and parents were quick to share just how unsurprised they were. Navigating public transportation in New York if you can't climb stairs is fraught. Less than 25 percent of subway stops have elevators, and the elevators that do exist are often out of order.[7] As anyone who has ridden a subway elevator can attest, the elevators that are in order are filthy and reek of urine, vomit, and feces, and are often sweltering. Every time a subway elevator door shuts behind me, I pray that I won't get trapped inside.

After Goodson died, the city comptroller, Scott Stringer, spoke out about the subway elevators. "As a parent, one of my biggest fears was navigating my kids' double stroller through our broken subway system," Stringer told *The Guardian*. When Stringer's office ran an audit of the limited number of elevators, they found that 80 percent didn't receive adequate maintenance.[8] New York–based publications have periodic pieces about the best way to travel around New York with a kid in a stroller.[9] The conclusions? Painfully.

Public transportation is one of many arenas in which disability access and parental access overlap. Parents using strollers for the first time are often struck by how inaccessible the world is for wheeled transportation. Before one uses a wheelchair or pushes a stroller, it's easy to assume that ramps are everywhere. If you don't need a ramp for access, it's natural to notice where they *are* but not where they *aren't*.

All parents need accommodations: spaces for breastfeeding, safe diaper changing areas, and storage for pumped breastmilk are all accommodations. Parents recovering from C-sections need car seats that aren't so heavy that they damage their surgical incisions. Using the restroom in public when the space won't fit a stroller can be impossible, and grocery shopping when a baby can't yet ride in the cart is cumbersome.

Working hours are often mismatched with daycare hours. Few parents have enough sick days to account for how often kids are sick. Summer break? Completely inaccessible for parents who work. Parenting, especially during the early years, is a perpetual attempt to shoehorn unwieldy family life into a rigid and productivity-based hyper-capitalist society. Fitting childcare into work life is like fitting an octopus into pants.

As I mentioned in chapter 5, for Stacy Cervenka, between being blind and having postpartum depression, it was nearly impossible for her to leave the house after her first child was born.[10] She entered a cycle of staying home because she was depressed and growing more depressed because she was staying home. She couldn't figure out how to be in the world as a blind person with a baby. It certainly didn't help that when she had expressed worry over her baby's latch in the hospital, a nurse had contacted child protective services with concerns over her parental fitness.

But, with her second baby, Stacy believed that, for her sanity, she needed to find a way to accept more risk and endure the discomfort of the unfamiliar. She started to experiment with the best way to wear her newborn. She tried countless carriers and wraps until landing on the Moby. It took her some time to learn, but, before too long, she found that she could strap her baby to her chest and negotiate the world almost like she had before becoming a parent. Her world expanded, and her mental health improved.

Once the carrier was no longer sufficient, Stacy and her husband found a jogging stroller that, with three wheels, could be used with one hand without fishtailing. This accessibility feature allowed them to navigate with their canes and pull a stroller behind them. Finding a way to make the world outside one's home tolerable as a disabled person isn't simply a matter of mindset. It wasn't only depression that formed a hurdle for Stacy to clear. Navigating the world as a blind person is full of accessibility hurdles. The National Federation for the Blind offers a guide to blind parenting to social workers and medical providers, which outlines some of the ways in which blind people can be accommodated.[11]

The guide is in response to substantial gaps in digital and physical parenting infrastructure. Digital accessibility is a problem for all blind people, including parents.[12] In Seattle, the math curriculum and online communications weren't accessible to blind staff, students, or parents after a 2012 software update. A blind parent filed a lawsuit with the National Federation for the Blind and prevailed in 2015 after asking the district to make changes for years. Seattle Public Schools updated their programs. But it took legal action to convince them to make the change.[13] Similarly, in British Columbia, an application that parents need to use to document absences is completely unusable for blind people.[14]

Josh Miele is a blind dad in California who has thought a lot about access. He was born sighted but became blind in 1973 when he was four and living in Park Slope in Brooklyn. One afternoon, his twenty-four-year-old neighbor rang his doorbell; Josh answered, and, for reasons that have never been fully explained, the neighbor poured acid on his face.[15]

Dr. Miele has a PhD in psychoacoustics from the University of California at Berkeley, worked for NASA, and is an avid inventor. He was a 2021 MacArthur Fellow. He is also an enthusiastic advocate for accessibility and has developed Braille maps for the Bay Area Rapid Transit system (BART). The maps are also usable using an audio smart pen. He is passionate about finding technological solutions to accessibility issues.

In a 2022 interview with PBS Newshour, he offered an important reminder that applies to parenting: "Most of us live in a heavily built environment, and most of the things that we interact with are human-made pieces of planning or infrastructure."[16] He elaborated using the example of stairs. It's well understood that people need assistance to access anything above or below ground level. For some, a rope might work, but, for most, climbing is inaccessible. For a larger group of people, stairs are adequate, but there are many for whom they don't work, including wheelchair users and those pushing strollers.

Yet, when we talk about disability, we often place the onus on the wheelchair user as someone who lacks the capacity to manage stairs. But we built the stairs. As Dr. Miele reminds us, we live in a human-built world. Instead of thinking of certain bodies or minds as deficient, we should take a step back and consider why our structures were built in this manner.

Dr. Miele offers,

So the question is, how was the infrastructure designed so that it resulted in you not being able to use it? . . . We have this long legacy culturally— and not just in our culture, but globally—of thinking that when a person's body is different from other people's bodies, it's lesser or not as valuable or less capable. If we design our tools and our systems to allow that person to interact equally, then that lets the person do it. But if we don't design those systems, [it's] because we don't believe that person actually has the right to do it. . . . It all comes back to the way we think about and value people with disabilities or whose bodies are different from the norm. If we don't value them, we won't build our systems to include them. And it's a self-perpetuating problem.

When interviewed, he brings the interviewer back to his underlying belief that disability is defined, largely, by a "configuration of social process and infrastructure." Dr. Miele loves technology and the access it provides, but he never forgets that changing cultural beliefs about disability will take much more than scientific innovation.

Dr. Miele and I emailed about his experience as a disabled parent.[17] I asked him about obstacles to being in public with his kids when they were young. He said that he used bells attached to their clothing and call-and-response. From the time his kids were very young, he made it clear that if he ever called to them, they had to respond. They did. Still, even with these techniques, he needed to be deliberate about what environments he visited alone with his kids. "I could really only give them freedom in well-fenced playgrounds where I could afford to lose track of them for a minute or two, or the environment needed to be quiet enough that I could be sure of hearing the bells or their responses. And, of course, they needed to be able to hear me call. Otherwise, I needed to keep a hand on them or to stay within arm's reach."

When I asked about his experience of disabled-parenting-as-spectacle he said that most often, strangers would make ill-informed comments like, "Be kind to your dad," or tell Dr. Miele that he was "miraculous." (What disabled person hasn't been complimented by a stranger for doing something totally mundane?) He said, "The thing that annoyed me the most was the folks who would talk to my young kids as though they were the ones in charge—they would never have spoken to a nondisabled parent's child like that."

It's my belief that ableism, internal and external, is born from a fear of need and a fear of death. And I agree with Dr. Miele that when society fails to accommodate a variety of bodies and minds in public and private spaces, it's an oversight that grows from ableism. To take the example from earlier in this chapter: the coffee shop near my Airbnb decided that enabling wheelchair users to enter their space was not worth the time and money it would take to build a ramp. When they were thinking about what chairs people would want to sit in and what drinks people would want to order, they didn't consider that disabled needs should be considered. That choice has an inherent implication: disabled people are not important.

The belief that it's worse to be disabled—which dictates a great deal of public and private life—thrives in part because disability is a reminder that bodies and minds fail, always. We build entire structures and belief systems around avoiding the reality of our collective fragility. Our governing ethos is that of independence and strength, not of need. When we request an accommodation—a lighter car seat, a ramp, a Braille edition of a book—we are admitting that we are needy. And when we have needs, we confess to something we wish weren't true, that we are mortal.

What makes our manic rejection of our mortality even more fraught is that, once we become parents, we must also find a way to delude ourselves that our kids are indestructible. It is intolerable to think about the reality that our kids will be hurt, physically and emotionally. We buy into the myth of safety, as we attempt to create a force field of invincibility around our family so that we can stay safe and happy forever.

All every parent wants is to inoculate their child from pain and loss. But, of course, we also know that every human suffers. When I imagine my child asking someone to play and getting rejected, the pain is more than I can bear. When she is off in the woods with her friends, my brain runs through all the ways she could be hurt.

Every time K coughs, my body remembers the paramedic, eyes bright with fear, saying the word "sepsis." I hate being reminded of K's fragility. At night before bed, when I cuddle her, I imagine a balloon stretching out of my chest and around her body. A shield that will always protect her. I want my love to do that, and I know it's not enough. One of the hardest things I do every day is let her leave my sight.

Every disabled person I spoke to while writing this book feels the same way. We want to keep our kids in a protective bubble, but we know they deserve the fullness that life has to offer. As Jessie Owen said, "We are meant to live big lives." When a disabled parent enters the world with their kids and endures inaccessibility and criticism, and the fear that someone will contact child protective services, we are acting from brave and expansive love. When a child's school adds a ramp or updates its communication so that it's accessible to screen readers, it's a way to honor that love.

Perhaps, when nondisabled people witness a blind parent at the playground listening for the bells on their kid's shoes, part of their concern is that they are forced to remember that none of this is guaranteed. That every safety consideration is a Band-Aid. That hardship is inevitable. When they wonder if another person's child is safe, they must consider that maybe their own children aren't as insulated as they'd like. The built world is sharp and hard and unwieldy for us all. Every child runs on concrete. Every car ride is a gamble. Every day at school is a chance to be bullied.

Reckoning with fragility often feels like the work of my life. My own body dislocates and injures often. Sometimes, part of the injuring action feels cosmically cruel—a hug can bump a rib out of place, and kissing my husband can injure my neck. It can feel impossible to both live fully and protect myself.

I learned early to err on the side of caution, which has been protective. But I've also learned that what others tell me is safe isn't always true, and what the world tells me is dangerous is also suspect. For example, taking a bowl from the cupboard is generally considered low risk. However, lifting my hand to the top shelf will trigger nerve pain for weeks. Also, speeding down the sidewalk in my 450-pound wheelchair with a toddler on my lap may invite criticism, but I, and disabled parents everywhere, know in our bones that it's where our babies are most at home.

In some ways, the pandemic illustrated that people will do almost anything to ignore how fragile we are. As I write this, the risk of long COVID is still pathologically ignored. Furthermore, catching COVID comes with a substantially increased risk of heart attack, stroke, and dementia. It can impact one's immune system long and short term. Between 10 and 45 percent of people who catch COVID will have long-term symptoms.[18] Yet the messaging and practices around COVID treat it like nothing more than a common cold.

But when the metrics being used to evaluate risk are shifted beyond the nondisabled norm, safety suddenly becomes paramount. In other words, the standards that disabled people are held to are inconsistent. We are receptacles for fear. It's perverse. We must find a way to live with the uncertainty that doesn't involve shoving all our fears onto those with minority bodies and minds. I am more than a reminder of your fragility.

When K was hospitalized with breathing issues, confronting the reality of her mortality was almost impossible. But the heartbreaking truth is this: K is mortal, and so am I. But here's what is also true: the admission that every person has unique needs is not some slippery slope to death and loss. In fact, it's the opposite. And that's the magic that disability culture has to offer. Disabled people have learned that caring for one another and offering access is life-giving. Our existence swells when the complexities of our bodies and minds are believed and respected.

Instead of worrying about safety when we see a baby riding on their parent's wheelchair, we should consider how we can create more spaces where wheelchair users are welcome. The picture disabled parents paint while in public with our kids is beautiful and offers permission. We are showing that there are countless ways to have bodies and minds and that it's OK to cross the border of what's expected. We are not reminders of death—we are reminders of how full life can be.

Chapter 7

MEDICAL CARE

The following chapter is expansive in scope and heavy in content. But it's vital. Without autonomy in healthcare, other parenting questions become moot. We must be alive to advocate for ramps into our children's schools.

For the first few months after I became disabled, I entered every new medical complex filled with trust and optimism—all I had to do was tell the truth about what I was experiencing, and a doctor would work with me to find an explanation and solution. I knew it might take some tests and time, but I saw every new provider as a potential teammate.

Here's what I knew I could offer during these early appointments: the details of what it felt like to live in my body and a memory of what it had felt like only a few months prior. And the doctors came with years and years of training and experience. Together, we could figure out why one day I was a runner and the next I wasn't able to get out of bed.

But here is what happened: the doctors were rushed and dismissive. They ordered basic bloodwork, and when the results returned close to normal, they suggested that anxiety was a probable explanation for my symptoms. Many said something along the lines of, "You'd be surprised what our brains can trick us into believing."

So, I worked harder to be a better teammate. I made spreadsheets about my symptoms and what helped and hurt my progress. But that seemed to alienate the doctors. When I shared the chronology of my symptom progression, they shook their heads. "See, this is what happens when you focus too much on your body."

Here is what I know now: all a doctor needed to do to give me an initial POTS diagnosis was to take my heart rate and blood pressure while lying flat. Have me stand upright. Retake my vitals five and ten minutes later. That's it. They would have seen that when horizontal, my heart rate hung out around 80, but within five minutes of standing, it topped 150. They would have seen that my blood pressure dropped precipitously. They would have realized that many of my symptoms could be explained by these wild orthostatic swings.

Despite my relentless pursuit of answers, it took two years for a doctor to mention POTS. During that time, I became a doubtful and tremulous shell of myself. Medical providers reiterated that my own hyper-focus was causing my symptoms, and, eventually, I believed it. So, when my vision faded and my hands shook, I not only endured physical agony but also berated myself for causing it.

Two years after the hike, I was in a psychiatrist's office in a strip mall near Duke Hospital asking for psychotropic medication. I confessed that I had somehow, through my own delusions, made myself so sick that I couldn't leave the house most days. I said that I felt like I was dying, but doctors told me it wasn't true, and I had to admit that, somehow, I had deceived myself into believing I was sick.

He listened closely and asked for details and clarifications. And after forty-five minutes, he offered his perspective. "I don't think you have a mood disorder or another condition that I can help with. I do think, however, that you may have a neurological and cardiovascular condition called POTS, which a patient of mine had years ago." He referred me for cardiovascular testing. He was right. I was diagnosed with POTS and saw a cardiac electrophysiologist who validated all the physical sensations I had experienced over the prior two years. The psychiatrist had saved my life.

I write this nearly a decade after my POTS diagnosis, and my interactions with medical care are still fraught. Although, in collaboration with my mental health providers, I have employed various therapeutic techniques to heal the trauma from the years of disregard, the profound humiliation and the self-doubt that formed during my early years of illness burrowed deep. Becoming suddenly disabled was painful and frightening, and my suffering was compounded when the systems I turned to for help told me I wasn't a reliable witness to my own body.

Now, when I have any medical appointment, starting the day before, my fingers tingle, and my limbs twitch with adrenaline. In every waiting room, even someplace as innocuous as an optometrist's office, I have trouble catching my breath. My nervous system shouts, "You are not safe here."

And, the truth is, I'm not. Disabled people experience staggering levels of medical mistreatment, particularly those who are multiply marginalized. Michael Hickson, who was Black and disabled, was the father of five kids in early 2020. He had been married to his wife, Melissa, for eighteen years. In 2017, while driving Melissa to work, he went into sudden cardiac arrest. The subsequent oxygen deprivation and CPR resulted in brain injuries, quadriplegia, and blindness. But he was very much still alive—videos from the years after his cardiac arrest show a joyful and engaged father—singing, laughing, and praying. His kids beam in their photos with him.[1]

Melissa, who was acting as his caregiver, applied for legal guardianship. That would give her the official capacity to make medical decisions for him. A move to Austin for more specialized medical treatment slowed that complex legal process. In February 2020, while awaiting a hearing to finalize her guardianship, Melissa received word that Michael's sister Renee, a doctor who lived in Washington, DC, was also requesting guardianship.

Michael and his sister spoke infrequently, and she had not visited him in years. According to Renee, she wanted to make his medical decisions because she believed that Melissa and Michael were not "living in reality" regarding his quality of life.[2] In 2019, Michael's doctors said he should be in a nursing home to receive palliative care, whereas Melissa believed he would be better served in a rehabilitation facility—she thought he could still acquire new skills. The director at Michael's nursing home wrote at that time that Melissa had "unrealistic expectations" as to the level of care her husband required.[3]

Jill Jacobs, a social worker and disability rights activist, who has spoken with Melissa and understands Michael's situation, told the *Washington Post* that she has found that courts tend to prefer guardians who "don't create waves—rather than those who would aggressively lobby for their loved one."[4] Jacobs suspects that Melissa's advocacy was an inconvenience and a financial burden to the hospitals where Michael was treated.

After Michael's sister petitioned to make her brother's medical decisions, a judge awarded temporary guardianship to an Austin nonprofit called Family Eldercare while the final guardianship was determined. The events of the next two months are detailed in court filings from 2021, from which many of these details are taken. In March 2020, Family Eldercare assigned Michael's care to one of their employees, Jessica Drake, who had only provisional status and was new to the field.[5] Against Michael and his wife's wishes, his care went from being managed by his best friend and partner of two decades to a stranger who met him three times and who had very limited experience coordinating complex medical care.

In the weeks before COVID hit Texas, Michael had been hospitalized with pneumonia and sepsis, from which he recovered without complications. After he was released, Family Eldercare placed Michael in a nursing home, and his visits with his family became limited because of COVID restrictions. Then, on May 8, 2020, Michael tested positive for COVID but, despite his wife's frequent requests for information, Jessica did not inform Melissa of his positive test until May 14, 2020. She also told Melissa that he was asymptomatic. Jessica then told Melissa that he tested negative on May 29.

Three days later, on June 2, 2020, an ambulance was called, and Michael was taken to Saint David's Hospital in Austin with acute respiratory illness.[6] At this hospital, he was diagnosed, once again, with sepsis, pneumonia, and a urinary tract infection. His doctors wrote in his medical records that he had a 70 percent chance of recovery. Fortunately, his doctors isolated the bacteria causing the infection and began administering antibiotics, to which he responded quickly. He was awake, verbal, and stable on minimal oxygen supplementation.

Unfortunately, one of the physicians who treated him in the emergency room, Dr. Steven Jennings, assessed his level of disability and suggested to his attending physician, Dr. Carlye Mabry Cantu, that he be placed in hospice and given a do-not-resuscitate (DNR) order.

Dr. Cantu agreed, and contacted palliative care, indicating that due to Michael's disabilities, he had a poor quality of life. She suggested a DNR. Michael and Melissa had not chosen a DNR. It was not what he wanted, which they told the hospital and Michael's newly appointed guardian. In his first few days in the hospital, he experienced improvements and setbacks, but his trajectory was good. On June 4, Jessica Drake emailed Melissa to let her know that he was stable and needed less oxygen. But, later that day, she emailed Melissa again to notify her that he had been moved to the ICU. She also indicated that they need to talk about his "code status."

After his admission into the ICU, his labs showed that the antibiotics were working. Despite this progress, Dr. Cantu requested palliative care again, and, with no written medical explanation, she stopped his antibiotics on June 5, 2020. Melissa went to the hospital to visit her husband and, upon arrival, learned that, per Jessica Drake's instructions, she could not see him unless she was accompanied by security. Melissa stood outside Michael's room and talked to him over FaceTime. He was alert and engaged. His kids joined the call, and he was thrilled to see him.

When Melissa got off the call, a nurse informed her that he was being moved from the ICU to hospice care. She asked to see his doctor, and the hospitalist on duty, Dr. Viet Vo, came to speak with her. She recorded this conversation, which I listened to in its entirety. He explained to her that they were stopping treatment because Michael wouldn't benefit from it. She asked why, since he was improving and was likely to survive. Dr. Vo explained that it was because, "as of right now, his quality of life, he doesn't have much of one." "What do you mean?" she asked, to clarify. "Because he's paralyzed with a brain injury, he doesn't have a quality of life?"

Listening to their conversation, I held my breath. Tears came when I heard Dr. Vo's reply.

"Correct."

All I could think for the rest of the conversation was that Melissa's composure was heroic. She didn't yell or cry. She asked his doctor, "Who gets to make that decision . . . if they have a disability that their quality of life is not good?"

Later in the conversation, Dr. Vo explained that the people who would benefit from additional treatment would be "walking and talking people."[7]

Later that day, Michael was transferred to hospice, and the hospital issued the DNR order that the admitting doctor had requested. His doctors also ordered that his medical team cease his IV nutrition and hydration. They took him off supplemental oxygen. They gave him only pain medication. The next days were frantic for Melissa and torturous for Michael. He was hungry and growing sicker without antibiotics and oxygen. Melissa tried everything. She contacted Family Eldercare many times each day.

She called the hospital. She tried to visit and was turned away. She tried to transfer Michael to a different hospital. She contacted attorneys. She encountered dead end after dead end. Only months before, she had been her husband's care provider, and now, she was powerless.

She begged for information. It came in slowly. The information she was able to glean horrified her. She emailed Jessica Drake on June 7: "I was stunned to find out on Saturday that the code status had been changed to DNR hospice. And even more stunned to find out Michael was in a cold room being starved to death. You have shown no regard for human life. Family Eldercare has shown no regard for the wishes of his wife to keep him alive."[8]

Melissa spoke with Dr. Cantu on June 8 and begged her to take her husband off hospice and treat his infections. Dr. Cantu said that Jessica Drake was the one permitted to make the request. Later that day, Melissa talked to her husband's nurse who told her that her husband was awake and saying that he was hungry. The doctors finally agreed to give him a "low trickle rate" of food. Melissa also learned that, despite no antibiotics or oxygen, his breathing had improved. His body was recovering.[9]

Melissa spent the 9th and 10th calling Family Eldercare and the hospital, begging them to treat her husband. On the 10th, without explanation, Jessica Drake told the hospital that they should no longer communicate with Melissa about his status and that his information should be kept confidential. Melissa had still not been able to see her husband over FaceTime.

Melissa contacted Jessica Drake almost hourly on the 11th, asking for permission to visit her husband. Drake told her to call the hospital. She called the hospital, and they told her that visits needed to go through Jessica Drake. She contacted Jessica that evening and again on the morning of the 12th, when she received an out-of-office reply. Melissa contacted Jessica's supervisor, asking to visit her husband. Melissa called the hospital again on the morning of June 12, hoping they would let her visit. The hospital, again, told her to call Jessica Drake.

What they didn't tell her, and couldn't tell her because of the new confidentiality requirements, was that Michael had been found dead at 10 p.m. the night prior, on June 11, 2020. Michael left behind five young children and his devoted wife.

After his death, his sister, whose request for guardianship set these tragic events in motion, spoke with the *Washington Post*. When asked about his quality of life, and why she believed that Michael and Melissa weren't living in reality, she explained that, "while he could carry on a conversation and remember facts such as her birthday and his social security number, there were many gaps. He could tell her how much he loved it when she snuck in gumbo, or chocolate, and put a few bits on his tongue. But he couldn't rattle off a list of breakfast food items when asked. He could help her pick a book to read—the most recent was Octavia E. Butler's award-winning science fiction novel *Parable of the Talents*—and tell her he enjoyed it. But he had no concept of time."[10]

Read that again. Michael, a disabled parent, loved food and his family and Octavia Butler and conversations. But, because a series of doctors and third-party guardians judged his quality of life as poor, he was left hungry and alone at the end of a hallway.

NPR and the *Washington Post* covered Michael's story after he died, and the articles were measured—cautious in saying what would have happened if he had been given antibiotics and proper care. Reluctant to identify the horror of what he experienced. What a moral dilemma! They lament.

If you have not personally experienced navigating the medical system while disabled, you may read Michael's story and assume that there are arguments I'm not including. Surely, in 2020, in a hospital with adequate staff and resources, a man would not be separated from his wife and denied food because strangers determined he would be better off dead.

But, based on all of the evidence I have access to, the story is as gruesome as I've described. I've scoured the court documents, I've read the interviews, I've listened to the tapes. As I discuss more in chapter 9, the widespread assumption that disabled lives are not worth living has brutal consequences. And what disabled people and those who love us fight so hard to prove is that we are valuable. A disabled person is far more likely to be happy with their life than nondisabled people assume.

When a life-threatening assumption is made about treating or not treating us, it's not made because we aren't happy; it's made because our collective obsession with perfection and productivity has convinced a group of people that there is a right way to have a body and mind, and that the bodies and minds that stray too far are worth less than the resources it would take to sustain them.

Untangling the systemic factors that contributed to Michael's death deserves its own book. But private equity, guardianship, for-profit hospitals, drug companies, and private health insurance create a system powered by profit and not compassion. I've referenced capitalism throughout the book; this is what I mean. For example, the chairman of the board at Family Eldercare is an attorney who specializes in representing private equity firms that purchase and consolidate nursing homes to make them more profitable through an economy of scale.[11] Although the hospital where Michael was treated, St. David's, is technically a nonprofit, it has partnered with a for-profit and publicly traded health management corporation, HCA, and no longer qualifies for tax-exempt status.[12] Notably, Michael's attending physician, Dr. Carlye Mabry Cantu, who pushed for days to put his DNR through, works at the "non-profit" hospital but actually works *through* a private-equity group, Hospital Internists of Texas (HIT).[13]

Michael's care team is emblematic of the haphazardly regulated glob that makes up our healthcare system—a system in which organizations motivated by an edict to maximize profits are intertwined with those that are not. In the last decade, private equity (an investment fund that takes over and often restructures companies) has increased its influence in the healthcare sector. Healthcare for profit has proven to be antithetical to disabled equity. The time and care disabled people need erases profit margins. Plus, we work less and cost insurance companies more. We are financially unproductive. But when you extract us from that context, our identity changes.

When a private equity firm takes over medical practices or systems, a few things tend to happen. First, the amount doctors charge increases. Second, "underperforming" practices close (often in poorer neighborhoods).[14] Third, they cut support staff in order to reduce costs. According to Dr. Robert Pearl, the former CEO of Permanente Medical Group and current columnist for *Forbes*, the goal of a private equity firm is to increase profits for three to five years and then sell the group of practices to a larger private equity firm for a profit.[15] This Russian doll profit chain continues until, often, a firm takes the company public.

The group that owns part of the hospital where Michael was treated is a great example. Hospital Corporation of America (HCA) was purchased by Bain Capital and other private equity firms in 2006 for $21 billion. By 2010, investors received $4.25 billion in dividends before going public in 2011, earning another $3.79 billion in profits. Bain Capital alone earned $750 million on their original $64 million investment. Buying and selling hospitals pays, but who suffers the cost?

Of course, medical injustice did not emerge with private equity's growth; the US has a long and sordid history of restricting its citizens' medical access and autonomy. As with many of the chapters in this book, the impact of healthcare on disabled parenting deserves a full book or series of books. This chapter will be, inevitably, incomplete.

Three of the ways that disabled parents are impacted by inadequate medical care are as follows: first, as was the case with Michael Hickson, healthcare discrimination can threaten the lives of parents. Second, getting pregnant and delivering a baby can be unnecessarily dangerous and complicated. And, third, reproductive autonomy, in general, is often fraught for disabled people. The rest of this chapter will address all three. And then, as I do in every chapter, I will consider how disabled obstacles are emblematic of those that all parents face. Because the United States and Canada have vastly different medical systems, I focus on the US, but let the failures in the US be a warning to Canada, which is increasingly embracing privatization.

The healthcare system, in general, often discriminates against disabled people. In 2022, Dr. Lisa Iezzoni, a disabled Harvard researcher, published the results of an interview-based study she had completed on doctors' attitudes toward disabled people. She knew, personally and from her research, that disabled people report inadequate care, but she had not evaluated the quality of care from the physician's perspective.

Her results were sobering: doctors admitted that they avoid taking on disabled patients. They explained that the time allotted for appointments doesn't provide enough room to make accommodations.[16] One complained about the cost of hiring a sign language interpreter. In other words, disabled patients are a medical burden.

In 2022, Meghan O'Rourke published *The Invisible Kingdom*, her account of her decades of chronic illness and what her path through the medical system taught her about how chronic illness is recognized and treated.[17] Her book received accolades from inside and outside the disability and chronic illness community for contextualizing her personal experience with an often-dehumanizing medical system. With more and more of the population experiencing long COVID, it's becoming common knowledge that our medical system is not equipped to treat those with poorly understood illnesses, particularly when those illnesses impact more women than men.

It's not surprising then, considering general access issues, that some disabled people encounter significant obstacles accessing pregnancy-related care. Dr. Jessi Elana Aaron knew she wanted to be a mother starting at the age of seven, when her baby brother was born. She had the first sense that she might encounter challenges when, at ten, she started menstruating.[18] Dr. Aaron, whom I have mentioned, has a nongenetic form of arthrogryposis multiplex congenita (AMC). After starting puberty, she needed assistance managing menstrual products. Those tasked with assisting her made it clear that her needs were a burden. When she was twelve, her doctors and mother suggested a hysterectomy, to bring an end to the inconvenience. She insisted that she needed her organs because she wanted to be pregnant one day. One of her mentors admonished her and said she couldn't get pregnant and keeping her organs was selfish because of how it impacted others.

When, around the same age, her peers took home economics to prepare for their future families, Dr. Aaron was diverted to a typing class because, her teachers explained, she wouldn't have a family. At thirty-five, as a Stanford graduate and professor, Dr. Aaron was ready to have a child. She was single and would need to work with a fertility clinic. The first clinic refused to treat her because of her disability.

She tried at-home insemination but was unsuccessful and decided to visit another fertility clinic. They were begrudging but willing, and, after a year of hurdles, she began IVF. She had the funds to cover one round of treatment, and the embryo was implanted on her thirty-ninth birthday. Her son was born eight months later.

Her medical hurdles weren't over. The nurses at the hospital called child protective services. Their concerns were unsubstantiated, and, at long last, Dr. Aaron brought her son home. (A note: The majority of the disabled parents I interviewed for this book had run-ins with child protective services in the hospital after giving birth. In most cases, a nurse or doctor flagged the disabled parent as potentially unfit because of their disability. We will explore disabled interactions with the child welfare system in chapter 8, but often the first encounter and first threat to parenting autonomy springs from an interaction with the medical system.)

The relationship between a pregnant person and their ob-gyn is vital. Those months are emotional and nerve-wracking, and it's essential that a pregnant person establishes mutual trust and respect with their providers. This is often not the case for disabled people. Unfortunately, medical care for pregnant, disabled people is, like many areas of disability care, underfunded and under-resourced. Moreover, information is sparse about the care itself because research on the underfunded care is, well, underfunded.

There have been a few qualitative interview studies that have found that disabled and pregnant people receive inadequate care. When researchers at the University of Washington interviewed five hundred obstetricians in 2018, they found that only 17 percent had received any sort of specialized training in caring for patients with disabilities.[19] It's not surprising, then, that a 2021 Canadian study found that pregnant people with disabilities were far more likely to experience severe maternal morbidity indicators, including postpartum hemorrhage, puerperal sepsis, and severe preeclampsia.[20] It's impossible to know how those health outcomes would change if medical providers were adequately trained to care for disabled people.

In 2021, Sonja Sharp, a disabled mother, wrote a piece for the *Los Angeles Times* on obstetric care for disabled people.[21] While researching the article, she discovered that, despite the paucity of research, disabled people get pregnant at the same rate as nondisabled people. Despite the frequency of disabled pregnancies, the care received, and the funding directed toward improving that care are wildly insufficient.

Sharp discovered that public health departments track disabled contraceptive use but not disabled pregnancy outcomes. Without research and attention, disabled people encounter what Sharp calls "cascade of harms that cannot be explained by medical complexity or anatomical difference." For example, "a blind woman is twice as likely as a sighted one to give birth by C-section. A wheelchair user . . . will typically go her entire pregnancy without being weighed. Mothers with intellectual disabilities are half as likely to breastfeed, while those with physical disabilities are at significantly increased risk for postpartum depression."

Dr. John Ozimek, a maternal-fetal medicine specialist at Cedars-Sinai Medical Center, told Sharp that disabled pregnancy complications are often a result of substandard care. "We do see an increased rate of complications, but it's not a result of the disability; it's a result of their not getting appropriate care. They're not getting *standard* pregnancy treatment."

Sharp also found that a great deal of medical harm occurs because of the widespread assumption that disabled people won't or don't want to get pregnant. Doctors constantly ask cis women between twenty and fifty if they may be pregnant—around 50 percent of pregnancies in the US are unintended. But they ask disabled people this question much less frequently, which can put the patient, since many medications and medical procedures are contraindicated for pregnant people.[22]

Disabled pregnant people often have difficulty finding an ob-gyn willing to take them on. Dr. Iezzoni, the medical researcher at Harvard mentioned earlier in this chapter, has found that many disabled patients must see between five and ten providers before they find one who can treat them. They often travel hundreds of miles for care.[23]

Disabled people who live in poorer neighborhoods face additional challenges because the specialists they need are concentrated in more affluent areas. Also, very few take public insurance. Sharp also found that medical racism compounds the care gap: "A disproportionate number of younger disabled women are Black and Indigenous." When it's time to give birth, disabled people are often scheduled for C-sections without a valid medical reason or a conversation about their options, which further compromises their right to medical self-determination.[24]

Sharp herself was not insulated from insufficient and disempowering medical care when she became pregnant. Early in her pregnancy, an assay revealed a possible neural tube defect, which could indicate spina bifida. Her doctors ordered an ultrasound, which was inconclusive. They encouraged Sonja to schedule an amniocentesis, but Sonja declined, explaining that she has many friends with spina bifida and she didn't need to know.

Her doctors were shocked and pushed harder. As Dr. Church explained, not testing quickly often means a patient is outside the window in which termination is possible. Sharp assured her doctors that she wouldn't proceed differently if the baby did have spina bifida. Sharp remembers, "They were so adamant that I didn't want a baby with this condition." Eventually, her providers acquiesced, but she had to sign a form acknowledging the risks she was taking. Her disability isn't all that different from spina bifida, and, like many disabled patients, she was being warned against creating a person with a life like her own.[25]

Disabled people face reproductive care hurdles far beyond pregnancy and delivery. The care gaps start with puberty, where data show that disabled people receive inadequate gynecological care and contraceptive counseling.[26] Doctors and patients cite inaccessible equipment, reduced appointment time, and bias as some of the reasons for the quality-of-care disparity. There are a few doctors in the United States who specialize in gynecological care for disabled people, but not enough to help a significant portion of the disabled population.[27]

Also, disabled people who need abortions encounter access obstacles. For one, since the Supreme Court overturned *Roe v. Wade* in 2023, people in many states have been forced to travel out of state for care. Often, having a disability can make traveling to another state difficult or impossible, and for some of these people, being unable to access abortion is life-threatening.[28] Because disabled people are more likely to live in poverty, the barriers to traveling are compounded.

Planned Parenthood twice told Roxanne Schiebergen, a disabled writer and actor in New York, that they could not give abortions to people in wheelchairs. She was forced to seek out care from a clinic that charged four times as much.[29] The reality is that Planned Parenthood does provide abortions to wheelchair users, but multiple people she spoke to were misinformed. Disabled people often face transportation obstacles when trying to obtain abortions; many of them rely on faith-based transportation services, and these services will not bring them to abortion appointments.[30]

While it's sometimes difficult for disabled people to access abortions, at other points, medical professionals assume they will have them. Jackie, an architect with genetic osteogenesis imperfecta, has been pregnant three times. She was told as a child that she would never be pregnant, and, because she assumed her doctors were right, she was surprised to see a positive pregnancy test in her twenties. She was not ready to be a parent, and before she had scheduled an abortion, she miscarried.

Years later, with her new husband, she decided she did want to have a baby. She would take on the risk. They talked about what help they would need and the financial position they would need to be in to support a family and decided to wait and try to get pregnant in a few years. They also wanted to live near loved ones before they grew their family. To their mutual surprise, they became pregnant shortly after marriage.

They considered their options and knew that they could not keep themselves and their baby safe and made the hard decision to terminate the pregnancy. Jackie continues to feel confident that it was the right decision. Years later, financially stable and living near family, they met with doctors about how Jackie could safely carry a baby.

They decided on IVF, and their providers assumed they would want to screen out embryos with osteogenesis imperfecta (often called OI). They did not. Jackie sees her life, and lives like hers, as worth living. She is in a Facebook group with other parents with OI, and this issue frequently arises. Care providers view OI as a tragedy that should be avoided if possible.

In the end, IVF was not financially feasible for Jackie and her husband, and they got pregnant without medical assistance. Once she was pregnant, her doctors assumed she would want an amniocentesis to screen for OI. Again, she declined. Her daughter does not have OI, but Jackie feels confident that they would have figured it out either way. I asked how it felt to be pressured to avoid having a child with a life like hers. "I understand [the perspective]," she replied, "but at the same time, my life has worth. The world is a better place because I'm in it. I bring good things to this place."

There is nothing quite as emblematic of reproductive oppression as forced sterilization. As I write this, the only states that explicitly ban forced disabled sterilization are North Carolina and Alaska. In thirty-one states, plus Washington, DC, it's legal to sterilize a disabled person against their will.[31] In the remaining eighteen states, the laws are unclear, but they don't ban it.[32] Take a second and read those sentences again. When the National Women's Law Center (NWLC) released their report on these laws in 2022, Ma'ayan Anafi, who authored the report and serves as general counsel for the NWLC, made it clear that these laws are not some obscure outdated legislation or an oversight but "are part of a larger, horrifying system that prevents disabled people from making basic decisions about their lives, their families, and their futures. These laws are part of a long history of state-sanctioned sterilizations, and are rooted in false, paternalistic assumptions about disabled people."

People with intellectual disabilities face the highest risk of forced sterilization. When the NWLC released its report, they created an accessible plain-language PDF outlining options and legal rights. The report explains that in the early 1900s, disabled sterilization grew from the eugenics movements as a method of purifying humanity. A Supreme Court ruling, *Buck vs. Bell*, in 1924 officially endorsed forced sterilization, and then, in the 1970s, Medicaid started funding nonconsensual sterilizations.[33] In many states, a judge is the person who determines if someone should be sterilized.[34] Pro-sterilization laws continue to be passed—as recently as 2019 in Iowa and Nevada.

A disabled person is more likely to be sterilized in a few scenarios. Guardianship and institutionalization increase the risk of sterilization.[35] Black, Latina, and Indigenous women are more likely to be sterilized against their wills.[36] Frequently, disabled people have had their medical autonomy compromised, including those with guardians. Not only can a guardian force disabled sterilization but they can also refuse to grant permission for a disabled person to obtain an abortion.[37]

Buck vs. Bell, the Supreme Court case that ruled that disabled people could be sterilized against their will, is indicative of the particularly cruel confluence of factors limiting disabled reproductive freedom. Carrie Buck was an institutionalized, intellectually disabled woman who was raped by a relative at seventeen.

Her story is not unique: one in three people with an intellectual disability will be sexually assaulted, and being institutionalized is the leading risk factor for assault.[38] Disabled people in institutions often lack access to sex education and are coerced into having abortions and using birth control without being adequately informed.[39]

Until very recently, it was assumed that a child born disabled would be put "in a home" instead of going home with their families. Care homes for the disabled were established as a solution to the common practice until that point: abandoning disabled people in hospitals or putting them in jail.[40] Over the past decades, there have been dozens of exposés revealing just how inhumane the conditions have been and continue to be in disabled institutional settings. In fact, the life expectancy for Down syndrome has almost doubled primarily because most people with Down syndrome no longer live in institutions. Unsurprisingly, if the care isn't good enough to keep someone alive, it rarely prioritizes reproductive and sexual autonomy.

Carrie Buck's mother was also considered disabled. She gave birth to a daughter, Vivian, who was also deemed disabled, and the institution where she lived, called Virginia Colony for Epileptics and Feebleminded, believed it would be best to sterilize Carrie Buck so that she didn't produce any more disabled kids. They prevailed. The Supreme Court's opinion made their understanding of disability clear. Justice Oliver Wendell Holmes wrote, "It is better for all the world, if instead of waiting to execute degenerate offspring for crime or to let them starve for their imbecility, society can prevent those who are manifestly unfit from continuing their kind . . . Three generations of imbeciles are enough."[41]

Carrie Buck's sister, Doris, who was not disabled, was also sterilized against her will after she was told she needed appendix surgery.[42] She later married and tried, for decades, to have kids. No one told her that she had been sterilized. The collective fear of disability was so strong that it was permissible to steal reproductive freedoms from even the relatives of disabled people.

Guardianship can also pave the way to forced sterilization. Sometimes, a judge will determine that a disabled person is unable to make sound decisions and will assign a guardian, often the disabled person's parent. In these cases, a guardian works with the disabled person's doctors to make medical decisions, including reproductive ones.[43] In some cases, for more medically risky decisions, a guardian will need a judge's approval. They do not need the disabled person's approval.

It's hard to deny that some disabled people might need assistance with decision-making. But, considering the history of institutionalization and forced sterilization, and the fact that *Buck v. Bell* has not been overturned, it's worth considering that guardianship, in its current state, is simply the next iteration of those depraved systems. Some states, encouraged by disabled advocates, are moving away from guardianship and toward "supported decision-making" in which some personal autonomy is preserved.[44] With 1.3 million disabled people under guardianship in the US, and limited oversight, politicians and disabled activists are pushing for a more humane and transparent system.[45]

Of course, it's not only disabled people who suffer under the current model of care. In the last decade, publishers have released numerous books that have shifted the collective consciousness about sexism, racism, and transphobia in medical care.[46] In *Doing Harm*, Maya Dusenbery describes how hard it is for a woman or trans person with a chronic illness to get diagnosed. She cites a few reasons for this difficulty, but a central factor is a long history of medical studies including only men.[47]

The gender gap in medical research is striking and, at times, absurd. Dusenbery refers to a study in the 1960s on estrogen supplementation, menopause, and heart disease—the researchers enrolled only men. Hormone therapy wasn't studied on women's bodies until 1991. Today, 70 percent of people with chronic illnesses are women, but 80 percent of the people studied are men.

In truth, while I am a disabled woman, I have fared better than most: I stayed insulated from the medical system's worst atrocities for so long only because I am white, cis, thin, and have always been at least middle class.

In *Medical Apartheid*, Harriet Washington outlines the appalling reality of medical abuse of Black bodies in the United States. She takes the reader through the gory history of grave robbing, racial eugenics, and medical experimentation. Critically, she explains how those practices have resulted in racial health deficits today.

Black people who give birth are three times more likely to die during childbirth, according to the Centers for Disease Control (CDC), and most of those deaths are preventable.[48] The CDC blames this disparity on "variation in quality healthcare, underlying chronic conditions, structural racism, and implicit bias." Healthcare settings magnify the social realities of marginalized people.

Fat people also face incredible hurdles when seeking care. In recent years, writers like Aubrey Gordon have managed to increase society's awareness of how inaccessible and cruel medical appointments can be for fat people. In her books, *What We Don't Talk About When We Talk About Fat* and *You Just Need to Lose Weight and 19 Other Myths About Fat People*, Gordon dismantles many of the false beliefs about fat people perpetuated, in part, by medical professionals.[49] Namely, she explains how statistics about the health risks of being fat can be misleading because many fat people experience adverse outcomes due to medical discrimination, not because of the size of their bodies. Numerous studies have explored the profound impact of medical bias and lack of access on long-term outcomes for fat people.[50]

Trans people, too, often have difficulty accessing the medical care they need. This is often due to a combination of discriminatory legislation and providers' lack of knowledge and education.[51] A large 2015 survey found that 23 percent of trans people avoid medical care because of a history of mistreatment. It's impossible to ignore the reality: medical care in the US and Canada is discriminatory. Statistically, the best way to receive consistently appropriate care is to be a wealthy, nondisabled, cis, white, thin, and straight man.

When it comes to pregnancy care, it's medically fraught for nearly every person, disabled and not. As Rachel Somerstein, who is not disabled, described in her 2024 book, *Invisible Labor: The Untold Story of the Cesarean Section*, giving birth in the US is complicated, dangerous, and littered with moments in which consent becomes a facade. As I mentioned in chapter 4, Rachel was told while laboring that a C-section was necessary. Warned that her baby was in danger, she had no choice but to consent. In Longreads, in 2019, she described the scene:

> I pushed for what seemed like a short time—but what doesn't seem short when you've been in labor for 24 hours?—when the midwife whispered into my ear, "I think it's time to call it. To do a C-section." She explained that, amid the pushing, the baby's heart rate wasn't returning to levels that seemed safe. Also, she said, I'd been in labor for so long. The baby and I were exhausted.
>
> I must have known something was going to go wrong, because I asked if I was going to die, if my baby was going to die. Oh, no, the midwife said, you're going to be fine. I signed papers, things I couldn't read because it was too loud in my head, which released the medical team from indemnities that would actually happen, but that I had never dreamed possible.

Then I waited. It took 40 minutes to pull together the surgical team. Some emergency!

Later the midwife would tell my husband, "I wonder, if we had just waited, if the baby would have slid out on her own. I wonder"—and, he told me, she didn't seem to wonder, but to be pretty certain—"if maybe we didn't need to do the C-section at all."

Rachel was rushed to the operating room, and the anesthesiologist could not effectively perform what's called a spinal block: the procedure that makes it so the birthing person does not feel the imminent major surgery. Instead, Rachel felt every moment of her abdomen being cut open. The surgery notes describe her kicking and bucking—nurses and her doula had to hold her down.

C-sections are performed for many reasons, but no one can deny that the rate (over 30 percent) is unnecessarily inflated in the United States. In *Invisible Labor*, Somerstein traces this rise through decades of racism, the medical shift from hands-on care to technology-centered care, and, most importantly, the nearly unchecked power of a profit-driven system. In the United States, around 1.2 million C-sections are performed annually. Of those, around 6 percent are performed without adequate anesthesia. That is 72,000 people held down on operating tables while their skin is cut, muscles are torn, and organs are rearranged.

America was built on a rejection of bodily autonomy—from the colonization of Indigenous land and culture to slavery to eugenics. We are a nation in which certain people assert their right to control the rights of other people. These structures stand today in the forms of mass incarceration, immigrant detention, and institutionalization, police brutality, and forced sterilization.

This chapter runs the risk of villainizing doctors, as if they are a group of people who endured nearly a decade of training and years of eighty-hour workweeks just so they could wrestle autonomy and dignity from their patients. That is, of course, not the case. Doctors are also suffering in this system.

Every few months, a major publication releases a story about the moral injury that doctors are enduring in our current medical system.[52] They are crumbling under the conflicting and inhumane demands placed by health insurance companies and medical systems controlled by profit-driven stakeholders. The number of patients they must see each day is untenable, and the treatments for which they are reimbursed are not those that improve patient outcomes. And, over all of it, the specter of lawsuits hovers.

Moreover, physicians are trained in a system and in a culture that values superhuman strength, objectivity, and, above all, ability. Within that system, the ability to comprehend and support choices based on a different value system suffers.

If doctors aren't the root of our diminishing and dehumanizing model of reproductive care, what is? The answer isn't simple, and it certainly encompasses far more than one section of one chapter of this book. But, in part, every person who enters the medical system and loses bodily autonomy can blame two things: one, a society that has historically acted as if some people do not have the right to their own bodies, and, two, a medical system that prioritizes profits over equity and access. It is simply not possible, without foundational changes, for a country built on slavery and eugenics to treat every person as if their rights matter. Along the same lines, a profit-based medical model cannot equally value all human lives. It simply costs too much money.

Because disabled people are at particular risk when accessing healthcare, disability culture is also a font of solutions. Disability justice invents and practices care structures that are antithetical to the existing inadequate systems. Before going forward, it's important to outline the difference between disability rights and disability justice.

The disability rights movement became influential in the middle of the twentieth century and focused on ensuring civil rights for disabled people. The meaningful and world-changing passage of the Americans with Disability Act (ADA) in 1995 is thanks to disability rights activists.[53] In 2005, a group of Bay Area disability activists called Sins Invalid saw a need for the movement to evolve. White and straight people had traditionally been the faces of the disability rights movement and, due to their privilege, held positions of power in various institutions. Sins Invalid, a group of women of color, observed the complex intersection of queer and racialized identities with disability and knew that for disabled people to access real equity, the leadership and structure of the movement would need to reflect those complexities.[54] The disability justice framework centers the experience of people of color, queer people, immigrants, unhoused people, those in prison, and Indigenous people. It considers how systems interact to perpetuate inequality and bases disability advocacy on those complex interactions.

In 2015, Patty Berne outlined the ten principles of the movement, which include intersectionality, leadership of the most impacted, anti-capitalist politics, cross-movement solidarity, the recognition of wholeness, sustainability, commitment to cross-disability solidarity, interdependence, collective access, and collective liberation.

One justice organization that is pursuing trust and equity solutions is Health Justice Commons, which was established in 2016. Like Sins Invalid, its founders were in the East Bay.[55] It's a health justice organization that takes an abolitionist approach to health reform and is oriented toward the disability justice movement. It calls the current healthcare system the medical industrial complex (MIC). The majority of the staff are queer people of color.

Organizations like Health Justice Commons (HJC) offer a desperately needed alternative to a system driven by profits. HJC runs a telehealth service they call Radical Telehealth Collective (RTC). RTC offers "free, accessible, multilingual urgent and essential care."[56] According to their website, the providers who offer care through RTC benefit because they can interact with people in the ways they have wished for but have been prevented from by the MIC. RTC prioritizes compassion, respect, and autonomy. They also honor the wisdom of the people with whom they work. Anyone who has fought to have their experience and knowledge respected in medical settings can imagine what a relief it would be to feel like your wisdom was respected. Providers working through RTC prescribe medications, advise on acute illnesses, assist with gender-affirming care, and help with resource navigation. The appointments are also accessible, which, as I've discussed, is often not the case for other medical visits. They include interpretive services, closed captioning, and ASL.

In addition to virtual care, Health Justice Commons offers online education on advocacy and medical system navigation. Their programs are for healthcare providers and patients who are in search of more equitable options. They also offer a robust curriculum for other health justice advocates.

HJC exemplifies how disability culture fosters a unique ability to conceive of and implement alternatives to a profoundly inhumane healthcare system. Navigating the world with our bodies and minds has helped us develop a needed perspective on care and humanity. And a disability-influenced system of care would benefit nondisabled people, too—one in which care is accessible and one's own experience and wisdom aren't disregarded. For nondisabled birthing people who have felt like they had to sacrifice most of their autonomy in order to receive care, a new structure would add dignity and, in all likelihood, improve outcomes.

The reproductive justice movement often intersects and overlaps with the disability justice movement. It strives to restore each person's right to their own body and mind. This concept, also called "self-determination," is a central premise in the disability justice movement as well and is a crucial component of fair and equitable medical care.

In Chicago in 1994, a group of women, predominantly white, met to hear more about President Clinton's healthcare reform plan. There were only a few Black women in attendance, and they grew concerned with presentations and conversations that seemed to avoid reproductive healthcare. They had hoped to hear more about prenatal care, postnatal care, and STI testing. They were also dismayed that the limited discussions about abortion and other reproductive choices didn't consider the impact of poverty and incarceration on reproductive care.[57]

Twelve of these Black women went into a conference room to discuss their observations and formed a coalition called, at the time, the Women of African Descent for Reproductive Justice. They collected over eight hundred signatures and paid for an ad in the *Washington Post* that demanded that health reforms include the concerns of Black women. It was from this movement that SisterSong Collective was formed in Atlanta in 1997. SisterSong describes the goal of the reproductive justice movement as advocating for "the human right to maintain personal bodily autonomy, have children, not have children, and parent the children we have in safe and sustainable communities."[58] The movement, which continues to be led by Black women and nonbinary people, demands that discussions about reproductive choice include the complex reality of the lives of people with reproductive systems. Reproductive justice is not just about whether or not abortion is legal but is a response to a web of factors, including race, disability, religion, sexual orientation, financial status, and immigration status. The reproductive justice movement considers what systems remove choice and strives to change those systems.

The disability justice movement and reproductive justice movement have shared beliefs and goals. That said, there have been ways in which pro-choice advocates have used arguments and frameworks that are harmful to disabled people.[59] When, in 2022, the Supreme Court overturned *Roe v. Wade*, pro-choice advocates used the stories of fetuses with genetic abnormalities to illustrate why having the right to an abortion is critical.

I will examine selective abortion more in chapter 9, but centering the "risk" of having a disability in an argument is a reliable way to alienate disabled people from the cause. At the same time, anti-abortion activists, including Justice Clarence Thomas, claim that their views on abortion grow from a desire to protect disabled people and disrupt "eugenic" practices.

The structure of this argument pits disabled people against those in favor of reproductive rights, when the reality is that disabled people have a long history of losing reproductive autonomy in a manner that mirrors those losses the reproductive justice movement fights against. When we see reproductive advocacy as a comprehensive indictment of the forces that disempower and dehumanize women, the overlap between the disability justice and reproductive justice movements becomes clear.[60]

The disability justice solutions would benefit everybody. The current medical system only works for a few—corporations. The distorted power and priority structure that left Michael Hickson to die alone at the end of a hallway hurts every person. Downstream of Michael's horrific death, one finds staggering maternal mortality rates, traumatic birthing experiences, and inadequate reproductive healthcare for everyone, not solely disabled people.

The chapters in this book all conclude with disabled solutions to wide-reaching problems. And, in many of those cases, the solutions can start at the individual level—acceptance instead of control, for example. But, in some cases, like the profound injustice of profit-driven medical care, the solutions are structural. There is no mindset or mentality that can fix this.

When I think about the pregnant people now, who fight to be heard and believed and, in many cases, to survive, I wish they could know that the disability community is here with our messy and painful bodies and minds, and we are fighting for them. We are fighting for the right to have babies, and the right to not.

Reproductive justice and disability justice have a shared vision. We all want to change the system. Disabled people are a vital part of that effort. And if you're new to the convoluted world of healthcare, while we all wait for things to change, we can show you the ropes.

Chapter 8

CHILD PROTECTIVE SERVICES

A faded sign outside boasted great rates and free local calls. The motel windows did nothing to block the West Oakland road noise. Sitting on the stained quilt, Natalie and her fifteen-year-old daughter Tara knew that they needed help. Natalie was starting to make less sense, and she had expressed a passing desire to hurt herself.[1]

Normally, Natalie had a support system in place through the Regional Center of the East Bay (RCEB), but, since she moved into the motel with Tara, it was harder to keep all the various parts of their lives in order. Natalie and Tara both have psychosocial disabilities, including schizophrenia. Tara is also intellectually disabled. Like many disabled people, Natalie lived with the threat that Tara would be taken away from her. After all, it's legal in twenty-two states to remove a child because their parent is disabled. In these states, the statutes include disability as one of the grounds for removal. In California, one reason a child can be removed is that "the parent or guardian is suffering from a mental disability."[2] While some laws say that the disability must impact care, in many cases there does not need to be evidence that it already has impacted care, just that someone predicts that it would. For example, Colorado's statute states a child may be removed if "emotional illness, mental illness, or mental deficiency of the parent [is] of such duration or nature as to render the parent unlikely within a reasonable time to care for the ongoing physical, mental, and emotional needs and conditions of the child."[3] Natalie knew that as a poor Black disabled woman, the stakes were high when she moved out of their stable housing.

Weeks before, in the house they shared with roommates, an older man made an aggressive sexual advance on Tara, which had frightened her. The astronomical housing costs in Oakland meant that finding housing with roommates had been their only option. The situation had felt tenable until Tara confessed what the older man had done. Natalie understood that the only reliable way to keep her daughter safe was to remove her from the situation. They left for the motel so that she could devise a plan.

Natalie and Tara, who are both Black, have always been particularly close and feel that they understand one another better than those outside their two-person family. Their overlapping disabilities help Natalie know what Tara needs when Tara is in emotional distress.

Natalie asked the Regional Center of the East Bay (RCEB) for help finding affordable and stable housing. RCEB was initially established to advocate for children and adults with developmental disabilities and has a close working relationship with Alameda County Social Services.[4] Unfortunately for Natalie, a disproportionate amount of the center's $500 million budget goes toward early interventions—programs for kids in the first three years of life—and they offer only anemic support for adults and parents with disabilities.[5] No assistance had materialized.

While she searched desperately for affordable housing that would be safe for Tara, she found it much more difficult to access the support and medical services on which she usually relied. Hunting for affordable housing disrupted her routine and occupied all of her time. At her motel, she started to feel less stable. They couldn't think of anywhere to turn except 911, so one of them called, and, within minutes, the police were at the door.

Once inside, they learned that Tara was a Regional Center client, which automatically flagged her as high risk for abuse and exploitation. The police weren't willing to consider Tara and Natalie's pleas to stay together and their explanation for the dynamic housing situation. Tara and Natalie insisted that they only needed help, not separation. Even so, the officers took Tara away that night.

Within hours, Alameda County Social Services had custody of Tara and began the search for a temporary guardian for her while they processed Natalie's case. But it is exceedingly difficult to find a foster home for any teenager. Children between the ages of eight and eleven make up around 50 percent of California's foster care population, yet 95 percent of group home residents are teenagers. Across the board, outcomes for foster children placed in group homes are worse than for those placed with families.[6] Few group homes have the capacity to care for disabled residents, and the closest option Tara's social workers could find was three hours away in Fresno.

Natalie begged the social workers to stop Tara's transfer. She knew that a group home setting, away from Natalie, would likely exacerbate some of Tara's more challenging symptoms. Without her mom's expert care, Tara was likely to struggle with hygiene and tasks of daily living. But, despite Natalie's efforts and Tara's appeals to be returned to her mother, Tara was sent to Fresno. Tara's social workers said that because of Tara's disability and unreliable housing, Natalie could not be granted custody.

Tara languished in the group home. She stopped washing and began soiling her bed. When staff members tried to help her, she lashed out, retraumatized by the bullying she had endured at school. The caregivers were poorly equipped to support Tara, whose mental health continued to deteriorate after being separated from her mom while Natalie worked tirelessly to find a safer option for Tara.

Without the means to visit her daughter regularly, Natalie spent her days parenting through phone calls with Tara and the people who ran the group home. Tara called her mom constantly and, from hours away, Natalie comforted her. Group home staff called Natalie, too, and she walked them through how they could comfort and talk to her daughter. The caregivers became reliant on Natalie's advice and guidance.

From three hours away, Natalie was still the person best suited to understand and meet Tara's needs.

And then, one night, Natalie and Tara's nightmare came true. Tara was abducted from the home and sexually assaulted. Her social workers weren't that surprised. Often, exploiters target group homes.[7] The very thing that Natalie had been working so hard to prevent happened after she was no longer her daughter's guardian.

After Tara's assault, social services categorized her as an even higher risk, and the requirements for her future caregivers became stricter. Social Services told the family court that a disabled teenager who had recently endured so much trauma needed more care than a disabled woman with unstable housing could provide. The judge agreed. The very fact that Tara was assaulted after the welfare system separated her from her mom meant that she could not be reunited with her mom.

Before Tara turned sixteen, the county terminated all of Natalie's parental rights, and she permanently lost custody of Tara.

When I spoke with Kavya Parthiban, an attorney who is well acquainted with Natalie and Tara's case, I said I wanted to make sure I told their story in a way that would keep them anonymous. I didn't want to put them in danger. Parthiban laughed wryly. "Situations like this occur so frequently here that there is no way that someone could isolate which specific case this is."

Parthiban, who is neurodivergent and was born in India, worked as a case manager in Alameda County right out of college. In that job, she observed the rampant bias and discrimination against disabled parents and, years later, as an attorney, returned to the East Bay to advocate for disabled parents who face losing custody of their children. She is, as far as she knows, the only attorney with this specialty in all of California. The demand for her specialty is so high that by consulting instead of representing, she has more time to help more people. Acting as the lead attorney on cases would end up narrowing the scope of who she can help. Instead, she works as an advisor to the attorneys representing disabled parents. Occasionally, she will join as co-counsel.

In her experience, the prospects for a disabled parent who has a custody case opened against them are dire, particularly if their child also has a disability. "If you are disabled and your child is disabled, your chances of separation are so high," Parthiban said. In fact, two-thirds of states permit parental rights to be terminated simply because of a parent's intellectual disability.

California has a reputation as a beacon of progress, but Parthiban explained that two appellate court rulings in 2000 actually made disabled parents' interactions with the welfare system more difficult there than in other states.[8] Those cases, which are still used as precedents, ruled that the Americans with Disabilities Act does not apply in dependency court. In other words, the laws that demand that disabled people have the right to reasonable accommodations become moot when they are at risk of losing their children. Ms. Parthiban hopes that one of the cases on which she advises may soon be heard by the appellate court, and, once it does, perhaps a new precedent could be set that would allow the ADA to be enforced in California family court.

Writing this chapter, I found myself sucked into the legal particulars of the child welfare system—as if untangling the knot of regulations and rulings would reveal a solution. And, in some ways, progress can be found in legislation. But I'm also convinced that the problem runs deeper than that. The injustice within the system is just one manifestation of the ways in which our dominant parenting structures are faulty. Our culture's deluded insistence that a nuclear family should be autonomous has far-reaching negative consequences, which include disabled parents losing custody of their kids.

Toward the end of our call, Parthiban asked to share the story of one of her clients in San Francisco. Annette is thirty and has an intellectual disability. Her mom is also disabled, and when Annette was a child, the county sent her to live with foster parents, Dan and Linda. The couple sexually and physically abused Annette throughout her childhood. Desperate to escape their cruelty, she ran away as an adolescent and experienced intermittent homelessness over the next decade. But when Annette, who is Black, became pregnant at twenty-nine, Dan and Linda convinced her to move in with them, and she did, eager to offer her baby stable housing. Once Annette was back in their home, they tormented her, demanding her Social Security Disability payments and threatening to call CPS once the baby was born.

While pregnant, Annette once again left the abusive couple and was able to secure housing in the Tenderloin for low-income and disabled residents. Annette was deeply committed to building a healthy life for the baby growing inside of her. But, even after she moved out, Dan and Linda continued to threaten Annette. They said that they would take away her baby. She was terrified.

She gave birth to a baby boy, Oliver, in a San Francisco hospital and said she fell in love immediately. She knew she would do anything to protect her son. But she couldn't relax; she kept looking at the door, waiting for Dan and Linda to come and take him. When it was time to sleep, she asked the nurses if Oliver could join her in bed. That way, she could make sure that no one stole her baby. The hospital told her that no, Oliver needed to sleep in a bassinet but that he would be safe.

Annette, after decades of abuse and manipulation, could not be comforted, and while she allowed them to place Oliver in the bassinet, on that first night, while recovering from the exhausting work of labor, Annette refused to sleep. She sat up in bed and watched her son. She wouldn't let them take him.

The nurses noted that Annette wasn't sleeping. Concerned with her preoccupation, healthcare providers contacted social services, filing a report that Annette was too fixated on her son. They suggested that maybe she was too disabled to be a parent. Tragically, Dan and Linda still had the power to manipulate Annette, and they convinced her to return to their house for her recovery. She did so, and, just as they had threatened to do, they called CPS and expressed concerns about Annette's capacity to parent.

A few days after giving birth, social services came into Dan and Linda's home, and, just like Annette had feared, they ripped Oliver from Annette's arms and took him away. They placed him with a couple who are "eager to adopt."

When I spoke to Parthiban, Oliver and Annette had been apart for nearly six months, and Annette's commitment to him had not wavered. She texts or calls her attorneys daily, updating them on her efforts to reunify with her son and asking for advice.

Parthiban is doing all she can to help Annette regain custody, but she is often pessimistic about the chances that they can be reunified. In her experience, as soon as a judge hears that a parent is intellectually disabled, they are much more likely to terminate the parent's rights. Most parents have a legal right to reunification services: a period of time in which they can follow the social worker's instructions and "earn" their children back.[9] But often a parent has not lost custody because of a lack of effort. The requirements are simply impossible without support.

In some cases, a county will petition to permanently terminate a parent's rights before their guaranteed reunification time has passed. For example, if a parent has previously lost custody of other children and there have been no significant changes in circumstance, a judge may determine that moving toward adoption is more beneficial for a child than working toward reunification. In Parthiban's experience, this approach is often taken with disabled parents. Once a disabled parent loses custody of one child, a judge is likely to circumvent reunification efforts and terminate a parent's rights before they have had any time to honor the social worker's requirements.

In Annette's case, Oliver is her first child, so the county is taking a different approach. They initially told the judge that Annette is simply too disabled to benefit from reunification efforts. If a judge terminates her rights to parent, that will pave the way for separations from any future children she may have.

According to Annette's counsel, her ability to obtain safe and stable housing and prepare for the birth of her child demonstrates that she is able to care for Oliver. Her behavior in the hospital was a result of the abuse she endured at the hands of the welfare system, not proof that she is unfit. Fortunately, the judge agreed that Annette deserves a chance to reunify with Oliver. Annette has been granted six months to prove that she can provide the stability and safety that Oliver needs. San Francisco CPS has specific metrics in place that will measure Annette's fitness, like stable housing and healthy relationships. For most of this case, Parthiban explains, it's been clear that Oliver's social workers are not earnestly pursuing reunification—they had, until recently, never tried to observe Oliver and Annette together.

A great deal of the social workers' reluctance was a result of insufficient disability accommodations. For months, they believed that Annette was refusing to provide information and answer the social worker's questions. However, her silence wasn't defiance but, instead, an outcome of their questions being too abstract. Annette couldn't process the questions in the form they were presented. But, once her counsel was able to explain the accommodations that Annette needed, the social workers began breaking down the questions into distinct parts, and, instantly, Annette became engaged and transparent.

The county uses Annette's IQ as evidence that she is unfit. Despite the fact that it's still used in practice, IQ testing has long been debunked as a test of parental fitness. In fact, it's not until IQ drops below fifty that there is any correlation to parenting ability.[10] Moreover, the IQ test itself is faulty and perpetuates racial discrimination.[11]

About a month after Parthiban and I first spoke about Annette, she updated me on the case. She had convinced Oliver's social worker to attend a visitation between Oliver and Annette. Every week, Annette has nine supervised hours with her son, divided over three days. It was the social worker's first time observing Oliver's connection with his mom.

Parthiban lights up when she describes Annette as a parent. Annette is teaching Oliver about body parts and purchased him a stuffed animal and uses it to make up songs. "This is bunny's ear," she sings. "This is Oliver's ear. This is Mommy's ear." Oliver is rapt and touches his own ear and then his mom's. It's impossible to deny the strength of their bond. "She focuses on him for every second of the three hours," Parthiban said.

Oliver's social worker has said that Annette cannot parent because her intellectual disability prevents her from parenting independently. Parthiban objected to this standard and challenged the original case plan and its requirements. She explained to me that demanding that someone parent without support is discriminatory. Parthiban prevailed, and Annette's case plan now allows for assistance and accommodations.

Annette has worked tirelessly to put these supports in place. The San Francisco waiting list for the disabled parenting classes she needed was so long that she went over to Oakland and asked for help there. Unfortunately, the East Bay agency that had space to provide services was unable to access adequate reimbursement from Annette's San Francisco agency. Anyone who has interacted with this kind of bureaucracy knows the utter frustration that it brings. It's like trying to navigate a corn maze blindfolded after spinning around a bat. But Annette persists.

Her case took a turn in March 2023 after she was approved for In-Home Supportive Services (IHHS), which would allow her access to supportive services while at home. The funding she received wasn't quite adequate, but a family friend stepped in and offered to supplement the paid-for support. If Annette provides this friend housing, she will help Annette care for Oliver.

Parthiban isn't surprised that a relationship is providing Annette with a way out. "She is very loyal to the people she considers family," Parthiban said. When Annette trusts someone, particularly a woman, she calls them a sister or an auntie. Parthiban explained, "All she has ever wanted are aunties to love her." She is loyal and kind and deeply appreciates the value of community. She is happy to share the housing she fought so hard to obtain.

For the first time since Oliver's birth, Parthiban thinks that they might be able to reunify, but she needs the social worker to stay convinced.

Annette's attorneys are not permitted to update the judge directly, so the social worker's interpretation of Annette's parenting carries the most weight. The social worker could change her mind at any moment. Parthiban is hesitant to express too much hope. "It's all so precarious."

Before becoming a foster parent, I had no knowledge of the inner workings of the child welfare system. For those who have not interacted directly with social workers and family court, the terminology can feel daunting. What follows is a cursory overview of what can be a completely convoluted tangle of contingencies and regulations. It's impossible to conceptualize what is wrong with the system without a basic understanding of its processes.

A family's interaction with social services begins when someone files a report expressing concern about a child's safety. Often, these reports are made by mandated reporters. A mandated reporter has a professional and ethical obligation to call child protective services (CPS) with concerns. Mandated reporters are usually people who have frequent interactions with children, including teachers, doctors, counselors, and law enforcement officers. When I became a social worker, I had extensive training on my obligations as a mandated reporter. If a mandated reporter fails to report suspicion of abuse, they can be prosecuted.[12]

It's this requirement that leads to what researchers call "exposure bias" in the welfare system. Exposure bias is one explanation for the overrepresentation of Black, Brown, Indigenous, and disabled families in the system; because these groups are, due to a history of discriminatory laws and practices, low-income, they interact with social workers, therapists, doctors, and other social service professionals more than their wealthier counterparts. These interactions increase the chances that a biased or uninformed person with power and the obligation to report will feel concerned about a family's dynamics.[13] In my own life as a disabled parent, I never let my guard down around a mandated reporter. I never forget how much power they have over me.

Once a report has been filed, a social worker visits the family. This first social worker looks at the evidence and the claim and determines if they should officially open a case. If they do, they also determine if a child is in immediate danger and needs to be removed at that time. If the child is removed, a placement social worker begins the process of searching for a foster home where the child can stay.

Those first few days are busy. The social workers must, within a designated amount of time (varies by state but usually twenty-four hours), find a place for the child to stay temporarily. Meanwhile, another social worker prepares documentation to present to a judge who must sign the removal order. Typically, if a judge does not sign within three days, the child returns home. If the judge signs the order, a few processes begin simultaneously.[14] First, social workers look for extended family members who can care for the child. Meanwhile, other social workers investigate the parent who has had their child removed and develop a plan for reunification. It's worth noting that all of the decisions along the way are judgment calls, which, by definition, emerge from both experience and bias.

After a few weeks, all parties return to court, and the social workers explain to the judge what they propose for the next steps. Often this includes what is called "concurrent planning," which is when parents simultaneously work toward reunification while the social workers look for other permanent options, like adoption.[15] At this point, the process varies widely. Some parents meet some of the reunification requirements and are granted extensions after an initial six-month period. Some do not meet any, and a social worker will request that parental rights be terminated after the initial six months.

If the judge agrees that terminating parental rights is the next step, they will schedule a date to do so: a termination of parental rights (TPR) hearing.[16] Usually, by this point, an alternative long-term guardian has been selected—either a relative or a nonrelated foster parent. In some cases, the county will determine that group homes are the best long-term option. After the TPR has been granted, the parent who has lost custody has no more rights as a guardian.

Our family has been through this process, as foster and then as adoptive parents in California. When we decided to become foster parents, we had not investigated the complicated history of the system we were joining. Looking back at those decisions now, my feelings are complicated. Being K's mom has been the greatest gift of my life. In K's case, there were no other options. The details of that are not mine to share, though. That said, as two people with space and income in Oakland, David and I were misguided in thinking that providing a home for foster kids was the best approach—as if those children were just floating, detached, and looking for a place to land. Each child in the system is bound to a complex web of injustice.

The stories that I heard from parents and their attorneys keep me up at night—the small moments and the profound heartbreak. But this isn't an anecdotal issue. According to Dr. Sharyn DeZelar, who spent decades researching disabled parents and the child welfare system, discrimination against disabled parents in the child welfare system is systemic.[17]

The primary statistic many people use to describe the child welfare's entrenched racism is the overrepresentation of Black families who have been under investigation by child protective services.[18] In the face of such stark numbers, it's impossible to deny the injustice. As I worked to track down the equivalent statistic for disabled parents, it proved to be more elusive.

During a call with Dr. DeZelar, I asked why that data was hard to find. She explained that every time Child Protective Services (CPS) opens a case against parents, they must file information about the case in the National Child Abuse and Neglect Data System (NCANDS).[19] While race and disability are both searchable in the national database, counties have set up their own system of logging cases.[20] Every county includes race on that platform, but many lack the option to mark that a parent is disabled. In those cases, a parent will show up in the national database as nondisabled. When researchers attempt to look at nationwide statistics, they must consider that many cases of disabled parents are being logged as not disabled.

Complicating the data further, for counties that do include disability, it's not a required field, and many who fill out the reports bypass that question. So even those counties lack accurate data. Surely there must be counties that reliably record the disability status of parents, I said. She explained that even in counties in which social workers regularly include disability when recording their cases, what they consider a disability varies significantly. Many activists consider substance use disorder a disability, but that is rarely categorized as such in NCANDS. Intellectual or psychosocial disabilities are also regularly excluded. Moreover, parents with chronic health issues or who are neurodivergent fail to show up in the statistics. The definition of disability is amorphous and expansive.

Yet even with a substantial undercounting of disabilities in NCANDS, disabled parents are *still* overrepresented in child welfare cases. Researchers estimate that 9.2 percent of parents are disabled, yet 19 percent of child welfare cases have parents with recorded disabilities (to reiterate: a significant undercounting). A 2020 study found that disabled parents were 36 percent more likely than nondisabled parents to have cases brought against them substantiated and to be separated from their children.[21] Dr. DeLezar can only imagine what accurate counts would reveal. Many researchers estimate that 70–80 percent of parents with intellectual disabilities are involuntarily separated from their children.[22]

Being able to identify the depth and breadth of the problem is a critical first step. The invisibility of disabled parents is part of the cruelty. When I asked Ms. Parthiban, the attorney, how frequently a parent separated from their children by CPS has a disability, she thought carefully. "Do you want the statistics?" she asked. I know those, I said; I asked for her observations instead.

She clarified that she considers substance use disorder and mental illness to be disabilities. Me, too, I assured her.

"Well, in that case, I have never heard of a parent who loses their kid who doesn't have a disability."

Some disability advocates believe that the child welfare system cannot be salvaged. The very nature of the system has, since its inception, brutally separated Black, Brown, and Indigenous kids from their families. Disabled parents have always lost their children without merit and at disproportionate rates. It has never been just.

Black activists have long called for the abolition of the child welfare system. In 2002, Dorothy Roberts, an attorney and a professor, wrote *Shattered Bonds: The Color of Child Welfare*, in which she proposed that the only option is to dismantle "what we now call child protection and replace it with a system that really promotes children's welfare."[23]

In her more recent 2022 book, *Torn Apart: How the Child Welfare System Destroys Black Families and How Abolition Can Build a Safer World*, she spells out how poverty and racism create a system that punishes Black families.[24] In some cities, 60 percent of Black children have had some interaction with CPS. According to her research, one-third of children in the foster system could be reunited with their parents if their parents could access adequate housing. Accessible and affordable housing is a primary barrier for both Natalie and Annette.

The mechanism and impact of racial bias within the system are intractable. Her claim from twenty years ago has not changed: the only option is abolition.

In 2021, echoing Roberts's groundbreaking work, Robyn Powell, a disabled attorney and an activist, published a paper in the *Yale Law Journal of Feminism*, repeating the calls for the abolition of the systems that separate children from their families. She refers to the current child welfare system as the "family policing" system and describes how the only just option is to replace it with "non-punitive supports and resources for families." The harms done to disabled people are "by design," she clarifies.[25]

In 2012, Powell served on the committee that wrote and published *Rocking the Cradle*, a 358-page document commissioned by President Obama, which proposed policies to bolster the rights of parents with disabilities. *Rocking the Cradle* centers largely on the child welfare system and the rate at which disabled parents lose custody without cause or merit. It proposed modest and incremental changes to the child welfare system.[26]

When I followed up with some of the other authors of *Rocking the Cradle*, I asked what changes they had seen in the decade-plus since its publication. They all said the same: very little. It's understandable that after decades of trying to fix a broken system, Powell considers it unsalvageable.

One couple I spoke to serve as a prime example of how the child welfare system is stacked against disabled families and how this version may be beyond repair. Cordelia and Joey are in their thirties and have been together since 2019. They are both autistic and white and live in New Jersey.[27] When Cordelia became pregnant during the pandemic, they started planning exactly what kind of parents they wanted to be. They would teach their infant sign language so that their baby could communicate early. They prepared their apartment for their baby's arrival.

As the due date approached, Cordelia had some health complications, including a stroke while pregnant, and a C-section was scheduled for August 10, 2021. As they left their apartment for the hospital, Cordelia felt sick and like she might throw up. Joey grabbed a bucket just in time. Joey wanted to clean out the bucket before they left—they knew how they wanted the apartment to be when their new baby came home—but worried about being late to the hospital. He brought it to their bathroom and put it in the tub, shutting the bathroom door so that the smell didn't permeate the rest of the apartment. Their apartment can get quite messy and they wanted to keep it clean for the baby.

Cordelia gave birth a few hours after arriving at the hospital, at 2:14 a.m. on August 11, and they named their new baby boy Finn. After a long night with no sleep, Cordelia and Joey both fell asleep around 7 a.m. in their recovery room. Around 10 a.m., a child welfare worker entered their room. They had been called because Cordelia received autism-related services from the county, making them a "family in need of services investigation." In other words, Cordelia's disability had flagged her as potentially unfit.

When the worker entered, Finn was out of the room getting measured, but, in the notes from that first morning, the social worker claimed that Joey had fallen asleep with Finn in his arms, which was unsafe. The worker asked to visit their apartment to ensure the baby had someplace safe to return to, but they didn't consent. Joey kept remembering the bucket of vomit in the bathroom.

Joey wasn't sure what was happening, but he knew enough to be suspicious. When he was three months old, his father physically abused Joey and his mother. Joey was removed from his home and sent to a foster home. His mother fought for seven years to regain custody but was unable. At seven years old, he was adopted by his foster parents. His childhood with his adoptive parents was unhappy. They were controlling and emotionally abusive. Their house was cluttered and overflowing with belongings. He was not safe and did not feel seen, and it wasn't until he met Cordelia that he was even screened for autism. He worried that one false move would damn his new baby to a similar fate.

Because there wasn't an official complaint against Cordelia and Joey, the social workers couldn't enter their apartment without permission. After Cordelia and Joey said no, the workers asked Cordelia's father, who is designated as Cordelia's guardian. Without understanding the context, he agreed. Joey was unsurprised to learn later that the vomit in the bathtub was the initial evidence that he and Cordelia were unfit parents.

The day after Finn was born, the social workers returned to the hospital and pulled Joey aside. They said they had some paperwork regarding

Finn's safety, and they needed him to sign it. He did. He has regretted that moment ever since. "All I want to do is burn that paper," he told me.[28]

No one had explained that the "safety plan" he was agreeing to with his signature gave his adoptive parents, who are nearing eighty, physical custody of Finn and put them on the path to legal guardianship of their grandson. After decades as foster parents, Joey's parents were close with many of the social workers and had been explaining that Finn would be in better hands with them. According to Cordelia and Joey, the social workers made that happen.

The three of us spoke for the first time for over an hour and then continued to talk by text. They both come across as detail-oriented and engaged, but they told me that it can be difficult for them to respond as expected in social situations. In other words, they are not very good at masking their autism.[29]

The weeks after Finn was born were exhausting and confusing for Joey and Cordelia. Finn was taken immediately to Joey's adoptive parents' house, and Joey was given permission to visit as often as he wanted. However, Cordelia had to stay in her apartment for her recovery. Cordelia was at high risk for additional strokes after leaving the hospital, and Joey had to be with her every twelve hours to administer injectable medication.

Immediately, Joey's parents began boxing him out of his son's life. They took Joey's car, making it nearly impossible to go back and forth between Finn and Cordelia, as he needed to. They lied about the baby's routine doctor appointment times, so Joey missed many appointments. Cordelia and Joey made it clear to me that since Finn was born, they have been extremely confused about the process and what they need to do to regain custody. When I asked about a reunification plan, they said, "That doesn't sound familiar."[30]

When I spoke with Cordelia's attorney for clarification, he echoed their sentiment. "The case *has* been confusing," he confirmed. CPS isn't the right fit here, he disclosed. "It's a square peg in a round hole."[31] Cordelia and Joey have been extensively questioned and examined by social workers and the court system, and, understandably, neither of them responds well to that pressure. According to her attorney, Cordelia's narratives become harder to follow when she's overwhelmed. He says it's hard to know what she really wants or needs.

I asked if any of the social workers were autistic or trained in autism and communication. He said no. "So it's like Cordelia and Joey are being forced to speak a second language and then being punished when they aren't fluent?" I asked. "That's exactly it," he agreed. "I hope you don't mind if I steal that to use in court."

At some point, Finn's legal guardians shifted from Joey and Cordelia to the county. From that day forward, Joey and Cordelia could only visit Finn for four hours a week at a neutral visitation center. Every visit is supervised. Since Finn's birth, they have not been alone with their son. When I asked why these visits must be supervised, they said they have asked that many times and no one will tell them.

During our call, it was obvious that they are very concerned about their son. They question Finn's safety with Joey's adoptive parents. Most of their time and energy is devoted to visitations, meetings with their attorneys, and attempts to obtain copies of the documents keeping their family apart. When I asked what the next steps were, they were quiet.

"No one will tell us."

I found myself wondering exactly what perpetuates these inequities within a system that is, often, staffed by people who care a great deal about justice. When Dr. Sharyn DeZelar and I spoke, she explained that her most current research focuses on disabled students in social work graduate programs. "So I've moved away from disabled parents and CPS," she revealed. Suddenly, the lingering stress of my own time in graduate school bubbled to the surface. I couldn't help sharing with her how difficult it was for me to complete my graduate degree in social work. I loved my MSW coursework and found that my perspective on justice shifted and grew while at Columbia.

However, in order to graduate, I had to complete 1,200 hours of internship fieldwork. The details of that requirement paused and almost halted my progress. Finding a placement that would accommodate my wheelchair and also had climate control was, to my great surprise, almost impossible. My first placement was at a middle school. On my first day of work, I was told that my wheelchair might take ramp space "from kids who needed it." The air conditioning at the school also didn't work, and when the temperature indoors exceeded 80, I developed heat exhaustion. I left that day, ill and demoralized, with 1,196 hours left to complete.

This was in 2018, and when I asked for a virtual placement, I was told that "social work never happens online." Two years later, during COVID lockdowns, that comment became almost comical in its rigidness. One administrator told me that maybe I was just too disabled to be a social worker. It was only because an influential faculty member took me under her wing and created an accessible placement that I was able to graduate.

As we continued to talk about disabled parents and custody cases, my experience in graduate school kept running through my mind. Finally, I wondered out loud if her research on social work education was, in fact, intimately connected to the child welfare system and custody. A tremendous amount of power rests with social workers in the foster care system. They are the professionals who make the recommendations to the courts about a parent's capacity to parent.

In my time studying disability justice, one of my most compelling realizations has been that humans, before becoming disabled, are generally terrible about predicting what a disabled life is like. We assign tragedy and incompetence when they are absent. We fail to conceptualize the degree of disabled creativity, community, and resourcefulness. In order words, we misjudge parental fitness. I thought of the time we attended one of K's hearings. A social worker warned me that the presiding judge had a bias against disabilities. "I know this isn't fair, but if possible, you might want to leave your wheelchair in the hall."

"Wouldn't the outcome of these cases change," I asked Dr. DeZelar, "if the person determining a parent's fitness was also disabled?"

She chuckled and said that maybe her two areas of focus were quite related after all.

As I've said, in twenty-two states, it is legal to forcibly separate a parent and their child *simply because* the parent is disabled. In thirty-five states, disability is one of the grounds for termination of parental rights.[32] Many of the attorneys and advocates I spoke to stressed the importance of state-by-state legislation changes. And I agree. The truth is that an entire book could be devoted to a study of the child welfare system from a legal perspective. And that book should exist. But, in this chapter, I am spending less time swimming around in appellate cases and proposed amendments and, instead, considering what solutions disability culture offers to widespread legalized family separation.

First, it's critical to recognize that separating children from their parents is harmful. There are cases in which it's the only option, but, even then, harm has occurred. If you find yourself wondering if this is *really* true, or if maybe it's actually good for children to be in "better" homes, then I would encourage you to spend more time with the work of adult adoptee advocates like Angela Tucker, Sam Collier, and Jessenia Parmer, all of whom speak about their complex experience as transracial adoptees.[33] It's widely understood that the process of splitting up a family is painful, even when it's necessary. Because of the importance of those first and primary connections, the goal of any child welfare system should be to provide services to keep families together.

If we can acknowledge that keeping a family together is the first and best solution, we have to consider what obstacles are standing in the way. From what beliefs and assumptions do those obstacles grow? What are the values that undergird a system that punishes parents and children because a parent has a body or mind that deviates too much from what society considers normal?

In many of the cases and studies I read, judges and social workers picked one parenting measure to be used as sort of a litmus test of parental fitness. In some cases, that was the ability to attend a parent-teacher conference; in others, like Annette's, it was IQ. Preceding each example of parental separation, there is one moment, action, or inaction that tips the scales away from the disabled parent. For Natalie, it was the hotel room, and for Annette, it was asking to sleep in bed with her baby. For Cordelia and Joey, it was the bucket of vomit.

But, as any parent, disabled or not, will tell you, we cannot determine our capacity to parent based on one moment. Every one of us has missteps driven by exhaustion or miscalculations or moments in which our patience runs dry. Yes, for sure, there are some behaviors that are inexcusable, but none of us would prevail if the standard of parenting were perfection.

Surely, every one of us can imagine having to spend some nights in a hotel and forgetting appointments in the chaos. Or feeling so delirious with the hormones of giving birth that we cannot imagine placing our baby a few feet away in a bed. Or rushing out the door and hiding vomit instead of cleaning it up. These are not inexcusable choices. But the system that witnessed those moments was ready to take drastic measures anyway.

In each of these examples, the cases were escalated within hours because a parent had a diagnosis and earlier interactions with publicly funded social services. Disabled parents are judged differently. In the examples I read and heard, doctors, nurses, and government employees assumed that a parent's disability indicates that it is the collective responsibility of those with power to monitor closely for mistakes and, if a mistake is spotted, to swoop in. One mother I spoke to, who is blind, had trouble breastfeeding the day that her daughter was born. She cried from exhaustion and discouragement. She wanted it to be easier. Her nurse called CPS. Ultimately, CPS decided to let her leave the hospital with the new baby, but she remains terrified of asking medical providers for advice.

So, to my earlier question, where do the assumptions that breed impossible standards and relentless observation originate? In part, I believe that they grow from the pernicious myth that corrodes every parent: our capacity to parent is measured by our ability to do it ourselves. It's the lie of individualism.

It's no coincidence that those who receive government assistance in the form of medical care, housing assistance, or disability income are more likely to lose custody. In practice, it's as if the natural conclusion is that if you need official help, your capacity to care for your children is suspect.

People access publicly funded programs for many reasons, but chief among those is poverty. Certain identities make someone much more likely to experience poverty, including disability and Blackness.[34] Those parents who, due to socioeconomic status, rely on federal and state funds for childcare, food, and housing, must spend their days in an ever-changing bureaucratic maze. At every turn, a mandated reporter waits, observing and judging their capacity to parent. And every misstep is seen through the lens of the parent's need for help feeding and housing their family.

Disabled parents who are unable to work also rely on a collage of inadequate and archaic social supports—less than $1,000 per month in income, inaccessible housing options, multiyear waitlists for childcare, doctors who don't take Medicaid, and overburdened mental health services.[35] And, for these parents, too, each step of the process involves an encounter with another person who is legally obligated to report concerns. And if a report is made, and CPS sees that, yes, this parent needs help managing their disability or that, last year, another person expressed concern about missed appointments (never mind that accessible public transport is incredibly unreliable), their case is escalated. This parent has a *history*.

It is essential that we fix the systems that unjustly separate so many children from their parents. It's critical that we change the policies that force so many disabled people to live below the poverty line. Of *course*, the law that allows employers to pay disabled people less than minimum wage must be repealed.

And we need to shift something even more foundational. We need to reconsider what it means to need assistance. We need to question the assumptions that make us suspicious of those who need help.

Because—and this is critical—every single parent needs help. Ask any parent, disabled or not, Black, Brown, Indigenous, or white, and they will admit that they do not parent alone. It is impossible. When people say that disabled people shouldn't be parents, what they seem to be saying is: disabled people won't be able to parent on their own. Underneath that claim is a sinister, society-rending assumption: people *should* be able to parent without help. What if, instead, we judged parents by how good they were at marshaling help for the sake of their children? If that were the metric, disabled parents would be among the best.

Black, Brown, and Indigenous writers have been advocating for more collective parenting for decades. In *Essential Labor*, Angela Garbes notes that there are many cultures in which we can find answers to our lonely isolation and impossible self-reliance. These are groups that have been exploited by capitalism and have, in practice, rejected capitalism's values. Garbes also points out that, at its essence, mothering *is* "human inter-dependence." She links the myth that one or two adults are enough to care for children to colonialism and the "coercion to adopt an isolated way of life."[36]

Dr. Dawn Dow, a Black sociologist at the University of Maryland, has studied collective parenting in Black culture and describes the dynamic as a "mother-centered" and "community-supported" activity.[37] A community is central to sustainable parenting. Another researcher at the University of Maryland, Patricia Hill Collins, has coined the term "other-mothering," which is the practice in Black cultures of looking out for all of the kids in your community, not just your own. She has observed that this type of collective parenting also leads to activism and broader civic engagement.[38]

Racialized parents have long been practicing and advocating for a more sustainable way to parent while having their children removed by Child Protective Services at a much higher rate than white parents. In her 2020 book, *How We Show Up*, Mia Birdsong, a Black writer and an activist, examines the practical details of collective parenting.[39]

The book was born from a conversation with her white friend, Johnny, who was having some difficulty managing work, parenting, and mental health. She found herself compelled to offer advice but, before doing so, realized her advice was targeted at ways that Johnny could improve his efficiency and time management—a way to do a better job on his own. When she reflected on her own family's culture, she realized that the answers didn't lie in optimization but in community. She went about exploring what collective communal parenting can look like on a daily basis.

Throughout her book, she considers exactly what it means to share burdens and which burdens need to be shared. For example, she reflects on how valuable it is for single parents to have people with whom they can make important decisions. The emotional toll of making all decisions alone is significant. Later, she celebrates and explores the role of the Black "auntie." The chapter I found to be the most meaningful came toward the end, as she examines how a community can serve to provide safety without resorting to incarceration. Interdependence and transformative justice—a framework that responds to violence without creating violence—can heal a community instead of just slowly removing its members. How might these concepts be applied to Child Protective Services?

It's not only Black, Brown, Indigenous, and disabled parents who are unable to parent in isolation. Every parent needs help. Wealthy and nondisabled parents often feel as if they *should* manage to do it on their own, though they are also reliant on support. As Jessica Grose laments in *Screaming on the Inside*, "It's been obvious for 40 years that you need to be on stimulants and never sleep to accomplish all the things expected of a modern American mother."[40]

White and wealthy families rarely lose custody of their children, simply because financial resources and access allow them to cobble together their own paid (and still usually inadequate) networks of support: nannies and private daycares and retired parents and so on. There is usually less paperwork but only barely; it can feel no less precarious. For those with means, their families stay together, but these parents are also drowning. The problem isn't that disabled people need too much help to parent safely. The problem is that society refuses to admit that everyone does. Like every other aspect of disabled parenting, the obstacles disabled parents face serve as a reflection of how parenting, for every person, is inhumane.

While writers Katherine Goldstein and Jessica Grose do acknowledge that parenting is unsustainable, they focus on legislative changes that would improve working conditions for breastfeeding people and increase access to affordable childcare. And, in some ways, I agree with them. But I think policy-focused solutions often overlook the powerful solutions that are already modeled in marginalized cultures such as mutual aid.

Mutual aid is a unique form of assistance—just because we ask for help does not mean we relinquish our inherent power. According to Dean Spade, a lawyer and trans activist, mutual aid is "collective coordination to meet each other's needs, usually from an awareness that the systems we have in place are not going to meet them. Those systems, in fact, have often created the crisis."[41] Mutual aid acknowledges that we all have needs and we all depend on one another. In the system of food and housing subsidies and the subsequent interactions with child welfare, there is a clear delineation between the service provider and the service receiver. And the former, from their position of power and false neutrality and rightness, is granted the power to judge. Within a disabled mutual aid system, that imbalance is eliminated.

The power that nondisabled people have wrested away from us is flimsy; it's not rooted in truth. Disabled people are not simply those who need your help. We are a critical part of a mutually beneficial web of care. This book is an example of mutual aid—an offering from my disabled body.

The first name that many in the disability justice movement think of when mutual aid is mentioned is Leah Lakshmi Piepzna-Samarasinha. In their most recent book, *The Future Is Disabled*, they share, through short anecdotes, what disabled mutual aid looks like in practice—on hikes, in Zoom meetings, and in new cities.[42] They describe how, early in the pandemic, disabled friends in densely populated cities weren't able to obtain N95 masks, but at a garden center near their home, they found some available, and checkout was available curbside. They set aside the money they could and purchased the masks to mail back to their friends in New York. They included some healing nettles in the envelope.

Piepzna-Samarasinha describes how mutual aid is detailed and practical, and complicated. They share this story:

> I remember my friend, a disabled, fat, mixed race queer and trans elder, texting because their PCA had come to work sick. . . . My friend, worried they'd been exposed to COVID, texted a bunch of people they knew and said, "Ok, we're going to set up a system, everybody sign up on this Google doc. I need someone to text me in the morning and at night, to make sure I'm responsive. Let's do it for the next four days, I'll get tested too but I want you to check in on me. If you don't hear back from me, I give you permission to call 911, let them know that I'm fat and they need to bring an accessible stretcher and this is where my apartment is.

Their approach is pragmatic and aspirational. They stress that any true disability justice movement must be led by queer, trans, Black, and Indigenous people of color (QTBIPOC). The "web of care" they describe is joyful and creative, but they don't shy away from the more practical obstacles of any care network. What happens if there are more needs than people to fill them? What if the community is too small? What if everyone gets sick at once?

Piepzna-Samarasinha understands that community isn't without struggles, but, like me, they believe that within its complications lies a structure that can save us all. They wonder, "What would a world radically shaped by disabled knowledge, culture, love, and connection be like?"

Mutual aid in the form of parenting would look different based on a community and its needs. It would grow from the wisdom and experience of marginalized cultures. Critically, no version of bodies or minds would be considered superior. A wealthy, white, and nondisabled person would recognize not only their capacities but also their needs.

You could argue that mutual aid, taken to its natural conclusion, would create a commune. In reality, it exists in a variety of interactions and to many degrees. That said, looking at official communal parenting structures in the United States can be a useful example of community in practice.

At Twin Oaks community, in Virginia, around one hundred residents live together, sharing labor, housing, food, finances, and parenting responsibilities. Valerie is in her mid-fifties and has lived there for decades. We spoke by phone for nearly an hour.[43]

She told me that at Twin Oaks, community members must labor for forty-two hours per week. Qualifying activities include upkeep of the grounds, cooking for the community, office work for the group's tofu business, and providing care to members in need. The definition of labor also includes caring for children—including the children of other community members. This structure creates a system in which the work of parenting is divided. Parents don't shoulder all of the burden, and nonparents are able to stay connected to children in a way they otherwise wouldn't. Parents at Twin Oaks fared very well during the early pandemic lockdown. In fact, very little changed in their daily life. Importantly, you cannot join Twin Oaks if you already have kids, and, in order to have your own children, you must first obtain the community's permission.

I asked Valerie what they do when a member gets sick or becomes disabled. She said that all community members have unlimited access to sick days. But, she admitted, there has been some concern about the policy because sick days are recorded publicly. Some community members see this structure as inherently ableist—that they are all being measured by their capacity to labor.

"What about when someone goes through something difficult and doesn't only need a break but also needs support?" I asked Valerie. She explained "care teams," which are formed in response to a crisis like cancer, a bad breakup, or a depressive episode. A care team is made up of three to six people and meets regularly with the person in crisis in order to come up with behavioral solutions for the person in crisis and to hold them accountable.

I was surprised by this approach and asked Valerie, "Does a care team ever turn away from a personal responsibility model and instead seek out community solutions for the person struggling?" She replied, "Maybe sometimes, but we want people to be self-managing."

I thought a lot about my call with Valerie. In some ways, their system does ease the burden on parents, but, in others, it leaves very little space for disability. I had imagined mutual aid as water poured into the space between people. And that as needs and capacities shift, the water moves and fills the gaps. But how do we structure in support so that one person is not left carrying more than they can bear?

If you ask about mutual aid and disability enough, someone is bound to bring up Camphill. There are more than one hundred Camphill communities worldwide. Each Camphill community is made up of a group of people divided into homes. There are different structures now, but, traditionally, in each Camphill home, people with intellectual disabilities live alongside nondisabled adults and their nondisabled children. The model serves to eliminate models of care that isolate disabled people. Many of the Camphill homes include a nondisabled couple, their children, two volunteers in their twenties, and then one or two intellectually disabled people.

I spoke with Maria McLaughlin, a nondisabled person who has lived in Camphill communities for over twenty years. In some ways, the structures they illustrated do break down the false division between care providers and care receivers. Disabled and nondisabled people do share projects and responsibilities. But in others, the distinction remains. Disabled people don't get paid for their labor, but the nondisabled people do. Which makes it even more strange that disabled people have historically been called residents, whereas nondisabled people were called volunteers. The first school that Maria worked at was called a "special school."[44]

I asked Maria if disabled people are ever parents, with the community supporting them. "I have never encountered that," she replied. "It's inspiring to hear how folks with disabilities are able to parent with people surrounding them."

I had hoped that Camphill would serve as an example of collective disabled parenting in practice, but, instead, I felt the familiar sting of being called inspiring for doing something that nondisabled people do every day.

There are other examples of communal parenting that don't include living together. At the Detroit Radical Childcare Collective, a group of childcare providers operates from a mutual aid and social justice framework. They accept bartering for their services, and all members are paid a living wage.[45] Discipline follows a restorative justice model. On social media, they alert followers to needs within the larger community. They offer those with means opportunities to provide funds to specific people in specific situations, prioritizing single, Black, and queer parents. Their model blurs the divide between those who need help and those who provide it. It becomes more of a web.

I think about Annette, Natalie, Cordelia, and Joey and how a mutually beneficial web of care could transform their situations. How Annette may be reunited with Oliver because she is expanding her family to include a trusted nonrelative. How things would be different if Natalie's roommate situation was less casual and more of a collective with safety and restorative justice.

The foster system is not filled with the children of disabled parents because disabled people are fundamentally less equipped to parent. It's filled because our legal standard of parenting is broken—those with money and access can patch the holes well enough to hide their struggles.

Changing the rigid laws and punitive responses won't fix the falsehoods on which child protective services is built. It also won't save the parents throughout the United States and Canada who are barely hanging on. We need to shift our focus to the wisdom of the cultures that value community and mutual aid above independence. We need to believe and practice on a daily, inconvenient basis, what is deeply true: we belong to each other.

Chapter 9

ABLEISM

I imagine telling my twenty-eight-year-old self about my life now. I picture walking up to her as she sits down for dinner in the city or speaking into her headphones as she's lacing up her shoes for a morning run. "Your life is going to change," I would tell her.

You will lose the ability to run and will even have trouble walking. This job you love? You will have to quit. Remember last summer, sunbathing on the beach with your friends before running into the water for "ocean beers"? Nearly every part of that moment will be out of your reach. Your marriage? It will dissolve. You will, for years, struggle financially. Every single day you will feel like you might faint. You will wake up clammy, and the food you love will nauseate you. You will, eventually, give up your driver's license. You will spend more hours on an adjustable memory foam mattress than anywhere else.

The younger version of me would pale, terrified. I can picture that time of my life so clearly, the way I clung to every fun and fancy and joyful thing in my life, like flotation devices. If you had asked me then, I would have said that letting it all go would make me drown.

And here is what I have spent years trying to understand: I would have been wrong.

The truth is, not only is my life in this disabled body still worth living, but it is also better. I mean that. I would pick this version of myself. I would pick this version of my days. The only way that I can explain this reality is that the standards by which I thought I should measure a life—by the diversity of experiences and absence of suffering and range of possibilities—were the wrong metrics.

My experience with well-being and disability is not unusual. In 1999, Dr. Gary L. Albrecht and Dr. Patrick J. Devlieger published a still-influential piece in the academic journal *Social Science & Medicine* called "The Disability Paradox: High Quality of Life Against All Odds."[1] In it, they consider data about disabled people and life satisfaction. Up until that point, and still today, on average, disabled people rate their life satisfaction and sense of well-being at equal or higher levels than nondisabled people. Albrecht and Devlieger struggled to reconcile those statistics with the widespread societal belief that "disabled individuals seem to live an undesirable daily existence."[2]

Why, if most people assume it is worse to be disabled than not to be disabled, are disabled people satisfied? To explain the paradox, they propose that our collective assumptions about what makes a life good are not based on what actually impacts satisfaction. Most people assume that quality of life is, at least in part, correlated with being in good health: "All that matters is our health." "I don't care if it's a boy or a girl, as long as it's healthy." "Without our health, we have nothing."

What if that's not true?

Devlieger and Albrecht posited, after dozens of interviews with disabled and nondisabled people, that, in fact, perceived quality of life is correlated more with integration between body, mind, and spirit than it is with objective health measurements. They call this a "balance theory."

In the decades since Devlieger and Albrecht published their article, philosophers and bioethicists have offered a range of explanations for the "disability paradox." In 2021, in *The Journal of Medicine and Philosophy*, Stephen Campbell, Sven Nyholm, and Jennifer Walter reflected on the 1999 article in their own editorial called "Disability and the Goods of Life."[3] They begin by asking the question posed in 1999—why are disabled people so much happier than nondisabled people expect?

They approached the question by exploring how disability impacts one's access to the "goods of life." If we can come up with a list of what makes life good, how does disability relate to each of those things? The authors proposed the following goods: happiness, rewarding relationships, knowledge, and achievement. This list consists of the items found over decades of research and interviews on well-being theories. Certainly, a list of four items is not definitive or universal but is, at the very least, a worthwhile exercise.

The authors then split disabilities into four categories: sensory, mobility, intellectual, and social. For each of the four "goods" they considered compatibility with each of the four disability categories. In general, they found that most disabilities are compatible with most goods. They concluded that trouble begins when we shift to a "perfectionistic" view of goodness. They concluded that if a list of objective goods defined well-being, disability does not make those "goods" unattainable.

In 2013 in the philosophy anthology *Disability and the Good Human Life*, Dr. Thomas Schramme, a philosophy professor in Liverpool, offered his own explanation in his chapter, "Disability (Not) as a Harmful Condition: The Received View Challenged."[4] Schramme starts by acknowledging that within philosophy, it is commonplace to work from the assumption that being disabled is worse than not being disabled. He explains the ripple effects of that assumption on bioethics and healthcare legislation.

Schramme's theory matches my own experience. He believes that when people compare their disabled life to an imagined nondisabled one, they assume a disabled life is worse. But when they take a "noncomparative" perspective and just see their life as it is, they find that they are satisfied. In his work, he has found that "people tend to be subjectively happy once they have adapted to the impacts of a medical impairment, even though they might have had fairly negative things to say about a possible disability some time before, and of course even though many other people within their environment see the condition as harmful." For many, it's comparing one's life to a hypothetical other life that reduces perceived well-being.

It's also important to consider what we mean by well-being, according to Schramme. Derek Parfit, the late British philosopher, said well-being could be explained in hedonistic terms, according to an objective list (as in the "goods of life" article), or by desire fulfillment. Aristotle equated well-being with a sense of "eudaimonia," or flourishing. It's anywhere from hard to impossible to define what makes a life good, but that doesn't stop most people from doggedly pursuing satisfaction. And when people, disabled or not, correlate well-being with not having a disability, they are oversimplifying the complex reality of being human.

Schramme points out that both sides of the disability argument (those who see disability as bad and those who do not) make the critical mistake of assuming commonality between people based on one aspect of their identities. He writes: "Our discussion of theories of well-being and their different assessments of disability has shown that the whole issue is diverse and should be dealt with accordingly. Not all disabilities are the same; not all people with disabilities are the same; not all societies in which people with disabilities live are the same." His point is essential. We are enacting a new kind of harm when we essentialize someone's life.

Along these lines, it's critical to remember that just because disabled people often have a high sense of well-being, not all disabled people do. Disability encompasses a wide range of conditions and, for some, the degree of pain, limitation, or unpredictability makes adjusting impossible. For others, the secondary losses (unreliable income, discrimination) reduce their quality of life. The key is that disabled people have the right to perceive the value of our own lives.

Ultimately, "well-being" is a fuzzy and subjective term that seems to grow even blurrier the more one tries to define it. The definition of "disability" has the same tendency. What remains critical is this: many disabled people love their lives. I am one of them.

Dr. Liza Iezzoni, who is disabled and was born in 1954, was in medical school at Harvard when she developed symptoms of multiple sclerosis. She became a doctor and is still at Harvard, where she researches medical care disparities for people with disabilities—in 2022, the *New York Times* published an article highlighting some of Dr. Iezzoni's research.[5] She found, through interviews with physicians, that many doctors are reluctant to provide care to disabled people.[6] She had suspected as much, from her own experiences and from her work with disabled people, but to have doctors admit it to her face in interviews was striking.

Also, she was shocked to discover that 82 percent of doctors interviewed believed that disabled people have a worse quality of life than nondisabled people. I have come to believe that this statistic is a crucial part of the dehumanizing reproductive medical care that disabled people encounter. I spoke with Dr. Iezzoni over Zoom one afternoon in June. She was cheerful and encouraging. I asked her about the 82 percent statistic. "Oh, boy. That number," she said.

She said she had been surprised that so many doctors admitted that they think disabled lives are worse. She had expected what's called a "positive response bias," with which interviewees nudge their answers closer to what they think the interviewer wants to hear. In this case, doctors felt so sure that being disabled is bad that they considered it a fact, not an opinion.

My own experience in healthcare since becoming a power wheelchair user reflects her study results. I never feel quite as pitied as when a doctor sees me. They often ask when I got my wheelchair as if it's when my life fell apart, not as if it's the time I was finally able to access freedom.

"What is the impact of this bias?" I asked Dr. Iezzoni. "We saw it during the early months of COVID when medical rationing was being discussed," she answered. She referred to the months when hospitals were coming up with which patients they would treat first and how they deprioritized those with certain disabilities because of a "lower quality of life." The triage decisions were so explicit, she remembered, that the Department of Health and Human Services had to issue an advisory to hospitals that they could not send people to the back of the line because of their "perceived quality of life."[7]

I remember that time well. David and I discussed that if I needed to be hospitalized in early 2020, I wouldn't bring my own wheelchair and would try to downplay my own disability. I was scared that someone would decide my life wasn't worth saving.

Dr. Iezzoni said that not all of the impacts are as explicit. When it comes to reproductive healthcare, doctors often make assumptions about their disabled patients' sex lives and family planning. Disabled people have more unplanned pregnancies than nondisabled people because we aren't offered contraception at the same rate, and we experience more sexual assault than nondisabled people.

She told me that in her work, she found that doctors are less likely to do cancer screenings on disabled people because of a "questionable benefit." In other words, if someone's life isn't worth living, why go through the trouble of saving it?[8] The irony is that disabled people are often well equipped to manage a cancer diagnosis. Dr. Iezzoni partnered with the National Institute of Health in 2021 to study the experiences of people with mobility disabilities who have cancer. The researchers found that disabled people were well prepared emotionally for cancer and had developed the skills they needed to navigate the medical system. While their cancer experiences were complex, Dr. Iezzoni was struck by the fact that disability serves as a protective factor.

I told her my findings about the first week of parenting—that disabled parents seemed to be able to adjust to this major life change with less internal disruption than nondisabled parents. She was not surprised. "Disabled people have an inherent practicality," she said. Her view, based on her decades of research, is that disabled people, out of necessity, develop the ability to problem-solve and navigate the complications that all people inevitably encounter. "We have learned to ride the waves?" I asked.

"Exactly."

It's easy to dismiss ableism in its purest form. Of *course* we shouldn't think that disabled people deserve less. Of *course* we shouldn't hate someone because they are disabled. But the fact is, pity lives near disdain. Believing that disabled lives are worse is just an inch away from believing that the people, themselves, are worse.

Ableism—and the assumptions and practices that hold it up—not only perpetuates all the ways that parenting while disabled is difficult, but it also contributes to the ways in which nondisabled parenting is unsustainable. Ableism calls us a deviation from the norm, that there is a best way to have a body and mind and that all of us disabled people are, to some degree, deficient. Ableism opens the door to inaccessibility, and exclusion, and disempowerment. Ableism provides the excuse to take our kids away. Ableism assumes that a child would be better off without us as a parent. Ableism assumes we'd be better off not existing in the first place.

And, just like homophobia and racism, ableism snakes its way into our minds and our hearts. As I mentioned in the introduction, my internalized ableism is how I became a writer. I saw nondisabled parenting as the norm against which I should measure my relationship with my child, and I fell short. I felt like an imitator. When we internalize the ableism surrounding us, we stop demanding what we deserve. We question our own instincts and perceptions. It's poison.

When the anatomy scan, done between weeks 18 and 22 of pregnancy, reveals what doctors call a "fetal abnormality," the next weeks are "like a conveyor belt," according to Dr. Paige Church, the Harvard antenatal physician with spina bifida I interviewed in chapter 3.[9] She explained that everything must be rushed because, in many states, the window in which the pregnant person can get an abortion is closing.

Doctors order additional testing and specialist consultations. They set up a time to counsel the parent or parents on their options. Sometimes, genetic counselors are called in. The goal is to help the parents-to-be decide if they want to terminate the pregnancy or try to set up antenatal care.

These weeks are excruciating for the family. They have spent months planning for a baby and imagining a future, and now their plans disintegrate. The future is hazy. Will there even be a baby? Parents must consider the viability of the pregnancy and the risk to the pregnant person. In many cases, the main consideration is if the baby, with a probable diagnosis, should be born.

A treating physician often calls Dr. Church to consult with these parents, particularly if the fetus has been diagnosed with spina bifida. Until Dr. Church published an editorial in *JAMA* in 2017, she was not public about her diagnosis. While she still doesn't mention it to expectant families, many have googled her or have come across her name in spina bifida support groups. They know she is advising from her own experience.

She is so careful when she tells the parents what life is like with spina bifida. She explains the common complications and what it is like to live with a neurogenic bladder. But her other message often goes unsaid; her presence does the talking. *Your baby can also be a Harvard physician.*

Despite that, parents often ride the conveyor belt right to pregnancy termination. I asked Dr. Church how she explains that choice. She said that she thinks it's because, in part, termination is often the solution the parents can picture. They can imagine that version of a future because it's "immediate and clean." A life with a disabled child is harder to visualize. "Sometimes I think it's all a failure of imagination," she said. "Picturing a new version of one's life is time-consuming, and these parents don't have time."

She thinks the medical system plays a large role, too. Doctors often believe that disabled lives are unequivocally worse than nondisabled lives. Their personal beliefs certainly influence the way in which they inform their patients.

When a parent decides if they should terminate a wanted pregnancy due to a fetal abnormality, it's not only the doctor's advice that influences their choice; it's how they have experienced disability up until that point.

Because of widespread professional and public inaccessibility, many non-disabled people have limited experience with disabled people. Disabled people are underrepresented in media and often reduced to flimsy inspirational characters or objects of pity. I think about Dr. Church's reflection on imagination, which seems true. How could a parent imagine a fulfilling and complex life for their disabled child if they haven't been exposed to that possibility?

It goes without saying that I think every pregnant person should be able to make the right decision for themselves about pregnancy termination. The tragedy is that when it comes to selective abortion, these decisions are strongly influenced by medical and social ableism and misconceptions. In some cases, a family wants to continue with the pregnancy, but because of inadequate social resources for disabled children, they make the hard decision to abort.

Some people simply cannot manage the additional complications that disability brings. Even if the information provided were truly objective and without ableism and bias, they would need to terminate the pregnancy. Parents have limited capacity and resources and should be able to make choices in light of that.

Many people, disabled and not, have hard lives and report low well-being levels. But just because a life is hard doesn't mean it's not worthy. Every person will suffer, and every life will have complications. Accurately predicting the degree of suffering is impossible, and that's true throughout the course of a life. Even if we knew that every disabled person would suffer, it's not an indication that their life is not worth having.

I asked Dr. Church how often, in these cases, the families are offered adoption services. "Probably ten percent," she answered. The doctors likely assume that a disabled fetus is a poor candidate for adoption. Again, the assumption that disabled lives are worse is pernicious.

Listening to her talk, I imagined going into consult rooms and leaving knowing that someone has determined that a life like yours isn't worth having. "What is the impact on your mental health?" I asked. She said that in recent years it has become easier because she reminds herself that it's not a judgment of her. Ableism and misperceptions of disability are so widespread that Dr. Church's existence would need to undo decades of messaging.

In 2020, Sarah Zhang published a reported piece in *The Atlantic* called "The Last Children of Down Syndrome" about the falling number of people with Down syndrome due to selective abortions. She traveled to Denmark because, since 2004, every pregnant person there has been offered prenatal Down syndrome screening. The result of nearly universal screening has been a stark drop in babies born with Down syndrome. Ninety-five percent of people who receive a positive test chose to abort.

During one of Zhang's interviews, she is at a café with a mother, Grete, and Grete's son, Karl Emil. Karl Emil was born in 2002 and has Down syndrome. While Grete and Sarah talk, Karl Emil is distracted with his mom's phone, taking selfies. At one point, Grete retrieves her phone to show Zhang an article about the Down syndrome abortion rate. Zhang observes, "When Karl Emil read over her shoulder, his face crumpled. He curled into the corner and refused to look at us. He had understood, obviously, and the distress was plain on his face."

Grete explained that Karl Emil can read and is aware of the debate about Down syndrome. As a child he felt proud of who he was but went through a period in adolescence when he wished he were more like his peers. But now he accepts his identity. The rate that people abort people like him feels like a judgment on his life.

In the near future, researchers will likely identify the genetic markers of my condition, hypermobile Ehlers-Danlos syndrome. I imagine amniocentesis revealing that abnormality and a genetic counselor or doctor explaining what it means. *Your child will be in pain every day of their life. They have a high likelihood of developing digestive and neurological complications. They should avoid most contact sports because of the risk of injury. They will need regular ocular and cardiovascular testing to monitor for additional complications. Many people with hEDS need to use wheelchairs at least some of the time. In some cases, pregnancy is dangerous for a person with hEDS. Many cannot work or the type of job they can do is limited.*

All of that is true. And, yet a description of my illness does not begin to describe the reality of my life. Prenatally, a doctor can articulate the details of what a diagnosis may mean, but they cannot predict the other details of a fetus's future life. There may be vague mentions of "people with this disability often have a rich and full life," but it would be impossible to give details.

She will live in Paris and Berkeley. She will marry a generous partner, and together they will adopt a baby who is joy personified. She will, in her late thirties, discover she's a writer and will find deep purpose and connection through that work. She will laugh easily and cry easily and will hate cooked carrots and will love clothes and have dozens of houseplants and will think about coffee as she's falling asleep at night and will read poetry every morning. She will hold on tightly to her friendships and when she turns forty, dozens of those friends will send voice recordings of themselves reading her favorite poems. She will tend toward optimism and hope.

Dr. Church's comments about imagination come from the work of the late Dr. Adrienne Asch, a blind bioethicist who first wrote about selective abortion in those terms. She saw selective abortion, in its current state, as a means of essentializing people to "a single aspect."[10] She believed it was the moral duty of the doctors and genetic counselors to provide a more complete picture of what a disabled life could be.

A doctor encounters a few hurdles if they try to accurately portray life with a disability. The first is that medical training reinforces that disability is to be avoided at all costs. As Dr. Church told me, "Death and disability are said in the same breath." The training is effective, as Dr. Iezzoni's interviews revealed. The vast majority of doctors believe that being disabled negatively impacts well-being. This is, of course, in contrast to the lived experience of disabled people.

Second, doctors are rarely disabled. The inaccessibility of university, medical school, and residency programs means that most doctors have not personally experienced disability. Twenty-five percent of the United States is disabled. Three percent of doctors are.[11] Doctors do not have an objective perspective of disability—they have a nondisabled one. It's easy to imagine that if disabled people were doing the informing, the outcomes might be much different.

Third, and this is particularly true with intellectual disabilities like Down syndrome, doctors, by the very nature of their profession, value cognitive capacity. Their very careers show they have lived lives that prioritize academic and professional success. Attempting to provide neutral guidance as a nondisabled physician is fraught. Particularly perplexing are the statistics around doctor well-being, suicide, and depression. Doctors, overall, have higher levels of burnout, depression, and suicidality than non-doctors.[12] It is, statistically, harder to be a doctor than it is to be disabled.

Further complicating the conversation about selective abortion and disability is that the anti-choice movement has co-opted some of the disability justice talking points.[13] Many conservatives claim to be against abortion because disabled people deserve to be born, yet the systems they advocate for offer little to no support for disabled people. Despite what those on the right say, it is possible to consider the disability implications of prenatal disability counseling without compromising a pregnant person's right to their own body. A small group's perversion of the conversation doesn't mean we should stop talking.

When disabled people express concerns that selective abortion, CRISPR, and genetic testing before IVF implantation are eugenic practices, we are often criticized for being dramatic. The fact is, many of these practices originated in the Eugenics movement in the 1930s. As I discussed in chapter 7, sterilizing disabled people became common during that time as a method of preventing additional disabled people from being born. The term "eugenics" fell out of favor, but in the 1970s in Denmark, when prenatal testing became more common, it was advertised as a way of cutting costs: aborting disabled fetuses was cheaper than the cost of institutionalizing them later.[14]

Denmark was the location of the first prenatal test in 1959. A pregnant woman who had passed hemophilia to her first son did not want to have another baby with hemophilia—her first baby had only lived for five hours. She knew that she could not pass it on to a daughter. Her obstetrician, Fritz Fuchs, had been developing a way of testing fetuses for biological sex by inserting a long needle attached to a syringe into the uterus and retrieving amniotic fluid. He knew that the test was risky but wrote up a report defending the choice because "the method seems to be useful in preventive eugenics."[15]

Abortion was not legal then but would have been acceptable under Danish law on "eugenic grounds" if the test had shown the fetus was male. For most of the twentieth century, there was a scientific consensus that finding a way to rid society of genetically inferior people was desirable. This belief manifested in widespread disabled sterilization in Denmark between 1911 and 1967.

Dr. Rosemarie Garland-Thomson is a disabled bioethicist at Emory University and a vocal opponent of healthcare that fall under the umbrella of what she calls "velvet eugenics." In 2021, in response to advancing gene editing technology (CRISPR) Garland-Thomson published an op-ed in *Scientific American* reflecting on the risk to disabled people.[16] In our current hyper-capitalistic structure, decisions about which babies should be born are inextricable from the commodification of humanity, she explains,

Velvet eugenics seems like common sense, yet it hides its violence and inequality behind claims of patient autonomy and under a veil of voluntary consent. Ultimately, market-driven velvet eugenics embodies a similar goal of purging unacceptable human variations that campaigns to eliminate the supposedly unfit and inferior have held in the past. Both enact a mandate to exclude people with disabilities from coming into the world.

In 2019, Garland-Thompson expressed a similar sentiment in the *Journal of American Bioethics*, where she links gene editing to capitalism. "From the early 19th century into 21st-century late capitalism," she writes, "human work transitions from producing food to producing products to producing people as products."[17] Her concerns are clear—when we judge a person's value under capitalistic metrics, the society we create is profoundly inhumane.

Once I learned more about the "disability paradox" and how reluctant society is to admit that disabled lives are often quite good, I had to consider why these assumptions about disability persist. If we keep saying that we are happy, what is stopping our doctors from believing us? Why, when Peter Singer said, and then said again, that it was morally permissible to kill disabled babies before a certain age, did he keep his job at Princeton?[18]

If disabled people keep testifying to our own satisfaction, why is it so common to assume that being disabled is a tragedy? It's because we aren't being judged on whether our life is good; we are being judged on whether we are productive. It's not about our happiness at all. Capitalism's tentacles and reach have created a system in which every person's value is determined by their ability to work and create wealth for themselves or corporations. What it means to be human has become flattened to a list of accomplishments. Our lives are in service of our output.

The irony is that humanity needs genetic diversity to flourish. As our world changes, our collective chance of survival increases with intraspecies variation.[19] Just as capitalism's insistence on profits over effective climate change policies promises extinction, our hyper-focus on perfecting humankind does the same. Eugenics with an eye toward a monoculture is more than immoral; it's also a losing battle.

Silicon Valley is emblematic of the cursed and toxic braiding of capitalism and eugenics. As Malcolm Harris explored in his 2023 book, *Palo Alto: A History of California, Capitalism, and the World*, not only is the economic culture of Silicon Valley dehumanizing, but its most highly regarded incubator, Stanford University, has an origin story bound up with explicit eugenic principles.[20] David Starr Jordan, the first Stanford University president, was a leader in the American eugenics movement.

According to the California Academy of Sciences, where he was also president, Jordan "believed that people with traits he deemed desirable deserve to have children. He thought that people he deemed 'unfit' should not reproduce and, in many cases, should undergo compulsory sterilization—or be surgically prevented from having children, even against their will."[21]

Eugenics, as a theory, was developed by Charles Darwin's half-cousin, Francis Galton, a polymath who advocated for a scientific explanation for racism as well as eugenics.[22] He advocated for the practice of "superior" humans mating to create a species that had weeded out those deemed "unfit." Starr was one of his followers. They both considered nonwhite people to be inferior, and eugenics as a belief system and practice was bound up with racism throughout the twentieth century.

Malcolm Harris coins the social structures that have formed around California's hub of business and innovation "the Palo Alto System." Silicon Valley's obsession with profit and innovation has created a microcosm of capitalism's downsides, in which people are machines valued for their ability to produce and purchase.

It's not surprising that alongside startup culture's obsession with innovation and profit, a parallel culture of physical optimization has developed—workers need to be able to keep up with the pace of progress. "Biohacking," the term for optimizing every function of one's body to increase physical capacity and longevity, is an obsession in Palo Alto.[23] It's there that CEOs and venture capitalists attempt to "disrupt" their own bodies' limits. It's a desperate hunt to find a way to live forever.[24] It's a continuation of the doomed attempt to outsmart our own mortality.

When we judge the value of a person based on their ability to produce, it's easy to see why other forms of medical pruning have developed. As I mentioned earlier, many doctors and scientists hope that CRISPR, the gene editing technology, will soon be used to alter a fetus's genetic makeup so that it can be born without a disability.

Disability activists have also expressed concern about doctor-assisted death (called Medical Assistance in Dying, or MAID, in many locations) in the context that it currently exists. In Canada, where I live, MAID is available not only for those with terminal conditions but also for those with chronic conditions. In 2022, a woman with my disability utilized MAID because she could not afford accessible housing and adequate medical care.[25] Many states in the US are considering expanding MAID to those with chronic conditions in addition to the terminally ill.

Healthcare is even harder to access in the US than in Canada, and the outcome of this changed legislation seems clear: disabled people will only be able to afford to die. In fact, when I asked Dr. Iezzoni about the impacts of physician's assumptions about disabled quality of life, she replied immediately, "You've heard of MAID, right?"

In early 2020, before COVID hit, the United Nations published a warning about the eugenic implications of MAID, prenatal testing, and genetic engineering,

> Current developments in medical research and practice may revive eugenic ideas if safeguards for those affected are not ensured. . . . If assisted dying is made available for persons with health conditions or impairments, but who are not terminally ill, a social assumption could be made that it is better to be dead than to live with a disability. . . . People have the right to live and to die with dignity, but we cannot accept that people choose to end their lives because of social stigma, isolation or lack of access to personal assistance or disability-related services.[26]

If disabled people could afford to live, and if society didn't systematically discriminate against us, then programs like MAID would truly be evidence of freedom. Every person should have the choice to live or not. But, as it stands, offering death instead of dignity is oppression.

Ableism—the assumption that a disabled life is worse and altogether different from a nondisabled one—has followed each of us from the beginning. It interacts with other forms of discrimination in profound and complex ways. For example, a Black disabled person has a much different experience than a white one.

In some ways, it's the myth that there is a clear line between disabled and not that is the most pernicious part of ableism. Humanity has been inaccurately divided into two categories: those who are broken and those who are whole. If you are not broken, the assumption is that you should be almost invincible. Nondisabled people live with the presumption that they should be able to hustle themselves into health, happiness, and success. Society assumes that disabled people are incapable of parenting and that nondisabled people's parenting should be superhuman. Everyone loses here.

The truth is, we all have fragile and mortal bodies and minds with profound needs. The exclusion disabled people encounter corrodes our self-esteem but so do impossible expectations. Our collective freedom will come from rejecting the rabid productivity focus of late-stage capitalism and living, together, with our shared needs.

Disabled people who decide to parent push against pervasive social messaging that it's a role they aren't equipped for. To start, disabled people receive inadequate reproductive healthcare and sexual education and it's common for a disabled person to be deemed asexual solely based on their disability. Next, until very recently, it has been easy to reach adulthood without witnessing a visibly disabled person parenting on TV or in movies. When a disabled person decides to get pregnant or adopt or be the partner to a pregnant person, they are often creating an identity from scratch. They decide to try to make a space for themselves in a hellish landscape. For those who need fertility assistance, finding a doctor willing to treat them can be difficult. Most fertility doctors are unwilling to take on that risk. The message that we've heard until this point—that it's worse to be us—slides easily into parenting—that it's worse to be parented by us. If we decide to do it anyway, it's because we find the quiet confidence deep inside that tells us that maybe everyone else is wrong.

Ableism also weaves itself around the decision to parent for nondisabled people. For nondisabled women, in particular, the expectation that they will get pregnant haunts them for decades.[27] Nondisabled ciswomen have to live with the fact that if they decide they don't want to parent, or aren't suited to it, they are an oddity. And for those people that do try to get pregnant and have difficulty, or experience pregnancy losses, they face overwhelming shame. There is no room in our culture for fragile bodies. Disabled or not, ableism dictates when and how you are expected to make the decision to parent and, in both cases, it's a trap.

Once a baby is born, or a parent adopts, ableism takes new forms. The disabled parents I interviewed experienced invasive judgment and skepticism around their capacity to parent. Nurses and social workers forced disabled people to prove that they could handle taking care of a baby. On top of the dramatic shift to parenthood, disabled people are forced to perform our aptitude.

Ableism also destabilizes new nondisabled parents. They have often spent their lives assuming and performing invincibility. The shift to parenthood is so dramatic that they cannot maintain that illusion. They are confronted with their own weakness and fear and physical frailty, particularly those who give birth.

As I found in the interviews discussed in chapter 4, nondisabled parents often look back on the first week of parenting as the hardest week of their lives. It's usually because the lived experience of giving birth and learning to take care of a baby differs considerably from the expectations placed on them by our wider culture. Also, if bodies are either broken or not, experiencing the physical exhaustion and suffering that accompanies labor in any form can feel like a threat to one's identity. "What if I always feel this way?" new parents wonder, and, in many cases, they are asking this: "What if I'm always disabled?"

Disabled parents are magicians at home. We take the baby products that the baby market creates, items that rarely work for our needs, and we adjust. The creativity we have spent decades honing allows us to care for our babies despite inaccessible cribs and highchairs. Instead of getting sucked into online product reviews and best-of lists, we ask our disabled peers for advice. While we deserve to have products made for us, our ingenuity finds other solutions. We know no choice is perfect.

On the other hand, some nondisabled people have been sucked into the consumeristic black hole of perfect parenting through perfect purchases.

Every choice is critical—how to feed, how to carry, how to sleep. Every parenting problem can be solved with the right purchase. All the burden is placed on the parents: to buy the right things, to develop the right schedule, to have the right mindset. Ableism lies and says that parenting correctly is possible. The truth is this: parenting at home is an opportunity to be honest about who your child is, who you are, and what you both need. It's a chance to come up with creative solutions with your community.

And then, in the world, ableism is a new kind of vice. When disabled parents leave the home, the pervasive belief that we are *less* takes the form of inaccessibility. We are stuck outside our kids' schools. We miss field trips. We struggle to find a way to push a stroller on a crowded sidewalk while in a wheelchair. But it's the judgment and the comments that sometimes cut the deepest. Strangers and acquaintances question our choices—they are "just worried about our kids' safety."

But those safety worries are born from ableism. And the myth of safety impacts nondisabled people, too. Ableism tries to convince us that we can escape our own frailty—that if we do everything perfectly, our children can avoid suffering. But suffering unites us as people, and our desperate attempt to avoid it only brings shame.

Ableism's impact on our perception of safety is a distortion more than a nudge in one direction or the other. It brings, simultaneously, a delusion of immortality and a hyper-focus on safety. It lies and says that we can plan our way out of mortality while offering false assurances of health. In general, humans are not skilled at predicting and reacting logically to risk. Ableism's ability to convince us that we can perform our way out of suffering, insistence on equating health with virtue, and rejection of our shared fragility harms us all.

Since ableism insists that disabled people are less valuable and worse off than nondisabled people, nondisabled healthcare providers have long stolen disabled agency in medical settings. As I discussed in chapter 7, reproductive healthcare is particularly brutal and fraught, including widespread (current) forced sterilization, withheld sex education, both inaccessible and coerced abortions, and more.

It's not only disabled people who are impacted by a medical system in which reproductive self-determination isn't a given. Ableism has created a system in which the right to one's body must be earned. It's a system where women and trans people are disbelieved, under-studied, and ignored. It amplifies the cruelties of medical racism.

Another of ableism's lies is that we should have the capacity to manage parenting on our own. When a disabled person needs a community to help them parent, it's seen as evidence that they are unfit. When we rank bodies on their level of independence, we are missing the whole point. As with the doomed pursuit of immortality, no one will ever achieve true autonomy.

We need each other, all of us. Just because disabled people and disability culture embrace interdependence doesn't mean we are the only ones who need help. Nondisabled parents are crushed as they attempt to make parenting in isolation work. Our ableist system tells them that they just aren't trying hard or well enough, not that isolation itself is unsustainable.

One way to describe ableism is that it's the lie that we can labor ourselves out of suffering. But our frailty and our suffering are what connect us. Suffering doesn't divide the broken from the whole. Yes, disabled people suffer, but all people suffer. When we try to distance ourselves from our physical fragility, we ignore what makes this life so precious: that it's temporary.

When I became disabled at twenty-eight, it took two years to admit I was sick and four more to call myself disabled. I didn't know that I had spent my life swimming in the waters of ableism and that I had internalized its messages. When doctors didn't believe me, I accepted their perspective. When my graduate school told me I was too disabled to get a degree, I worried they were right. When everything I read about parenting featured nondisabled parents, I assumed that was for a reason.

My internalized ableism didn't only come out in specific moments. It infiltrated all of my thoughts. Believing that my body makes me less valuable is just another way of describing shame. When I wrote my first essay about feeling like an imposter, I described how every moment that I had to ask for help or could not perform a parenting-related task, I was hearing the message "You aren't a real parent" or, more broadly, "You aren't good enough."

Writing this book has transformed me. Through the lives of the disabled people I've interviewed, I've had the incredible honor of witnessing just how beautiful disabled parenting is. Disabled parenting is a beacon.

Disabled parenting is a path forward. Disabled parenting is evidence that this all could be different.

I am convinced that ableism is a way for us to try to outrun our own deaths. To try to shop and work and optimize our way out of pain. Having a child is an unbelievable risk. When a doctor tells a parent about all the suffering a disability might entail, it can sound insurmountable. But, the truth is, suffering is promised for every single one of us and every single one of our children. The secret is figuring out how to survive the inevitable. Disability culture has some answers: we accept, we create, we adapt, we advocate, and we join together. Disabled people also know that we cannot innovate ourselves out of the truth of our finitude.

Our lives are limited. And we want more. We crave more. And, because our demand for our lives vastly exceeds the supply, they are even more precious.

A few weeks ago, K had a birthday party. Around thirty people met us at the park near our house for pizza and cupcakes. The kids climbed on the playground and ran through the field, picking dandelions. My wheelchair bounced through the grass, and every few seconds, I had to change positions so that I didn't sink down and get stuck.

The weekend before the party, K's old nanny came over, who, since she worked here, has been diagnosed with autism. She was joined by her husband, who is also autistic. K, who is autistic, told her nanny she was excited about her party but was scared she might get overwhelmed and wouldn't know what to do. K's nanny and her husband stopped to think and asked K a few questions.

Together with K, they came up with a plan. If the party started to feel like too much, K would say a code word or signal so that I could know she needed help. "ET!" K suggested, as the word.

"What do you want me to do if you say 'ET'?" I asked.

"Put me on your wheelchair and take me away," she answered. "And when I put one finger up like ET, it means I'm ready to go back to the party."

About fifteen minutes into the party, as I stood laughing with neighbors, I heard a small voice. "ET! ET!" it whispered.

"Excuse me," I said to Ann and Nikki, and I went right to K. She clambered onto my lap, her long body leaning to the side so I could see around her head, and we rode away together, quiet, K gripping my arms.

Once we were alone, I turned the chair away from the crowd, and reclined the backrest. K's grip loosened, and she leaned back, taking deep breaths. "I'm proud of you for telling me," I whispered. "I'm here if you need me."

After a few minutes, she lifted her left hand, and her pointer finger stretched out in front of her. We turned around and reentered the crowd. She jumped down and ran off with her friends. Twice more during the party she called, "ET," and twice more I dropped what I was doing and went to her, and twice more we left together. We escaped to where we could be alone and quiet and where my perfect kid could rest her head on my chest, safe.

Epilogue

MARCH 2024

K has been the beating heart of this book. But, after I finished the first draft and before it went to press, we had a second child. Another beating heart. Jo, someone we love, had long offered to be a surrogate for us and in 2022 we started the process with her. In January 2024, we traveled to North Carolina, where she lives, to wait for our second baby to arrive.

We rented an old ranch-style home in a wooded neighborhood about five minutes from where I went to high school. During our first weeks in town, David and K endured an endless and unrequested tour of my teenage years. "That's where my car ran out of gas." "That's where I learned to drive stick shift." "That was the Bojangles that got shut down because of rats." We were proximate to an earlier version of me—obsessed with achievements, shiny, young, and, notably, not disabled.

A few weeks after arriving, we drove to the local Target for some new board games for K and to pick up cake pops at the in-store Starbucks. We placed an order online in advance, but when we arrived, it was delayed. After a few minutes of waiting for an alert that our order was ready, David and K got out of the car to walk around.

I flagged down a store employee and asked about our order timing, and she told me that she wasn't allowed to tell me (strange). I texted David and suggested we go across the street to a different nearby Starbucks (the suburbs!) and pick up the cake pops there.

We pulled out of the sprawling big-box complex and pulled onto the four-lane highway—the highway where, with other honor roll kids, I snuck cigarettes in my teens inside my parents' minivan—and turned into the Starbucks parking lot. And there, behind us, a cop turned on his lights. We stopped, he parked, and he motioned for me to roll down my window.

I cannot remember his exact words. I do remember the way I felt. At first, slight annoyance that David had made an illegal turn and now we'd need to pay a ticket. And then, I heard the word "kidnapping." And the word "suspicious." And the question, "Is she your daughter?" A tingling wave of terror crashed over my body. My heart was racing, my hands shaking.

He said someone at Target had called 911 because we were acting suspiciously, and it didn't seem like K wanted to be with us. He noted our Ontario tags and asked what we were doing there.

I imagined the officer taking K—which is what he would need to do if we couldn't prove that we were her parents. She could be in custody for a few minutes, an hour, days. What could happen to my Black autistic child during that time? In a small conservative town in the South?

My mind was racing. The mayor of my small town used to be the bike cop at our high school and was friends with a guy I dated senior year. Could that help? The attorney who helped me with my disability case partnered with a man who had once run for president. I could call him.

I saw my way in.

"I'm actually from here," I told the officer. "I went to the high school right up the road." I smiled at him and leaned into my Southern lilt.

I'm one of you, I begged him to believe.

He wrote down our information and asked questions, and, eventually, he was satisfied that we were K's parents. We pulled out of the parking lot and onto the highway, where a pickup truck pulled up next to us, matching our pace. Another pulled up close behind us. I thought of vigilantes in the South. Of racism and child removal and all of the bigoted laws that could destroy our family.

And then the trucks sped away. Probably nothing.

K asked, "What would you do if they took me?"

The sob rose from my chest into my throat, and I held it down.

"We would get you back. We would do whatever it took. I promise."

Two days later, our surrogate went into labor.

As I've discussed, K's appearance in our lives was sudden. In some ways (legally), I became her mom slowly, but in others (attachment), it happened all at once. With F, it was a series of countdowns.

First Jo offered to be our surrogate.

And then we waited for the results of David's semen analysis. Then we waited for the day that Jo would try to become pregnant. Then we waited for the results of the pregnancy test. And then the countdown to the first ultrasound. Then the countdown to the second. Then the countdown to viability. And then to our trip to North Carolina to wait for F to be born. And then, finally, the countdown to his birth.

I am, pathologically, impatient. I did not handle the waiting well. I had multiple notebooks with various methods for marking this time as it passed. Filling in hearts in one, crossing through a printed calendar in another.

After the long wait, Jo began labor on a Thursday night. We drove her to the hospital. I filled out the preliminary birth certificate and other paperwork and only later learned I had filled out sections wrong, including David's name and the year of his birth.

That first night, labor progressed slowly, and Jo's doctors said it might be a while. We left and returned to the hospital early the next morning, after a sleepless night. Jo's nurse greeted us and said F's appearance seemed imminent. Jo had a friend with her for support, Steph. I had thought I would be there for every moment, but it was more complicated than I had predicted. Jo was suffering, and my baby was inside her, and we both needed space to feel all of our feelings without tamping them down to protect the other.

The hospital staff put David and me in our own small room in the OB emergency department. We watched a muted Bob Ross, ate biscuits, used the bathroom, and sanitized our hands. To everyone's surprise, the hours kept passing without a baby. F's heart rate dropped but then seemed OK again. Labor stalled. Jo was exhausted. We ordered more food. Peed again. And then it was evening. They moved us to a different room to sleep.

Jo slept some, we slept some, and then it was Saturday at 4 a.m. "It's almost time," Steph said. "She's pushing. I'll tell you when to come." But it wasn't time. Hours passed again. "She's taking a break from pushing."

And then more hours. And then, thirty-nine hours after labor began, Jo texted. *I need a C-section.*

Weeks before, Jo had asked which of us would come to a C-section. We had decided on David because my body can be unpredictable, and my wheelchair is large. I wanted an agile person who doesn't have waves of dizziness to be there for those vital moments.

But none of us had pictured what that moment would feel like or how exhausted and scared everyone would be. Jo asked Steph to join her in the operating room instead. We understood. And still, I wept. I couldn't catch my breath. I wanted David to be there to make sure F was okay.

Jo's surgeon came to talk to us. I made him promise that Jo and F would be fine. He did. He said his only regret was that we hadn't moved to a C-section sooner. I asked him over and over again if he was worried. No. He promised.

Once in the surgical suite, Steph texted me multiple times per minute. She sent photos of the room, every tiny update. And then, shortly after the C-section began, she sent a photo of F in the air above Jo's body. The surgeon grinned. *Is he breathing?* I texted back. She didn't reply.

Minutes passed.

They were endless.

And then.

They are working on him.

David grabbed my hand.

So no, he wasn't breathing.

What about now? I texted.

The NICU team is here. He has our favorite nurse practitioner.

My baby, all the countdowns, and he wasn't breathing.

And, finally, five minutes after he exited Jo's body,

He's pinking up.

And then, a minute later.

Looks like he's breathing now.

He's ok? I texted.

I think so. He's crying.

Thank god, I said.

How's Jo? I asked.

She is good, Steph texted.

For the next few minutes, I asked, in a dozen different ways, how they both were. And in a dozen different ways, she said they were fine.

Incredibly, forty-five minutes after F entered the world, not breathing, with an APGAR of 1, a nurse brought him into our room.

We held him. We cried. We fed him. We loved him.

I texted Steph.

How's Jo?

She didn't reply.

I asked again. And again.

An hour passed.

I knew something was wrong. I told David. He said everyone was probably just resting.

We FaceTimed K, at home with her nanny.

Three hours after F was born, we still didn't have news about Jo. We ordered Chipotle to the hospital, and I went out front to wait for it. On the way back, I saw Jo's surgeon.

He looked like hell. He was drawn and had dried blood on his clothes.

"She's stable," he said, panting.

And then, I saw Steph.

She was also colorless, and her eyes were huge, spooked.

"How's Jo?" I asked.

"OK, now," she said. "How much do you know?"

She explained that, after the C-section, things had become quite bad quite quickly. And the details of what happened in that room are not mine to share. In fact, this whole story is complicated because it's mine and not mine. It's our baby in another person's body.

Here's the part that happened to me: someone I love very much had been in danger and had suffered so that we could have a baby.

As I barreled my wheelchair back into our room, burritos in hand, I was sobbing. I told David what had happened, and then I looked at little F. And shame and guilt crashed around me. We had wanted this baby so badly that we were willing to let someone else endure what Jo had just endured. How could I live with that?

Hours passed. Nurses and doctors visited. F was tested and checked. We fed him and changed his diaper.

I went to see Jo. She was puffy and as white as the sheets on her hospital bed. We cried, and we laughed, and I said that I was sorry, and she said not to feel guilty.

And there, in the middle of the most emotional day of my life, I was still disabled. My body had started to let me know that I couldn't push it for another night. The nurses would be in to check F every hour. I knew that if I spent a third night awake, I would be doing harm to myself that would take months to undo.

I booked a hotel room next to the hospital. At 8 p.m., I left the hospital, David, Jo, and F, and crossed the sprawling parking lot. It was freezing, and my gloveless hand locked up around the joystick. The empty lobby flickered with fluorescent lighting. In the elevator, a child's handprint on the door looked like it had been made with blood.

Dark stains covered the frayed carpet in the dated room. The heater roared. I took off my mask and hospital clothes and planned my morning. Every day, when I wake up, I roll over to take my medicine, drink water and coffee, and eat. Even with all these things, it takes about an hour to stand up and move around. Without all four, I become clammy and weak, unable to function.

I dug through my purse and found the remaining bits of food: two sticks of beef jerky and a package of hospital graham crackers. I set them on the wobbly nightstand with water and my morning medicine.

I awoke the following morning at 5:30, physically and emotionally miserable. *How are you?* I texted Jo. *How's F?* I texted David. I was gagging with nausea, and my body was covered in a cold sweat. I took my medicine, finished the food, and realized that I needed more. I needed coffee. My blood pressure was low, my heart rate high, and I would never make it back to the hospital without more nourishment and some caffeine to boost my blood pressure. I called the front desk to ask if they could bring up food if I ordered it, but it wasn't that kind of hotel, not the kind where they answer phones—it rang and rang.

I imagined getting into my wheelchair and going downstairs to meet a delivery driver but knew that my body simply could not. I could not make it that far.

I opened DoorDash and saw that Dunkin Donuts was open. I took a chance, ordering a bagel and coffee. Once they assigned a driver, I messaged him. I asked if I could pay him extra to park and place my food outside my hotel room. And then a tiny bit of grace.

Of course, he replied.

With food and coffee en route, I thought about Jo and I thought about F and I thought about the day ahead and all I could think was this:

We will never be OK.

And, also, a tiny voice inside.

We will all be OK.

I texted my friends, Jenna and Casey, and my therapist and said that I was not OK. I drank my coffee and ate my bagel and, after an hour, made it back to the hospital. I visited Jo and I fed F and asked his doctors questions and FaceTimed K and her nanny, and knew, at every moment, that I was swimming through hardening concrete of trauma.

They discharged F and I visited Jo again and we made the ten-minute drive back to K and, still, all I could think about was Jo's pain. Every time I was in a room alone, I wept.

Jenna and Casey checked in and asked what I needed, practically. Food? Childcare? Strangely, only an hour before, K had discovered a dead opossum under our rental house's deck, feet from where F slept. In my state, I simply could not imagine what it would take to get rid of a decomposing animal.

So, I answered my friends, *Can you please get rid of the dead opossum under our deck?*

Hours later, Jenna replied, *OK! Someone from Pest Solutions will be at your place in about an hour to remove the opossum. It's all paid for. They should just take it and leave. Hugs to you today!!*

Next, my friend Lauren asked what I needed. I wasn't sleeping. They are a musician and so I asked them to please find something to listen to that could help me sleep. White noise was giving me anxiety. They did. And I slept.

My friend Ann Marie checked in. She had given birth a few months earlier. She had sent a box of her son's old clothes for F. I texted a two-sentence version of F's birth story. She called. Again, I wept. And she did something I didn't know that I needed. A brilliant cardiologist herself, she talked through every moment of F's birth and Jo's recovery and explained it all. She made it make sense, and the medical events all became less scary. They were both always going to be OK, she assured me, and, remarkably, I believed her.

And then, in her familiar bluster, she told me that my guilt was simply illogical. You made good decisions, she promised. She said that F isn't only mine, and the decision wasn't only mine, and that there is love all around his story.

We hung up, and she called back.

"You have a therapist, right?"

And then Jo was discharged. David picked her up at the hospital and helped her inside. And my heart stopped seizing quite as much.

———

The months around F's birth were a return to an uncanny valley version of home. I was back with the tall trees of my childhood, back to the place where I once believed that effort yields happiness. As a teen, I thought I could mold myself into someone who could thrive in that very particular culture. It wasn't true, but it almost worked. But now, with my wheelchair and needs and Black autistic daughter, North Carolina is a shoe that no longer fits. But it's not only North Carolina that I've outgrown; my early delusions of fairness no longer fit. I will never strive myself into invincibility. I am needy all the way down. We all are.

During those North Carolina months, I was afraid for one child and then the next. I was afraid for Jo. I was afraid for myself. There was great pain around F's birth. There was also great beauty because he became ours. And because—crucially—there were people who loved and cared for us during those days.

There was Victoria, an expert on feeding babies who was on call for two weeks to answer all my F-specific questions. Jenna, who was available to babysit K when we thought Jo was in labor early and who brought food and who always tested for COVID before seeing us and who wore a mask and who took care of the opossum. Casey, who drove forty-five minutes to talk in the driveway in the rain, since she had the sniffles and didn't want to pass a cold on to F. Preston, who flew across the country for an afternoon on the deck. Heather and Matt who masked and tested and tested and tested and then cleaned our rental after we left. Scottie and Bob, who brought comfort and dinner. Vicki and Dave, who were generous and kind and who mailed our packages and hung a pride flag in their front yard. Ann, who watered our plants back at home and filled our fridge and left muffins and baby clothes. Mona, who washed the sheets on our beds in Canada because they were covered in construction dust from a basement renovation. Ben, who checked our Canadian mail and opened anything time-sensitive. Ames, who set up air purifiers to clean the construction dust out before we arrived. Mark, our handyman, who cleaned F's room and K's room and washed the rest of the sheets. Julie, who has checked in every few days, and has never expected a reply. And Brittany, who rested her hand next to F to feel his breathing for all eighteen hours of the drive home and who loves our kids with her whole heart.

And here's what's amazing: this account isn't even comprehensive. There were other gifts, other N95-clad visitors. There has been more generosity and support than I can list.

And, of course, there is the grace of F, who is a miracle, because we are all miracles, but also in his own unique ways. Who is hungry. Who curls up on my chest like K but also, more often, prefers to face out, taking in the world.

And, most of all, there is Jo. Who offered and offered again to carry our baby. Who did so because she believed that my wants mattered. Who risked her life. Who believed that a disabled mom is a good-enough mom. Who, with her entire self, reminded me of what I have spent the last decades learning again, and again. We need each other.

People have asked what we will tell our kids about their early days. In part because our family was formed in an atypical way but also because of the loss woven into both of their stories. Our answer? The truth.

The first days of life, and of parenting, aren't meant to be a pristine canvas that we should avoid marring for as long as possible. It begins as it will be—with suffering and need.

Our lives are shorter than we would like and more painful than we think we can bear. This world is woven with unfairness and injustice. Our bodies and our minds fall short. We must spend our days balancing the impossible: working to repair something that will always be broken.

I believed, for so long, that I could love my life only if it were perfect, or, rather, only if I was perfect. I thought my own effort could eclipse my mortality. My disability introduced me to a body and a culture that rejects that premise. Disability has taught me an enormous amount, but in essence it comes down to this: these bodies and minds are fragile—in fact, our entire lives are. But we don't have to spend our whole lives outrunning that reality because, miraculously, a very good life can be found when everything breaks. What a gift to learn that we are terrible at predicting what will give us meaning and joy.

And, so, I will tell my kids this.

There was suffering at the beginning. Your early days were complicated. And this pain and difficulty will never end. But there was love there, and truth. We held you and other people held us, and other people held them, and that web of people could hold the whole world.

ACKNOWLEDGMENTS

As I made a list of all the people who contributed in some way to writing this book, I thought about other big projects in my life—graduate school, moving to California alone, getting a diagnosis—and how I could make a similar list for each of those.

We don't do anything alone.

But what a gift that there is a tradition of concluding books with a section devoted to thanks. Gratitude is an antidote, and I am so very thankful to the people who supported me while writing *Unfit Parent*.

To start, this book would not be what it is without the disabled parents and nondisabled parents who spent hours sharing their stories with me. Thank you to Cordelia, Jessie, Jessi Elana, Joey, Joshua, Jourdan, Kelly, Lee, Maria, Rachel, Stacey, Tianna, and Valerie, among others.

And thank you to the researchers, journalists, doctors, attorneys, and other professionals who took the time: Theodore Baker, Dr. Paige Church, Dr. Sharyn DeZelar, Dr. Lisa Iezzoni, Kavya Parthiban, Renée Racik, and Sonja Sharp.

To my friends and loved ones: you are a lifeline and a center, and every hard thing I have done is thanks to you. Thank you Amanda, Amelia, Ames, Andrea, Angela, Ann, Ann Marie, Antwon, Caroline, Carter, Casey, Critter, Aunt Donna, Hillary, James, Jenna, Joanna, Kate, Lauren, Lee, Maggie, Mandy, Michi, Nataly, Nikki, Preston, Roxy, Tianna, and Wolffie.

I found my vocation late in life and have asked for help from people I respect at every step. To Irene, thank you for telling me eleven years ago that I should consider writing a book and for all of the other ways you have helped me find my path. To Dr. Shear, thank you for the additional nudge.

Jacqueline Alnes, thank you for the publishing tutorial. Alice Wong, thank you for including me in *Disability Visibility*. Jenny Pritchett, thank you for answering so many questions. To the late Judy Heumann, thank you for introducing me to Jill. Emily Ladau, I want to emulate your generosity and openness. Nat and Evan, thank you for your advice and support.

Since becoming a writer, I have met other writers and thinkers who inspire me. Thank you Elizabeth Barnes, Alyssa Blask-Campbell, Victoria Facelli, Aubrey Gordon, Jessica Grose, Erin Lane, Jennifer Natalya Fink, Meghan O'Rourke, Erin Rafferty, and Sarah Wheeler.

Other than David, no one has read more of my writing than my writing group. Thank you, Allison, Elaine, Mardi, and Shelley for your thoughtfulness and understanding. My writing is better thanks to you.

At different stages, people have read *Unfit Parent*, which has helped me be brave enough to release it more widely. Thank you, Amelia, Amy, Angela, Brittany, Caroline, Carter, Heather, Jenna, Lee, and Megan for taking the time.

I wrote this book in Canada, where we moved in 2020, and I am thankful to those who have helped make this home. Thank you, Ann, Kevin, Mona, Monica, Peggy, Tianna, and the homeschool crew.

No working mom accomplishes anything without childcare. Thank you Brittany, Stacey, Monica, Leah, Angie, Chelsea, and Elizabeth.

Thank you, Laylin, for your hard work on the endnotes.

Early in the process of writing this book, I posted on Facebook asking if there were other authors with a nonfiction deadline who would want to stay in touch. Thank goodness Rachel Somerstein responded. She read the first draft of every chapter and the last. Our twice-monthly calls made my work better and stopped me from unraveling. Thank you for your astute eye and for your friendship.

Thank you to my family: Mom, Dad, Megan, Amy, Heather, Donna, Johnny, Angela, the Monaghans, Ben, Ryleigh, Avery, Matt, Chrisiana, Maya, Amaya, Toni, Jamie, and Jenny.

Joanna Green, your intellectual rigor and commitment to excellence have made this work better. Thank you for dreaming this up with me and ushering it through.

Jill Marr and SDLA, thank you for connecting me with an editor like Joanna. This book would not exist without your advocacy.

K and F. You are both magic. I love you. Honeypuppy and Pebbles, you are cute.

David: You are an editing savant. I trust you implicitly with my work, and I can't believe I get to live with the best thinker I know. Thank you for reading and talking through every bit of this book. Thank you for this life—the spreadsheets and the beauty. I love you.

NOTES

A NOTE ON SOURCES

This book was created using a combination of my own personal story; interviews with disabled parents, nondisabled parents, doctors, researchers, attorneys, and other writers, and text-based research. In all but a few cases, the names and locations of the people I interviewed have remained unchanged. But, when requested, some have been anonymized to allow for more transparency and protection.

INTRODUCTION

1. Elizabeth Barnes, *The Minority Body: A Theory of Disability* (Oxford: Oxford University Press, 2017).

2. Sonja Sharp, "For 'Disabled Oracle' Alice Wong, Rest Is a Radical Act," *Los Angeles Times*, September 5, 2022, https://www.latimes.com/california/story/2022-09-05/for-disabled-oracle-alice-wong-rest-is-a-radical-act.

CHAPTER 1: DISABILITY & ME (& YOU)

1. Shigeki Shibata, Qi Fu, Tiffany B. Bivens, Jeffrey L. Hastings, Wade Wang, and Benjamin D. Levine, "Short-Term Exercise Training Improves the Cardiovascular Response to Exercise in the Postural Orthostatic Tachycardia Syndrome," *Journal of Physiology* 590, no. 15 (2012): 3495–505.

2. Elizabeth Barnes, *The Minority Body: A Theory of Disability* (Oxford: Oxford University Press, 2017).

3. Susan Sontag, *Illness as Metaphor: AIDS and Its Metaphors* (New York: Doubleday, 1990).

4. Kitty Cone, "Short History of the 504 Sit-In," Disability Rights Education & Defense Fund, April 4, 2013, https://dredf.org/504-sit-in-20th-anniversary/short-history-of-the-504-sit-in.

5. Abigail Scott, "Disability Activism History: The Capitol Crawl," *Accessible Web*, July 25, 2022, https://accessibleweb.com/history/when-disability-activists-influenced-history-the-capitol-crawl.

6. Sally Haslanger, "Gender and Race: (What) Are They? (What) Do We Want Them to Be?" *Noûs* 34, no. 1 (2000): 31–55.

7. Eli Clare, *Exile and Pride: Disability, Queerness, and Liberation* (Durham, NC: Duke University Press, 2015).

8. Eli Clare, *Brilliant Imperfection: Grappling with Cure* (Durham, NC: Duke University Press, 2017).

9. Alison Kafer, *Feminist, Queer, Crip* (Bloomington: Indiana University Press, 2013).

10. Andrew Pulrang, "5 Questions to Think About This #DisabilityPrideMonth," *Forbes*, July 15, 2021, https://www.forbes.com/sites/andrewpulrang/2021/07/15/5 -questions-to-think-about-this-disabilitypridemonth/?sh=57dd3c5e1417.

11. Julie Rehmeyer, *Through the Shadowlands: A Science Writer's Odyssey into an Illness Science Doesn't Understand* (New York: Harmony/Rodale, 2017); Laura Hillenbrand, "A Sudden Illness," *New Yorker*, July 7, 2003, 56; Nasim Marie Jafry, *The State of Me* (New York: HarperCollins Publishers, 2010); Meghan O'Rourke, *Sun in Days: Poems* (New York: W. W. Norton, 2017).

12. Nancy L. Eiesland, *The Disabled God: Toward a Liberatory Theology of Disability* (Nashville: Abingdon Press, 1994).

13. Maya Dusenbery, *Doing Harm: The Truth About How Bad Medicine and Lazy Science Leave Women Dismissed, Misdiagnosed, and Sick* (New York: HarperCollins, 2018).

14. Rosemarie Garland-Thomson, "Disability Gain," Avoidance and the Academy Conference, September 2013, Liverpool Hope University, Liverpool.

CHAPTER 2: WE, PARENTS

1. "Commentary: COVID-19 Has Driven Millions of Women out of the Workforce. Here's How to Help Them Come Back," *Fortune*, February 13, 2021, https://fortune.com/2021/02/13/covid-19-women-workforce-unemployment -gender-gap-recovery.

2. Alice Wong, *Disability Visibility: First-Person Stories from the Twenty-First Century* (New York: Knopf, 2020).

3. Rajan Sonik, Susan Parish, Monika Mitra, and Joanne Nicholson, "Parents with and Without Disabilities: Demographics, Material Hardship, and Program Participation," *Review of Disability Studies* 14, no. 9 (2018): 1–20.

4. Roosa Tikkanen, Munira Z. Gunja, Molly FitzGerald, and Laurie Zephyrin, "Maternal Mortality and Maternity Care in the United States Compared to 10 Other Developed Countries," Commonwealth Fund, November 18, 2020, https:// www.commonwealthfund.org/publications/issue-briefs/2020/nov/maternal -mortality-maternity-care-us-compared-10-countries.

5. Krystin Arneson, "Why Doesn't the US Have Mandated Paid Maternity Leave?" BBC, June 28, 2021, https://www.bbc.com/worklife/article/20210624 -why-doesnt-the-us-have-mandated-paid-maternity-leave.

6. Sarah A. Donovan, *Paid Family Leave in the United States*, updated May 29, 2019, Congressional Research Service, https://hdl.handle.net/1813/79152.

7. Angela Garbes, *Essential Labor: Mothering as Social Change* (New York: Harper Collins, 2022).

8. Evan K. Rose, "The Rise and Fall of Female Labor Force Participation During World War II in the United States," *Journal of Economic History* 78, no. 3 (2018): 673–711.

9. Lawrence Mishel, Josh Bivens, Elise Gould, and Heidi Shierholz, *The State of Working America*, 12th ed. (Ithaca, NY: Economic Policy Institute/ILR Press, 2012).

10. Eve Rodsky, *Fair Play: A Game-Changing Solution for When You Have Too Much to Do (and More Life to Live)* (New York: Penguin, 2019).

11. Jennifer Ervin, Yamna Taouk, Ludmila Alfonzo, Belinda Hewitt, and Tania King, "Gender Differences in the Association Between Unpaid Labor and Mental Health in Employed Adults: A Systematic Review," *Lancet Public Health* 7 (2022): e775-e786, doi: 10.1016/S2468–2667(22)00160–8.

12. Jessica Grose, *Screaming on the Inside: The Unsustainability of American Motherhood* (New York: HarperCollins, 2022).

13. Grose, *Screaming on the Inside.*

14. Rachel Somerstein, *Invisible Labor: The Untold Story of the Cesarean Section* (New York: HarperCollins, 2024).

CHAPTER 3: DECIDING TO PARENT

1. Akanksha Sood and Muhammad Akhtar, "T-Shaped Uterus in the 21st Century (Post–DES Era)—We Need to Know More!" *Journal of Human Reproductive Sciences* 12, no. 4 (2019): 283–86, doi: 10.4103/jhrs.JHRS_101_19.

2. US Department of Health and Human Services, *AFCARS Foster Care Annual User's Guide*, 2021, https://www.acf.hhs.gov/sites/default/files/documents/cb/afcars-report-29.pdf; "America's Children: Key National Indicators of Well-Being, 2021–Demographic Background," *Childstats*, https://www.childstats.gov/americaschildren/demo.asp, accessed July 17, 2023.

3. University of Nevada, Reno, "Transracial Adoption: Statistics and Social Challenges," https://onlinedegrees.unr.edu/blog/transracial-adoption-statistics, accessed July 7, 2022.

4. National Association of Black Social Workers, "Position Statement on Transracial Adoptions," 1972, https://cdn.ymaws.com/www.nabsw.org/resource/collection/E1582D77-E4CD-4104-996A-D42D08F9CA7D/NABSW_Trans-Racial_Adoption_1972_Position_(b).pdf.

5. Morgan E. Cooley, Brittany P. Mihalec-Adkins, Heather M. Thompson, and Aakansha Mehrotra, "Motivation to Foster Among Single Foster Parents," *Child Welfare* 99, no. 2 (2021): 55–76.

6. T. E. MacGregor, S. Rodger, A. L. Cummings, and A. W. Leschied, "The Needs of Foster Parents: A Qualitative Study of Motivation, Support, and Retention," *Qualitative Social Work* 5, no. 3 (2006): 351–68, https://doi.org/10.1177/1473325006067365.

7. "How Many Kids Are in Foster Care?" All4Kids, December 26, 2023, https://www.all4kids.org/news/blog/how-many-kids-are-in-foster-care.

8. "The Evolution of Foster Parent Recruitment and Training," *The Imprint*, June 7, 2016, https://imprintnews.org/analysis/evolution-foster-parent-recruitment-training/18556.

9. Jessie Owen, author interview, phone call, Canada, December 8, 2022.

10. P. T. Church, "A Personal Perspective on Disability: Between the Words," *JAMA Pediatrics* 171, no. 10 (2017): 939, doi:10.1001/jamapediatrics.2017.2242.

11. Hope B, author interview, phone call, Canada, August 18, 2022.

12. Mayo Clinic, "Ehlers-Danlos Syndrome—Symptoms and Causes," August 25, 2022, https://www.mayoclinic.org/diseases-conditions/ehlers-danlos-syndrome /symptoms-causes/syc-20362125.

13. Jourdan F., author interview, phone call, Canada, September 2, 2022.

CHAPTER 4: THE FIRST WEEK

1. Thomas Curran and Andrew P. Hill, "Perfectionism Is Increasing Over Time: A Meta-Analysis of Birth Cohort Differences from 1989 to 2016," *Psychological Bulletin* 145, no. 4 (2019): 410, doi.10.1037/bul0000138.

2. Thomas Curran, "Over-Stressed and Under Pressure: The Problem with Being Perfect," London School of Economics and Political Science, January 18, 2021, https://www.lse.ac.uk/research/research-for-the-world/health/over-stressed -and-under-pressure-the-problem-with-being-perfect.

3. Will Coldwell, "The Rise of Perfectionism and the Harm It's Doing Us All," *The Guardian*, June 4, 2023, https://www.theguardian.com/society/2023/jun/04 /the-rise-of-perfectionism-and-the-harm-its-doing-us-all.

4. Renée Racik, author interview, phone call, Canada, December 7, 2022.

5. Alessio D'Angelo et al., "Pregnancy in Women with Physical and Intellectual Disability: Psychiatric Implications," *Rivista Di Psichiatria* 55, no. 6 (2020): 331–36, doi:10.1708/3503.34890.

6. Jessie Owen, author interview, phone call, Canada, December 8, 2022.

7. Rachel Somerstein, author interview, phone call, Canada, December 7, 2022.

8. Tianna E., author interview, phone call, Canada, December 13, 2022.

9. Wiruntri Punchuklang et al., "Total Failure of Spinal Anesthesia for Cesarean Delivery, Associated Factors, and Outcomes: A Retrospective Case-Control Study," *Medicine* 101, no. 27 (July 8, 2022), doi:10.1097/MD.0000000000029813.

10. Lee P., author interview, phone call, Canada, December 15, 2022

11. Racik, author interview, phone call, Canada, December 7, 2022.

12. Shruti Nagaraj and Victoria Facelli, *Feed the Baby: An Inclusive Guide to Nursing, Bottle-Feeding, and Everything in Between* (New York: W. W. Norton, 2023).

CHAPTER 5: PARENTING AT HOME

1. Julia N. Daniels, "Disabled Mothering? Outlawed, Overlooked and Severely Prohibited: Interrogating Ableism in Motherhood," *Social Inclusion* 7, no. 1 (2019): 114–23.

2. Aislinn Thomas, "Disability, Creativity, and Care in the Time of Covid-19," *Akimbo*, https://akimbo.ca/akimblog/disability-creativity-and-care-in-the-time-of -covid-19-by-aislinn-thomas, accessed May 3, 2024.

3. Marta Russell, *Capitalism and Disability: Selected Writings by Marta Russell* (Chicago: Haymarket Books, 2019).

4. Social Security Administration, "SSI Federal Payment Amounts for 2023," https://www.ssa.gov/oact/cola/SSI.html, accessed June 28, 2023.

5. Nanette Goodman, Michael Morris, and Kelvin Boston, "Financial Inequality: Disability, Race and Poverty in America," National Disability Institute, 2017, https://www.nationaldisabilityinstitute.org/wp-content/uploads/2019/02/disability-race-poverty-in-america.pdf.

6. Robyn M. Powell et al., "Adaptive Parenting Strategies Used by Mothers with Physical Disabilities Caring for Infants and Toddlers," *Health & Social Care in the Community* 27, no. 4 (2019): 889–98, doi:10.1111/hsc.12706.

7. Jessi Elana Aaron, author interview, phone call, Canada, March 26, 2022.

8. Stacy Cervenka, author interview, phone call, Canada, March 28, 2022.

9. Kelly Peterson, author interview, phone call, Canada, March 30, 2022.

10. Through the Looking Glass, "A Short History of TLG," https://lookingglass.org/history, accessed May 3, 2024.

11. Ronald John Seiler, *Assistive Technology for Parents with Disabilities: A Handbook for Parents, Families, and Caregivers* (Moscow: Idaho Assistive Technology Project, Center on Disabilities and Human Development, University of Idaho, 2003).

12. Katherine Chiles, "Risks, Fears, and Misconceptions: How Supplemental Security Insurance Traps People in Poverty," Symposium of University Research and Creative Expression, May 18, 2020, https://digitalcommons.cwu.edu/source/2020/CEPS/2.

13. Kate McIlvanie, "Seeking Equality in Wages for Employees with Intellectual and Developmental Disabilities," *Northern Illinois University Law Review*, Rev. 40 (2019): 70.

14. New Horizons Un-Limited, "Home Modification Assistance," https://new-horizons.org/houmod.html, accessed May 3, 2024.

15. Shruti Nagaraj and Victoria Facelli, *Feed the Baby: An Inclusive Guide to Nursing, Bottle-Feeding, and Everything in Between* (New York: W. W. Norton, 2023).

16. Christina Caron, "Breast-Feeding or Formula? For Americans, It's Complicated," *New York Times*, July 14, 2018, https://www.nytimes.com/2018/07/14/health/trump-breastfeeding-history-nyt.html.

17. Linda Rodriguez McRobbie, "Perfect Prams for Perfect Parents: The Rise of the Bougie Buggy," *The Guardian*, March 20, 2018, https://www.theguardian.com/news/2018/mar/20/bugaboo-luxury-pram-baby-buggy-stroller-parenting.

18. "Should Parents Push or Carry Their Infants?" Northwestern Early Intervention, https://ei.northwestern.edu/should-parents-push-or-carry-their-infants, accessed May 3, 2024.

CHAPTER 6: IN THE WORLD

1. Jessie Owen, author interview, phone call, Canada, December 8, 2022.

2. Emily Ladau, *Demystifying Disability: What to Know, What to Say, and How to Be an Ally* (Emeryville, CA: Clarkson Potter/Ten Speed, 2021).

3. Rebekah Taussig, *Sitting Pretty: The View from My Ordinary Resilient Disabled Body* (New York: HarperCollins, 2020).

4. US Access Board, "Where Ramps and Curb Ramps Are Required," ADA Standards, https://www.access-board.gov/ada/guides/chapter-4-ramps-and-curb-ramps, accessed June 29, 2023.

5. Jessi Elana Aaron, author interview, phone call, Canada, March 26, 2022.

6. Erin Durkin, "New York Subway: Woman Dies While Carrying Baby Stroller on Stairs," *The Guardian*, January 29, 2019, https://www.theguardian.com/us-news/2019/jan/29/new-york-subway-woman-dies-baby-stroller-stairs.

7. "Stringer Audit Reveals Serious Gaps in MTA's Maintenance and Repair of Elevators and Escalators," press release, New York City Comptroller Brad Lander, May 1, 2017, https://comptroller.nyc.gov/newsroom/stringer-audit-reveals-serious-gaps-in-mtas-maintenance-and-repair-of-elevators-and-escalators.

8. "Stringer Audit Reveals Serious Gaps in MTA's Maintenance and Repair of Elevators and Escalators."

9. Jen Chung, "Ask a Native New Yorker's Mom: Must You Bring Your Stroller on the Subway?" *Gothamist*, February 13, 2015, https://gothamist.com/news/ask-a-native-new-yorkers-mom-must-you-bring-your-stroller-on-the-subway, accessed June 29, 2023.

10. Stacy Cervenka, author interview, phone call, Canada, March 28, 2022.

11. National Federation of the Blind, *Parenting Without Sight: What Attorneys, Social Workers, and Parents Should Know About Blindness*, https://nfb.org/images/nfb/publications/brochures/blindparents/parentingwithoutsight.html, accessed June 29, 2023.

12. Gus Alexiou, "Blind People Stagnating at Work Due to Inaccessible Technology, Says New Study," *Forbes*, February 22, 2022, https://www.forbes.com/sites/gusalexiou/2022/02/22/blind-people-stagnating-at-work-due-to-inaccessible-technology-says-new-study/?sh=a1c934d716e7.

13. Paige Cornwell, "Blind Parent Wins Battle for Access to Online Seattle School Resources," *Seattle Times*, September 24, 2015, https://www.seattletimes.com/seattle-news/education/blind-parent-wins-battle-to-get-access-to-online-school-resources.

14. Jules Knox, "Accessibility in the Digital Age: Okanagan Parent Voices Concern," *Global News*, February 25, 2019, https://globalnews.ca/news/4996759/accessibility-digital-age-okanagan-parent-voices-concern.

15. Wendell Jamieson, "The Crime of His Childhood," *New York Times*, March 2, 2013, https://www.nytimes.com/2013/03/03/nyregion/40-years-after-an-acid-attack-a-life-well-lived.html.

16. Bella Isaacs-Thomas, "This Researcher Builds 'Cool Stuff for Blind People.' He's Also Trying to Help Transform Society," PBS, October 26, 2022, https://www.pbs.org/newshour/science/how-this-innovator-is-making-sure-the-tech-that-drives-daily-life-doesnt-leave-out-people-with-disabilities.

17. Joshua Miele, author interview by email, May 15, 2023.

18. John Donne Potter, "Long COVID Puts Some People at Higher Risk of Heart Disease: They Need Better Long-Term Monitoring," *The Conversation*, March 29, 2023, https://theconversation.com/long-covid-puts-some-people-at-higher-risk-of-heart-disease-they-need-better-long-term-monitoring-202596.

CHAPTER 7: MEDICAL CARE

1. Joseph Shapiro, "One Man's COVID-19 Death Raises the Worst Fears of Many People with Disabilities," NPR, July 31, 2020, https://www.npr.org/2020

/07/31/896882268/one-mans-covid-19-death-raises-the-worst-fears-of-many
-people-with-disabilities.

2. Ariana Eunjung Cha, "Quadriplegic Man's Death from Covid-19 Spotlights
Questions of Disability, Race and Family," *Washington Post*, July 5, 2020, https://
www.washingtonpost.com/health/2020/07/05/coronavirus-disability-death.

3. Cha, "Quadriplegic Man's Death from Covid-19 Spotlights Questions of
Disability, Race, and Family."

4. Cha, "Quadriplegic Man's Death from Covid-19 Spotlights Questions of
Disability, Race, and Family."

5. Hickson et al. v. St. David's Healthcare Partnership, L.P., LLP et al., Justia
Dockets & Filings, June 10, 2021, https://dockets.justia.com/docket/texas/txwdce
/1:2021cv00514/1137111.

6. *Hickson et al. v. St. David's Healthcare Partnership.*

7. Britney Wilson, "Crisis Standards of Care May Discriminate Against
Patients with Disabilities," *Regulatory Review*, November 1, 2021, https://www
.theregreview.org/2021/11/01/wilson-crisis-standards-of-care-may-discriminate
-against-patients-with-disabilities.

8. "RD Seeks Justice for Michael Hickson, Files Lawsuit Against Guardianship
Program," Robbins DiMonte Ltd., March 17, 2021, https://robbinsdimonte.com
/news/press-releases/robbins-salomon-patt-ltd-seeks-justice-for-michael-hickson
-files-lawsuit-against-guardianship-program.

9. *Hickson et al. v. St. David's Healthcare Partnership.*

10. Cha, "Quadriplegic Man's Death from Covid-19 Spotlights Questions of
Disability, Race and Family."

11. Amy, "Guest Blog—M&A of Long-Term Care Facilities in Texas," Senior
Living Investment Brokerage, July 20, 2011, https://www.seniorlivingbrokerage
.com/guest-blog-ma-of-long-term-care-facilities-in-texas; MacDonald Law
Group, "Cory Macdonald," https://www.mrfirm.legal/cory-macdonald-1, accessed
July 31, 2023.

12. St. David's HealthCare, "About St. David's HealthCare," https://stdavids
.com/about, accessed May 3, 2024.

13. "Ep. 90: Luke Redman, CEO, Hospital Internists of Texas—Investors &
Operators," *Investors & Operators*, 51 Labs, June 17, 2020, https://investorsand
operators.captivate.fm/episode/ep-90-luke-redman-ceo-hospital-internists
-of-texas.

14. Eileen Appelbaum, "How Private Equity Makes You Sicker," *American
Prospect*, October 7, 2019, https://prospect.org/health/how-private-equity-makes
-you-sicker.

15. "Private Equity and the Monopolization of Medical Care," *Forbes*, February 20, 2023, https://www.forbes.com/sites/robertpearl/2023/02/20/private-equity
-and-the-monopolization-of-medical-care/?sh=14090f202bad.

16. Gina Kolata, "These Doctors Admit They Don't Want Patients with Disabilities," *New York Times*, October 19, 2022, https://www.nytimes.com/2022/10
/19/health/doctors-patients-disabilities.html.

17. Meghan O'Rourke, *The Invisible Kingston: Reimagining Chronic Illness* (New
York: Penguin Random House, 2022).

18. Jessi Elana Aaron, "Reproductive Rights Are More Than Birth Control and Abortion," *Medium*, May 22, 2020, https://medium.com/@jessi.elana.aaron /reproductive-rights-are-more-than-birth-control-and-abortion-8965584e8c4.

19. Laura Taouk et al., "Provision of Reproductive Healthcare to Women with Disabilities: A Survey of Obstetrician–Gynecologists' Training, Practices, and Perceived Barriers," *Health Equity* 2, no. 1 (2018): 207–15.

20. Hilary K. Brown et al., "Association of Preexisting Disability with Severe Maternal Morbidity or Mortality in Ontario, Canada," *JAMA Network Open* 4, no. 2 (2021): e2034993-e2034993.

21. Sonja Sharp, "Disabled Mothers-to-Be Face Indignity: 'Do You Have a Man? Can You Have Sex?'" *Los Angeles Times*, September 30, 2021, https://www .latimes.com/california/story/2021-09-30/how-modern-medicine-neglects -disabled-mothers.

22. Sharp, "Disabled Mothers-to-Be Face Indignity."

23. Sharp, "Disabled Mothers-to-Be Face Indignity."

24. Alex Battler, "Studies Find Health-Care System Often Fails People with Disabilities Who Give Birth in Ontario," University of Toronto Scarborough News, March 30, 2023, https://utsc.utoronto.ca/news-events/breaking-research /studies-find-health-care-system-often-fails-people-disabilities-who-give-birth.

25. Sonja Sharp, author interview, phone call, Canada, May 23, 2023.

26. Sarita Sonalkar et al., "Gynecologic Care for Women with Physical Disabilities: A Qualitative Study of Patients and Providers," *Women's Health Issues*: Official Publication of the Jacobs Institute of Women's Health 30, no. 2 (2020): 136–41, doi:10.1016/j.whi.2019.10.002.

27. Elizabeth Heubeck, "Most OB-GYN Practices Fall Short in Caring for Women with Disabilities," Connecticut Health Investigative Team, November 26, 2019, https://c-hit.org/2019/11/26/most-ob-gyn-practices-fall-short-in-caring -for-women-with-disabilities.

28. Jamie Ducharme, "For People with Disabilities, Losing Abortion Access Can Be a Matter of Life or Death," *Time*, January 25, 2023, https://time.com /6248104/abortion-access-people-with-disabilities.

29. Katherine Rosman, "For a Woman in a Wheelchair, Abortion Access Was One More Challenge," *New York Times*, July 14, 2022, https://www.nytimes.com /2022/07/14/style/abortion-accessibility-planned-parenthood.html.

30. National Partnership for Women and Families, *Access, Autonomy, and Dignity: Abortion Care for People with Disabilities*, September 2021, https://national partnership.org/wp-content/uploads/2023/02/repro-disability-abortion.pdf.

31. National Women's Law Center, "New NWLC Report Finds over 30 States Legally Allow Forced Sterilization," press release, January 25, 2022, https:// nwlc.org/press-release/new-nwlc-report-finds-over-30-states-legally-allow-forced -sterilization.

32. National Women's Law Center, "Forced Sterilization of Disabled People in the United States," press release, January 24, 2022, https://nwlc.org/resource /forced-sterilization-of-disabled-people-in-the-united-states.

33. Alexandra Minna Stern, "Forced Sterilization Policies in the US Targeted Minorities and Those with Disabilities—and Lasted into the 21st Century," *The*

Conversation, August 26, 2020, https://news.yahoo.com/forced-sterilization-policies -us-targeted-122042074.html.

34. Henan Li et al., "Female Sterilization and Cognitive Disability in the United States, 2011–2015," *Obstetrics & Gynecology* 132, no. 3 (2018): 559–64, https://doi.org/10.1097/aog.0000000000002778.

35. Ashwin Roy et al., "The Human Rights of Women with Intellectual Disability," *Journal of the Royal Society of Medicine* 105, no. 9 (2012): 384–89, doi:10 .1258/jrsm.2012.110303.

36. "National Women's Law Center, "Forced Sterilization of Disabled People in the United States."

37. National Partnership for Women and Families, *Access, Autonomy, and Dignity.*

38. Raluca Tomsa et al., "Prevalence of Sexual Abuse in Adults with Intellectual Disability: Systematic Review and Meta-Analysis," *International Journal of Environmental Research and Public Health* 18, no. 4 (2021): 1980, doi:10.3390 /ijerph18041980.

39. United Nations Girls' Education Initiative (UNGEI), *Women and Young Persons with Disabilities: Guidelines for Providing Rights-Based and Gender-Responsive Services to Address Gender-Based Violence and Sexual and Reproductive Health and Rights,* 2018, https://www.ungei.org/publication/women-and-young-persons -disabilities-guidelines-providing-rights-based-and-gender.

40. André Felix, "Persons with Disabilities: Locked Up in Institutions, Forgotten by Governments," EQUINET: European Network of Equality Bodies, May 25, 2020, https://equineteurope.org/persons-with-disabilities-locked-up -in-institutions-forgotten-by-governments.

41. Shankar Vedantam, "How a Family Became a Test Case for Forced Sterilizations," transcript, *Hidden Brain,* NPR, April 23, 2018, https://www.npr.org /transcripts/604926914.

42. Vedantam, "How a Family Became a Test Case for Forced Sterilizations."

43. Nicole Agaronnik et al., "Ensuring the Reproductive Rights of Women with Intellectual Disability," *Journal of Intellectual & Developmental Disability* 45, no. 4 (2020): 365–76, doi:10.3109/13668250.2020.1762383.

44. Emily DiMatteo, Osub Ahmed, and Vilissa Thompson, *Reproductive Justice for Disabled Women: Ending Systemic Discrimination,* Center for American Progress, April 13, 2022, https://www.americanprogress.org/article/reproductive-justice -for-disabled-women-ending-systemic-discrimination.

45. Emily DiMatteo, Vilissa Thompson, and Osub Ahmed, *Rethinking Guardianship to Protect Disabled People's Reproductive Rights,* Center for American Progress, August 11, 2022, https://www.americanprogress.org/article/rethinking -guardianship-to-protect-disabled-peoples-reproductive-rights.

46. Paul Hudson and Michelle A. Williams, "People Are Much Less Likely to Trust the Medical System If They Are from an Ethnic Minority, Have Disabilities, or Identify as LGBTQ+, According to a First-of-Its-Kind Study by Sanofi," *Fortune,* January 31, 2023, https://fortune.com/2023/01/31/people-trust-health -medical-system-ethnic-minority-disabilities-identify-lgbtq-study-sanofi-hudson -williams.

47. Maya Dusenbery, *Doing Harm: The Truth About How Bad Medicine and Lazy Science Leave Women Dismissed, Misdiagnosed, and Sick* (New York: HarperCollins, 2018).

48. Centers for Disease Control and Prevention, "Working Together to Reduce Black Maternal Mortality," Health Equity Features, April 8, 2024, https://www.cdc.gov/healthequity/features/maternal-mortality/index.html.

49. Aubrey Gordon, *What We Don't Talk About When We Talk About Fat* (Boston: Beacon Press, 2020).

50. S. M. Phelan et al., "Impact of Weight Bias and Stigma on Quality of Care and Outcomes for Patients with Obesity," *Obesity Reviews: An Official Journal of the International Association for the Study of Obesity* 16, no. 4 (2015): 319–26, doi:10.1111/obr.12266.

51. Joshua D. Safer et al., "Barriers to Healthcare for Transgender Individuals," *Current Opinion in Endocrinology & Diabetes and Obesity* 23, no. 2 (2016): 168–71, https://doi.org/10.1097/med.0000000000000227.

52. Eyal Press, "The Moral Crisis of America's Doctors," *New York Times*, June 15, 2023, https://www.nytimes.com/2023/06/15/magazine/doctors-moral-crises.html.

53. Hailey Hudson, "Moving from Disability Rights to Disability Justice," World Institute on Disability, https://wid.org/moving-from-disability-rights-to-disability-justice, accessed May 3, 2024.

54. "What Is Disability Justice?" Sins Invalid, June 16, 2020, https://www.sinsinvalid.org/news-1/2020/6/16/what-is-disability-justice.

55. Health Justice Commons, "HJC," https://www.healthjusticecommons.org, accessed May 3, 2024.

56. Health Justice Commons, "Radical Telehealth Collective," https://www.healthjusticecommons.org/rtc, accessed May 3, 2024.

57. Abigail Abrams, "'We Are Grabbing Our Own Microphones': How Advocates of Reproductive Justice Stepped into the Spotlight," *Time*, November 21, 2019, https://time.com/5735432/reproductive-justice-groups.

58. Abrams, "'We Are Grabbing Our Own Microphones.'"

59. DiMatteo, Ahmed, and Thompson, *Reproductive Justice for Disabled Women*.

60. DiMatteo, Ahmed, and Thompson, *Reproductive Justice for Disabled Women*.

CHAPTER 8: CHILD PROTECTIVE SERVICES

1. Kavya Parthiban, author interview, phone call, January 23, 2023.

2. Elizabeth Lightfoot, Katharine Hill, and Traci LaLiberte, "The Inclusion of Disability as a Condition for Termination of Parental Rights," *Child Abuse and Neglect* 34 (2010): 927–34.

3. Lightfoot, Hill, and LaLiberte, "The Inclusion of Disability as a Condition for Termination of Parental Rights," 927–34.

4. Regional Center of the East Bay (RCEB), "About RCEB," https://www.rceb.org/about-us, accessed June 29, 2023.

5. RCEB, "Performance, Finance, Policies—Regional Center of the East Bay," https://www.rceb.org/about-us/public-information/transparency, accessed June 29, 2023.

6. Kathryn Hurd, "How California's Big Effort to Help Abused Children Left Some with Nowhere to Go," *Los Angeles Times*, May 28, 2023, https://www.latimes

.com/california/story/2023–05–28/california-law-foster-children-shortage-group
-homes.

7. Helping Survivors of Sexual Assault and Abuse, "Sexual Abuse Within
the Foster Care System," https://helpingsurvivors.org/foster-care-sexual-abuse,
accessed May 3, 2024.

8. In re Diamond H., 82 Cal.App.4th 1127, 98 Cal. Rptr. 2d 715 (Cal. Ct. App.
2000); In re Anthony L., 43 Cal.App.5th 438, 256 Cal. Rptr. 3d 688 (Cal. Ct. App.
2019).

9. Alameda County Social Services, "Reunification," https://www.alameda
countysocialservices.org/our-services/Youth/resource-families/tabs/reunification,
accessed May 3, 2024.

10. Claire Chiamulera, "Representing Parents with Disabilities: Best Practice,"
Child Law Practice Today 34 (February 2015), https://www.americanbar.org/groups
/public_interest/child_law/resources/child_law_practiceonline/child_law_practice
/vol-34/february-2015.

11. Lawrence G. Weiss and Donald H. Saklofske, "Mediators of IQ Test Score
Differences Across Racial and Ethnic Groups: The Case for Environmental and
Social Justice," *Personality and Individual Differences* 161 (2020): 109962.

12. National Association of Mandated Reporters (NAMR), "What Is a Mandated Reporter?" https://namr.org/news/what-is-a-mandated-reporter, accessed
May 3, 2024.

13. Brett Drake et al., "Surveillance Bias in Child Maltreatment: A Tempest in
a Teapot," *International Journal of Environmental Research and Public Health* 14, no.
9 (2017): 971, doi:10.3390/ijerph14090971.

14. Family Law Education for Women (FLEW)/Femmes Ontariennes et
Droit de La Famille, "Child Protection and Family Law," Family Law for Women
in Ontario, https://impekacdn.s3.us-east-2.amazonaws.com/onefamilylaw.ca
/content/user_files/2023/08/29143149/FLEW-Child-Protection-Booklet-update
-2019-final.pdf, accessed May 3, 2024.

15. FLEW, "Child Protection and Family Law."

16. Joseph F. Rice School of Law, University of South Carolina, "Termination
of Parental Rights Hearing," https://sc.edu/study/colleges_schools/law/centers
/childrens_law/publications_and_resources/abuse_neglect_benchbook/tpr
_hearing/index.php, accessed May 3, 2024.

17. Sharyn DeZelar and Elizabeth Lightfoot, "Use of Parental Disability as
a Removal Reason for Children in Foster Care in the US," *Children and Youth
Services Review* 86 (2018): 128–34; Traci LaLiberte et al., "Child Protection
Services and Parents with Intellectual and Developmental Disabilities," *Journal
of Applied Research in Intellectual Disabilities* 30, no. 3 (2017): 521–32; Ella Callow,
Kelly Buckland, and Shannon Jones, "Parents with Disabilities in the United
States: Prevalence, Perspectives, and Proposal for Legislative Change to Protect
the Right to Family in the Disability Community," *Texas Journal on Civil Liberties
& Civil Rights* 17 (2011): 9.

18. Arthur Horton and Jerry Watson, "African American Disproportionate
Overrepresentation in the Illinois Child Welfare Systems," *Race, Gender & Class*
22, nos. 1–2 (2015), https://www.jstor.org/stable/26505324.

19. Sharyn DeZelar, author interview, phone call, February 2, 2023.

20. Children's Bureau, "National Child Abuse and Neglect Data System (NCANDS)," June 16, 2023, https://www.acf.hhs.gov/cb/data-research/ncands.

21. Elizabeth Lightfoot, Mingyang Zheng, and Sharyn DeZelar, "Substantiation of Child Maltreatment Among Parents with Disabilities in the United States," *Journal of Public Child Welfare* (2020), DOI: 10.1080/15548732.2020 .1773369.

22. National Council on Disability, *Rocking the Cradle: Ensuring the Rights of Parents with Disabilities and Their Children*, September 27, 2012, https://www.ncd .gov/report/rocking-the-cradle-ensuring-the-rights-of-parents-with-disabilities -and-their-children.

23. Dorothy Roberts, *Shattered Bonds: The Color of Child Welfare* (Sydney: ReadHowYouWant, 2010).

24. Dorothy Roberts, *Torn Apart: How the Child Welfare System Destroys Black Families—and How Abolition Can Build a Safer World* (New York: Basic Books, 2022).

25. Robyn M. Powell, "Achieving Justice for Disabled Parents and Their Children: An Abolitionist Approach," *Yale Journal of Law & Feminism* 33 (2021): 37.

26. National Council on Disability, *Rocking the Cradle*.

27. Cordelia and Joey, author interview, phone call, February 3, 2023.

28. Cordelia and Joey, author interview.

29. Jill Feder, "Examples of Autism Masking," Accessibility.com, May 20, 2022, https://www.accessibility.com/blog/examples-of-autism-masking.

30. Cordelia and Joey, author interview, phone call, February 3, 2023.

31. Theodore Baker, author interview, phone call, February 27, 2023.

32. S. M. Albert, R. M. Powell, and J. Rubinstein, "Barriers and Solutions to Passing State Legislation to Protect the Rights of Parents with Disabilities: Lessons from Interviews with Advocates, Attorneys, and Legislators," *Journal of Disability Policy Studies* 33, no. 1 (2022): 15–24, https://doi.org/10.1177/10442073211006394.

33. Angela Tucker, *"You Should Be Grateful": Stories of Race, Identity, and Transracial Adoption* (Boston: Beacon Press, 2023).

34. Scott Winship et al., *Long Shadows: The Black-White Gap in Multigenerational Poverty*, Brookings, June 10, 2021.

35. Social Security Administration, "Supplemental Security Income (SSI)," https://www.ssa.gov/ssi, accessed May 3, 2024; Justin Schweitzer, Emily DiMatteo, and Nick Buffie, "Administrative Burdens: How the Social Safety Net Is Failing Disabled People," Center for American Progress, December 5, 2022, https:// www.americanprogress.org/article/administrative-burdens-how-the-social-safety -net-is-failing-disabled-people.

36. Angela Garbes, *Essential Labor: Mothering as Social Change* (New York: HarperCollins, 2022).

37. Dawn Marie Dow, *Mothering While Black: Boundaries and Burdens of Middle-Class Parenthood* (Oakland: University of California Press, 2019).

38. Evelyn Nakano Glenn, Grace Chang, and Linda Rennie Forcey, eds., *Mothering: Ideology, Experience, and Agency* (Abingdon: Taylor & Francis, 2016).

39. Mia Birdsong, *How We Show Up: Reclaiming Family, Friendship, and Community* (New York: Hachette Books, 2020).

40. Jessica Grose, *Screaming on the Inside: The Unsustainability of American Motherhood* (New York: HarperCollins, 2022).

41. Dean Spade, *Mutual Aid: Building Solidarity During This Crisis (and the Next)* (London: Verso Press, 2020).

42. Leah Lakshmi Piepzna-Samarasinha, *The Future Is Disabled: Prophecies, Love Notes and Mourning Songs* (Vancouver: Arsenal Pulp Press).

43. Valerie, author interview, phone call, March 8, 2023.

44. Maria McLaughlin, author interview, phone call, March 13, 2023.

45. Melinda Clynes, "Detroit Radical Childcare Collective: Not Your Typical Babysitters," Model D Media, September 18, 2018, https://www.modeldmedia .com/features/detroit-radical-childcare-091718.aspx.

CHAPTER 9: ABLEISM

1. G. L. Albrecht and P. J. Devlieger, "The Disability Paradox: High Quality of Life Against All Odds," *Social Science & Medicine* 48, no. 8 (1999): 977–88, doi:10.1016/s0277-9536(98)00411-0.

2. Samuel R. Bagenstos and Margo Schlanger, "Hedonic Damages, Hedonic Adaptation, and Disability," *Vanderbilt Law Review* 60 (2007): 745.

3. Campbell et al., "Disability and the Goods of Life," 704–28.

4. Campbell et al., "Disability and the Goods of Life," 704–28.

5. Gina Kolata, "These Doctors Admit They Don't Want Patients with Disabilities," *New York Times*, October 19, 2022, https://www.nytimes.com/2022/10 /19/health/doctors-patients-disabilities.html.

6. Tara Lagu et al., "'I Am Not The Doctor for You': Physicians' Attitudes About Caring for People with Disabilities," *Health Affairs* 41, no. 10 (2022): 1387–95, doi:10.1377/hlthaff.2022.00475.

7. US Department of Health and Human Services, "FAQs for Healthcare Providers During the COVID-19 Public Health Emergency: Federal Civil Rights Protections for Individuals with Disabilities under Section 504 and Section 1557," https://www.hhs.gov/civil-rights/for-providers/civil-rights-covid19/disabilty-faqs /index.html, accessed May 3, 2024.

8. Lisa I. Iezzoni, "Cancer Detection, Diagnosis, and Treatment for Adults with Disabilities," *Lancet Oncology* 23, no. 4 (2022): e164–e173, doi:10.1016/S1470 -2045(22)00018-3.

9. Cleveland Clinic, "20-Week Ultrasound (Anatomy Scan)," https://my .clevelandclinic.org/health/diagnostics/22644-20-week-ultrasound, accessed May 3, 2024.

10. Adrienne Asch and David Wasserman, "Where Is the Sin in Synecdoche? Prenatal Testing and the Parent-Child Relationship," in *Quality of Life and Human Difference: Genetic Testing, Health Care, and Disability*, ed. David Wasserman, Jerome Bickenbach, and Robert Wachbroit (Cambridge: Cambridge University Press, 2005).

11. Zakia Nouri et al., "Estimated Prevalence of US Physicians with Disabilities," *JAMA Network Open* 4, no. 3 (2021): e211254, doi:10.1001/jamanetworkopen .2021.1254.

12. Molly C. Kalmoe et al., "Physician Suicide: A Call to Action," *Missouri Medicine* 116, no. 3 (2019): 211–16.

13. Eli Rosenberg, "Clarence Thomas Tried to Link Abortion to Eugenics. Seven Historians Told the *Post* He's Wrong," *Washington Post*, May 30, 2019,

https://www.washingtonpost.com/history/2019/05/31/clarence-thomas-tried-link
-abortion-eugenics-seven-historians-told-post-hes-wrong.

14. Henri Goldstein, "Health and Social Security Services for People with
Down's Syndrome in Denmark: Economic Considerations," *International Journal
of Mental Health* 20, no. 2 (1991): 29–46, http://www.jstor.org/stable/41344584.

15. Wolfgang Saxon, "Dr. Fritz Fuchs, 76, Who Advanced Obstetrics," *New
York Times*, March 4, 1995, https://www.nytimes.com/1995/03/04/obituaries/dr
-fritz-fuchs-76-who-advanced-obstetrics.html.

16. Sandy Sufian and Rosemarie Garland-Thompson, "The Dark Side of
CRISPR," *Scientific American*, February 16, 2021, https://www.scientificamerican
.com/article/the-dark-side-of-crispr.

17. Rosemarie Garland-Thomson, "When Better Becomes Worse," *American
Journal of Bioethics* 19, no. 7 (2019): 24–26, doi:10.1080/15265161.2019.1619345.

18. Kevin Toolis, "The Most Dangerous Man in the World," *The Guardian*,
November 6, 1999, https://www.theguardian.com/lifeandstyle/1999/nov06
/weekend.kevintoolis.

19. Richard Frankham et al., "Loss of Genetic Diversity Reduces Ability to
Adapt," in *Genetic Management of Fragmented Animal and Plant Populations*, ed.
Richard Frankham et al. (Oxford: Oxford Academic, 2017; online ed.), https://
doi.org/10.1093/oso/9780198783398.003.0004.

20. Malcolm Harris, *Palo Alto: A History of California, Capitalism, and the World*
(New York: Little, Brown, 2023).

21. Kate Montana, "The Problematic Legacy of David Starr Jordan," IBSS
Seminar series, California Academy of Sciences, YouTube video, 1:02:20, June 9,
2022, https://www.youtube.com/watch?v=ZwTl73j6pBc.

22. Dominique Aubert-Marson, "Sir Francis Galton: Le fondateur de
l'eugénisme" [The father of eugenics], *Medecine Sciences* 25, nos. 6–7 (2009):
641–45, doi:10.1051/medsci/2009256–7641.

23. Nick Bilton, "'They Present a Version of Themselves That Isn't Real': Inside
the Dark, Biohacked Heart of Silicon Valley," *Vanity Fair*, April 9, 2021, https://www
.vanityfair.com/news/2021/04/inside-the-dark-biohacked-heart-of-silicon-valley.

24. Tad Friend, "Silicon Valley's Quest to Live Forever," *New Yorker*, April 3,
2017, https://www.newyorker.com/magazine/2017/04/03/silicon-valleys-quest
-to-live-forever.

25. Penny Daflos, "'Easier to Let Go' Without Support: B.C. Woman Approved for Medically Assisted Death Speaks Out," British Columbia CTV News,
June 7, 2022, updated June 8, 2022, https://bc.ctvnews.ca/easier-to-let-go-without
-support-b-c-woman-approved-for-medically-assisted-death-speaks-out-1.5937496
?fbclid=IwAR2IaaTUGx247MyyoNvjRQkO2D2FRHUY2ZCfrfleX_TweCW6
qTfkP25M30k.

26. UN Human Rights, Office of the High Commissioner, "New Eugenics:
UN Disability Expert Warns Against 'Ableism' in Medical Practice," press release,
February 28, 2020, https://www.ohchr.org/en/press-releases/2020/02/new
-eugenics-un-disability-expert-warns-against-ableism-medical-practice.

27. Erin S. Lane, *Someone Other Than a Mother: Flipping the Scripts on a Woman's Purpose and Making Meaning Beyond Motherhood* (New York: Penguin Publishing Group, 2022).

INDEX

Aaron, Jessi Elana, 53–54, 68, 89–91, 108
ableism: as fear of mortality, 96, 161–62, 167; focus on accomplishment, 160–61; internalized, 2–3, 166; and marginalization, 5, 19, 84, 101, 116, 145, 154; pervasiveness of, 13–14, 163; underlying assumptions, 10, 95, 105–6, 154–56. *See also* capitalism; perfectionism trap; shame feelings
abortion, selective, 94, 121, 155–59
acceptance, 5, 39–42, 50, 63, 121
accessibility: adaptive equipment, 66–70, 72; challenges for the nondisabled, 91–92; importance of, 86; infrastructure design/built environments, 94, 97–98; jogging stroller, 93; and risks of leaving the house, 81, 84–86; suggestions for improving, 86–87; as visibility, 4, 39, 51, 62, 84, 86–87; and vulnerability, 87–91. *See also* creative adaptation; shame feelings; wheelchairs
air travel, challenges of, 62, 80–81
Alan (Jessie Owen's partner), 33
Albrecht, Gary L., 150
All Our Families: Disability Lineage and the Future of Kinship (Fink), 51 xxx
ambulance rides, 82–83

Americans with Disabilities Act (ADA), 12, 118, 126
anatomy scans, 154–55. *See also* abortion, selective
Annette and Oliver, and the California child welfare system, 127–30, 140
Aristotle, concept of "eudaimonia," 151
arthrogryposis multiplex congenita (AMC), 53, 108
Asch, Adrienne, 158
The Atlantic, Zhang article on Down syndrome, 157
Austin, Texas, Hickson's medical trauma, 101–3

baby care equipment, modifying, 67–68, 72–74
"bad difference" model of disability, 12, 14
Bain Capital, 107
balance theory, 150–51
Barnes, Elizabeth, 4, 11–14
Bay Area Rapid Transit, Braille maps, 93
Berne, Patty, 119
biohacking (genetic engineering), 161
Birdsong, Mia, 143
Black people: collective parenting approaches, 142–43; death during childbirth, 115; threats of child removal, 123–24